Journey Into
The Heart Of Magic
With
Carlos Castaneda

**"One can't exaggerate the significance
of what Castaneda has done."**
—*The New York Times*

Books by Carlos Castaneda

The Eagle's Gift
The Fire from Within
Journey to Ixtlan: The Lessons of don Juan
The Power of Silence: Further Lessons of don Juan
The Second Ring of Power
A Separate Reality: Further Conversations with don Juan
Tales of Power
The Teachings of don Juan: A Yaqui Way of Knowledge

Published by
POCKET BOOKS/WASHINGTON SQUARE PRESS

The Teachings
of
Don Juan

A YAQUI WAY
OF KNOWLEDGE

by

CARLOS CASTANEDA

WASHINGTON SQUARE PRESS
PUBLISHED BY POCKET BOOKS

New York   London   Toronto   Sydney   Tokyo   Singapore

A Washington Square Press Publication of
POCKET BOOKS, a division of Simon & Schuster Inc.
1230 Avenue of the Americas, New York, NY 10020

ISBN: 0-671-72791-5

First Washington Square Press trade paperback printing December 1990

10 9 8 7 6 5 4 3 2 1

For don Juan—
and for the two persons who shared
his sense of magical time with me

Acknowledgments

I wish to express profound gratitude to Professor Clement Meighan, who started and set the course of my anthropological fieldwork; to Professor Harold Garfinkel, who gave me the model and the spirit of exhaustive inquiry; to Professor Robert Edgerton, who criticized my work from its beginning; to Professors William Bright and Pedro Carrasco for their criticisms and encouragement; and to Professor Lawrence Watson for his invaluable help in the clarification of my analysis. Finally, I am grateful to Mrs. Grace Stimson and Mr. F. A. Guilford for their assistance in preparing the manuscript.

Contents

Foreword

This book is both ethnography and allegory.

Carlos Castaneda, under the tutelage of don Juan, takes us through that moment of twilight, through that crack in the universe between daylight and dark into a world not merely other than our own, but of an entirely different order of reality. To reach it he had the aid of *mescalito, yerba del diablo,* and *humito*—peyote, datura, and mushrooms. But this is no mere recounting of hallucinatory experiences, for don Juan's subtle manipulations have guided the traveler while his interpretations give meaning to the events that we, through the sorcerer's apprentice, have the opportunity to experience.

Anthropology has taught us that the world is differently defined in different places. It is not only that people have different customs; it is not only that people believe in different gods and expect different postmortem fates. It is, rather, that the worlds of different peoples have different shapes. The very metaphysical presuppositions differ: space does not conform to Euclidean geometry, time does not form a continuous unidirectional flow, causation does not conform to Aristotelian logic, man is not differentiated from nonman or life from death, as in our world. We know something of the shape of these other worlds from the logic of native languages and from myths and ceremonies, as recorded by anthropologists. Don Juan has shown us glimpses of the world of a Yaqui sorcerer, and because we see it under the influence of hallucinogenic substances, we apprehend it with a reality that is utterly different from those other sources. This is the special virtue of this work.

Castaneda rightly asserts that this world, for all its differences of perception, has its own inner logic. He has tried to explain it from inside, as it were—from within his own rich and intensely personal experiences while under don Juan's tutelage—rather than to examine it in terms of our logic. That he cannot entirely succeed in this is a limitation that our culture and our own language place on perception, rather than his personal limitation; yet in his efforts he bridges for us the world of a Yaqui sorcerer with our own, the world of non-ordinary reality with the world of ordinary reality.

The central importance of entering into worlds other than our own—and hence of anthropology itself—lies in the fact that the experience leads us to understand that our own world is also a cultural construct. By experiencing other worlds, then, we see our own for what it is and are thereby enabled also to see fleetingly what the real world, the one between our own cultural construct and those other worlds, must in fact be like. Hence the allegory, as well as the ethnography. The wisdom and poetry of don Juan, and the skill and poetry of his scribe, give us a vision both of ourselves and of reality. As in all proper allegory, what one sees lies with the beholder, and needs no exegesis here.

Carlos Castaneda's interviews with don Juan were initiated while he was a student of anthropology at the University of California, Los Angeles. We are indebted to him for his patience, his courage, and his perspicacity in seeking out and facing the challenge of his dual apprenticeship, and in reporting to us the details of his experiences. In this work he demonstrates the essential skill of good ethnography—the capacity to enter into an alien world. I believe he has found a path with heart.

Walter Goldschmidt

*Para mi solo recorrer los caminos que tienen
corazon, cualquier camino que tenga corazon.
Por ahi yo recorro, y la unica prueba que
vale es atravesar todo su largo. Y por ahi
yo recorro mirando, mirando, sin aliento.
(For me there is only the traveling on paths
that have heart, on any path that may have
heart. There I travel, and the only worthwhile challenge is to traverse its full length.
And there I travel looking, looking, breathlessly.)*

—DON JUAN

*... nothing more can be attempted than to
establish the beginning and the direction of
an infinitely long road. The pretension of
any systematic and definitive completeness
would be, at least, a self-illusion. Perfection
can here be obtained by the individual
student only in the subjective sense that he
communicates everything he has been able to see.*

—GEORG SIMMEL

Introduction

In the summer of 1960, while I was an anthropology student at the University of California, Los Angeles, I made several trips to the Southwest to collect information on the medicinal plants used by the Indians of the area. The events I describe here began during one of my trips. I was waiting in a border town for a Greyhound bus, talking with a friend who had been my guide and helper in the survey. Suddenly he leaned toward me and whispered that the man, a white-haired old Indian, who was sitting in front of the window was very learned about plants, especially peyote. I asked my friend to introduce me to this man.

My friend greeted him, then went over and shook his hand. After they had talked for a while, my friend signaled me to join them, but immediately left me alone with the old man, not even bothering to introduce us. He was not in the least embarrassed. I told him my name and he said that he was called Juan and that he was at my service. He used the Spanish polite form of address. We shook hands at my initiative and then remained silent for some time. It was not a strained silence, but a quietness, natural and relaxed on both sides. Though his dark face and neck were wrinkled, showing his age, it struck me that his body was agile and muscular.

I then told him that I was interested in obtaining information about medicinal plants. Although in truth I was almost totally ignorant about peyote, I found myself pretending that I knew a great deal, and even suggesting that it might be to his advantage to talk with me. As I rattled on, he nodded slowly and looked at me, but said nothing. I avoided his eyes and we finished by standing, the two of us, in dead silence. Finally, after what seemed a very long time, don Juan got up and looked out of the window. His bus had come. He said goodbye and left the station.

I was annoyed at having talked nonsense to him, and at being seen through by those remarkable eyes. When my friend returned he tried to console me for my failure to learn anything from don Juan. He explained that the old man was often silent or noncommittal, but the disturbing effect of this first encounter was not so easily dispelled.

I made a point of finding out where don Juan lived, and later visited him several times. On each visit I tried to lead him to discuss peyote, but without success. We became, nonetheless, very good friends, and my scientific investigation was forgotten or was at least redirected into channels that were worlds apart from my original intention.

The friend who had introduced me to don Juan explained later that the old man was not a native of Arizona, where we met, but was a Yaqui Indian from Sonora, Mexico.

At first I saw don Juan simply as a rather peculiar man who knew a great deal about peyote and who spoke Spanish remarkably well. But the people with whom he lived believed that he had some sort of "secret knowledge," that he was a "brujo." The Spanish word *brujo* means, in English, medicine man, curer, witch, sorcerer. It connotes essentially a person who has extraordinary, and usually evil, powers.

I had known don Juan for a whole year before he took me into his confidence. One day he explained that he possessed a certain knowledge that he had learned from a teacher, a "benefactor" as he called him, who had directed him in a kind of apprenticeship. Don Juan had, in turn, chosen me to serve as his apprentice, but he warned me that I would have to make a very deep commitment and that the training was long and arduous.

In describing his teacher, don Juan used the word "diablero." Later I learned that diablero is a term used only by the Sonoran Indians. It refers to an evil person who practices black sorcery and is capable of transforming himself into an animal—bird, a dog, a coyote, or any other creature. On one of my visits to Sonora I had a peculiar experience that illustrated the Indians' feeling about diableros. I was driving at night in the company of two Indian friends when I saw an animal that seemed to be a dog crossing the highway. One of my companions said it was not a dog, but a huge coyote. I slowed down and pulled to the side of the road to get a good look at the animal. It stayed within range of the headlights a few seconds longer and then ran into the chaparral. It was unmistakably a coyote, but it was twice the ordinary size. Talking excitedly, my friends agreed that it was a very unusual animal, and one of them suggested that it might be a diablero. I decided to use an account of the experience to question the Indians of that area about their beliefs in the existence of diableros. I talked with many people, telling them the story and asking them questions. The three conversations that follow indicate what they felt.

"Do you think it was a coyote, Choy?" I asked a young man after he had heard the story.

"Who knows? A dog, no doubt. Too large for a coyote."

"Do you think it may have been a diablero?"

"That's a lot of bull. There are no such things."

"Why do you say that, Choy?"

"People imagine things. I bet if you had caught that animal you would have seen that it was a dog. Once I had some business in another town and got up before daybreak and saddled up a horse. As I was leaving I came upon a dark shadow on the road which looked like a huge animal. My horse reared, throwing me off the saddle. I was pretty scared too, but it turned out that the shadow was a woman who was walking to town."

"Do you mean, Choy, that you don't believe there are diableros?"

"Diableros! What's a diablero? Tell me what a diablero is!"

"I don't know, Choy. Manuel, who was riding with me that night, said the coyote could have been a diablero. Maybe you could tell me what a diablero is?"

"A diablero, they say, is a brujo who changes into any form he wants to adopt. But everybody knows that is pure bull. The old people here are full of stories about diableros. You won't find that among us younger people."

"What kind of animal do you think it was, doña Luz?" I asked a middle-aged woman.

"Only God knows for sure, but I think it was not a coyote. There are things that appear to be coyotes, but are not. Was the coyote running, or was it eating?"

"It was standing most of the time, but when I first saw it, I think it was eating something."

"Are you sure it was not carrying something in its mouth?"

"Perhaps it was. But tell me, would that make any difference?"

"Yes, it would. If it was carrying something in its mouth it was not a coyote."

"What was it then?"

"It was a man or a woman."

"What do you call such people, doña Luz?"

She did not answer. I questioned her for a while longer, but without success. Finally she said she did not know. I asked her if such people were called diableros, and she answered that "diablero" was one of the names given to them.

"Do you know any diableros?" I asked.

"I knew one woman," she replied. "She was killed. It happened when I was a little girl. The woman, they said, used to turn into a female dog. And one night a dog went into the house of a white man to steal cheese. The white man killed the dog with a shotgun, and at the very moment the dog died in the house of the white man the woman died in her own hut. Her kin got together and went to the white man and demanded payment. The white man paid good money for having killed her."

"How could they demand payment if it was only a dog he killed?"

"They said that the white man knew it was not a dog, because other people were with him, and they all saw the dog stood up on its legs like a man and reached for the cheese, which was on a tray hanging from the roof. The men were waiting for the thief because the white man's cheese was being stolen every night. So the man killed the thief knowing it was not a dog."

"Are there any diableros nowadays, doña Luz?"

"Such things are very secret. They say there are no more diableros, but I doubt it, because one member of a diablero's family has to learn what the diablero knows. Diableros have their own laws, and one of them is that a diablero has to teach his secret to one of his kin."

"What do you think the animal was, Genaro?" I asked a very old man.

"A dog from one of the ranches of that area. What else?"

"It could have been a diablero!"

"A diablero? You are crazy! There are no diableros."

"Do you mean that there are none today, or that there never were any?"

"At one time there were, yes. It is common knowledge. Everybody knows that. But the people were very afraid of them and had them all killed."

"Who killed them, Genaro?"

"All the people of the tribe. The last diablero I knew about was S——. He killed dozens, maybe even hundreds, of people with his sorcery. We couldn't put up with that and the people got together and took him by surprise one night and burned him alive."

"How long ago was that, Genaro?"

"In nineteen forty-two."

"Did you see it yourself?"

"No, but people still talk about it. They say that there were no ashes left, even though the stake was made of fresh wood. All that was left at the end was a huge pool of grease."

Although don Juan categorized his benefactor as a diablero, he never mentioned the place where he had acquired his knowledge, nor did he identify his teacher. In fact, don Juan disclosed very little about his personal life. All he said was that he had been born in the Southwest in 1891; that he had spent nearly all his life in Mexico; that in 1900 his family was exiled by the Mexican government to central Mexico along with thousands of other Sonoran Indians; and that he had lived in central and southern Mexico until 1940. Thus, as don Juan had traveled a great deal, his knowledge may have been the product of many influences. And although he regarded himself as an Indian from Sonora, I was not sure whether to place the context of his knowledge totally in the culture of the Sonoran Indians. But it is not my intention here to determine his precise cultural milieu.

I began to serve my apprenticeship to don Juan in June, 1961. Prior to that time I had seen him on various occasions, but always in the capacity of an anthropological observer. During these early conversations I took notes in a covert manner. Later, relying on my memory, I reconstructed the entire conversation. When I began to participate as an apprentice, however, that method of taking notes became very difficult, because our conversations touched on many different topics. Then don Juan allowed me—under strong protest, however—to record openly anything that was said. I would also have liked to take photographs and make tape recordings, but he would not permit me to do so.

I carried out the apprenticeship first in Arizona and then in Sonora, because don Juan moved to Mexico during the course of my training. The procedure I em-

ployed was to see him for a few days every so often.
My visits became more frequent and lasted longer during
the summer months of 1961, 1962, 1963, and 1964.
In retrospect, I believe this method of conducting the
apprenticeship prevented the training from being successful, because it retarded the advent of the full commitment I needed to become a sorcerer. Yet the method
was beneficial from my personal standpoint in that it
allowed me a modicum of detachment, and that in turn
fostered a sense of critical examination which would
have been impossible to attain had I participated continuously, without interruption. In September, 1965,
I voluntarily discontinued the apprenticeship.

Several months after my withdrawal, I considered for
the first time the idea of arranging my field notes in a
systematic way. As the data I had collected were quite
voluminous, and included much miscellaneous information, I began by trying to establish a classification system. I divided the data into areas of related concepts
and procedures and arranged the areas hierarchically
according to subjective importance—that is, in terms
of the impact that each of them had had on me. In that
way I arrived at the following classification: uses of
hallucinogenic plants; procedures and formulas used in
sorcery; acquisition and manipulation of power objects;
uses of medicinal plants; songs and legends.

Reflecting upon the phenomena I had experienced, I
realized that my attempt at classification had produced
nothing more than an inventory of categories; any attempt to refine my scheme would therefore yield only a
more complex inventory. That was not what I wanted.
During the months following my withdrawal from the
apprenticeship, I needed to understand what I had experienced, and what I had experienced was the teaching
of a coherent system of beliefs by means of a pragmatic
and experimental method. It had been evident to me
from the very first session in which I had participated
that don Juan's teachings possessed an internal cohesion. Once he had definitely decided to communicate

his knowledge to me, he proceeded to present his explanations in orderly steps. To discover that order and to understand it proved to be a most difficult task for me.

My inability to arrive at an understanding seems to have been traceable to the fact that, after four years of apprenticeship, I was still a beginner. It was clear that don Juan's knowledge and his method of conveying it were those of his benefactor; thus my difficulties in understanding his teachings must have been analogous to those he himself had encountered. Don Juan alluded to our similarity as beginners through incidental comments about his incapacity to understand his teacher during his own apprenticeship. Such remarks led me to believe that to any beginner, Indian or non-Indian, the knowledge of sorcery was rendered incomprehensible by the outlandish characteristics of the phenomena he experienced. Personally, as a Western man, I found these characteristics so bizarre that it was virtually impossible to explain them in terms of my own everyday life, and I was forced to the conclusion that any attempt to classify my field data in my own terms would be futile.

Thus it became obvious to me that don Juan's knowledge had to be examined in terms of how he himself understood it; only in such terms could it be made evident and convincing. In trying to reconcile my own views with don Juan's, however, I realized that whenever he tried to explain his knowledge to me, he used concepts that would render it "intelligible" to him. As those concepts were alien to me, trying to understand his knowledge in the way he did placed me in another untenable position. Therefore, my first task was to determine his order of conceptualization. While working in that direction, I saw that don Juan himself had placed particular emphasis on a certain area of his teachings— specifically, the uses of hallucinogenic plants. On the basis of this realization, I revised my own scheme of categories.

Don Juan used, separately and on different occasions, three hallucinogenic plants: peyote *(Lophophora williamsii),* Jimson weed *(Datura inoxia* syn. *D. meteloides),* and a mushroom (possibly *Psilocybe mexicana).* Since before their contact with Europeans, American Indians have known the hallucinogenic properties of these three plants. Because of their properties, the plants have been widely employed for pleasure, for curing, for witchcraft, and for attaining a state of ecstasy. In the specific context of his teachings, don Juan related the use of *Datura inoxia* and *Psilocybe mexicana* to the acquisition of power, a power he called an "ally." He related the use of *Lophophora williamsii* to the acquisition of wisdom, or the knowledge of the right way to live.

The importance of the plants was, for don Juan, their capacity to produce stages of peculiar perception in a human being. Thus he guided me into experiencing a sequence of these stages for the purpose of unfolding and validating his knowledge. I have called them "states of nonordinary reality," meaning unusual reality as opposed to the ordinary reality of everyday life. The distinction is based on the inherent meaning of the states of nonordinary reality. In the context of don Juan's knowledge they were considered as real, although their reality was differentiated from ordinary reality.

Don Juan believed the states of nonordinary reality to be the only form of pragmatic learning and the only means of acquiring power. He conveyed the impression that other parts of his teachings were incidental to the acquisition of power. This point of view permeated don Juan's attitude toward everything not directly connected with the states of nonordinary reality. Throughout my field notes there are scattered references to the way don Juan felt. For example, in one conversation he suggested that some objects have a certain amount of power in themselves. Although he himself had no respect for power objects, he said they were frequently used as aids by lesser brujos. I often asked him about such objects, but he seemed totally uninterested in discussing them.

When the topic was raised again on another occasion, however, he reluctantly consented to talk about them.

"There are certain objects that are permeated with power," he said. "There are scores of such objects which are fostered by powerful men with the aid of friendly spirits. These objects are tools—not ordinary tools, but tools of death. Yet they are only instruments; they have no power to teach. Properly speaking, they are in the realm of war objects designed for strife; they are made to kill, to be hurled."

"What kind of objects are they, don Juan?"

"They are not really objects; rather, they are types of power."

"How can one get those types of power, don Juan?"

"That depends on the kind of object you want."

"How many kinds are there?"

"As I have already said, there are scores of them. Anything can be a power object."

"Well, which are the most powerful, then?"

"The power of an object depends on its owner, on the kind of man he is. A power object fostered by a lesser brujo is almost a joke; on the other hand, a strong, powerful brujo gives his strength to his tools."

"Which power objects are most common, then? Which ones do most brujos prefer?"

"There are no preferences. They are all powerful objects, all just the same."

"Do you have any yourself, don Juan?"

He did not answer; he just looked at me and laughed. He remained quiet for a long time, and I thought my questions were annoying him.

"There are limitations on those types of powers," he went on. "But such a point is, I am sure, incomprehensible to you. It has taken me nearly a lifetime to understand that, by itself, an ally can reveal all the secrets of these lesser powers, rendering them rather childish. I had tools like that at one time, when I was very young."

"What power objects did you have?"

"Maíz-pinto, crystals, and feathers."

"What is maíz-pinto, don Juan?"

"It is a small kernel of corn which has a streak of red color in its middle."

"Is it a single kernel?"

"No. A brujo owns forty-eight kernels."

"What do the kernels do, don Juan?"

"Each one of them can kill a man by entering into his body."

"How does a kernel enter into a human body?"

"It is a power object and its power consists, among other things, in entering into the body."

"What does it do when it enters into the body?"

"It immerses itself in the body; it settles on the chest, or on the intestines. The man becomes ill, and unless the brujo who is tending him is stronger than the bewitcher, he will die within three months from the moment the kernel entered into his body."

"Is there any way of curing him?"

"The only way is to suck the kernel out, but very few brujos would dare to do that. A brujo may succeed in sucking the kernel out, but unless he is powerful enough to repel it, it will get inside him and will kill him instead."

"But how does a kernel manage to enter into someone's body?"

"To explain that I must tell you about corn witchcraft, which is one of the most powerful witchcrafts I know. The witchcraft is done by two kernels. One of them is put inside a fresh bud of a yellow flower. The flower is then set on a spot where it will come into contact with the victim: the road on which he walks every day, or any place where he is habitually present. As soon as the victim steps on the kernel, or touches it in any way, the witchcraft is done. The kernel immerses itself in the body."

"What happens to the kernel after the man has touched it?"

"All its power goes inside the man, and the kernel is free. It becomes just another kernel. It may be left at the site of the witchcraft, or it may be swept away; it does not matter. It is better to sweep it away into the underbrush, where a bird will eat it."

"Can a bird eat it before the man touches it?"

"No. No bird is that stupid, I assure you. The birds stay away from it."

Don Juan then described a very complex procedure by which such power kernels can be obtained.

"You must bear in mind that maíz-pinto is merely an instrument, not an ally," he said. "Once you make that distinction you will have no problem. But if you consider such tools to be supreme, you will be a fool."

"Are the power objects as powerful as an ally?" I asked.

Don Juan laughed scornfully before answering. It seemed that he was trying hard to be patient with me.

"Maíz-pinto, crystals, and feathers are mere toys in comparison with an ally," he said. "These power objects are necessary only when a man does not have an ally. It is a waste of time to pursue them, especially for you. You should be trying to get an ally; when you succeed, you will understand what I am telling you now. Power objects are like a game for children."

"Don't get me wrong, don Juan," I protested. "I want to have an ally, but I also want to know everything I can. You yourself have said that knowledge is power."

"No!" he said emphatically. "Power rests on the kind of knowledge one holds. What is the sense of knowing things that are useless?"

In don Juan's system of beliefs, the acquisition of an ally meant exclusively the exploitation of the states of nonordinary reality he produced in me through the use of hallucinogenic plants. He believed that by focusing on these states and omitting other aspects of the knowledge he taught I would arrive at a coherent view of the phenomena I had experienced.

I have therefore divided this book into two parts. In the first part I present selections from my field notes dealing with the states of nonordinary reality I underwent during my apprenticeship. As I have arranged my notes to fit the continuity of the narrative, they are not always in proper chronological sequence. I never wrote my description of a state of nonordinary reality until several days after I had experienced it, waiting until I was able to treat it calmly and objectively. My conversations with don Juan, however, were taken down as they occurred, immediately after each state of nonordinary reality. My reports of these conversations, therefore, sometimes antedate the full description of an experience.

My field notes disclose the subjective version of what I perceived while undergoing the experience. That version is presented here just as I narrated it to don Juan, who demanded a complete and faithful recollection of every detail and a full recounting of each experience. At the time of recording these experiences, I added incidental details in an attempt to recapture the total setting of each state of nonordinary reality. I wanted to describe the emotional impact I had experienced as completely as possible.

My field notes also reveal the content of don Juan's system of beliefs. I have condensed long papers of questions and answers between don Juan and myself in order to avoid reproducing the repetitiveness of conversation. But as I also want to reflect accurately the overall mood of our exchanges, I have deleted only dialogue that contributed nothing to my understanding of his way of knowledge. The information don Juan gave me about his way of knowledge was always sporadic, and for every spurt on his part there were hours of probing on mine. Nevertheless, there were innumerable occasions on which he freely expounded his knowledge.

In the second part of this book I present a structural analysis drawn exclusively from the data reported in the first part. Through my analysis I seek to support the following contentions: (1) don Juan presented his teachings as a system of logical thought; (2) the system made sense only if examined in the light of its structural units; and (3) the system was devised to guide an apprentice to a level of conceptualization which explained the order of the phenomena he had experienced.

PART ONE

The Teachings

1

My notes on my first session with don Juan are dated June 23, 1961. That was the occasion when the teachings began. I had seen him several times previously in the capacity of an observer only. At every opportunity I had asked him to teach me about peyote. He ignored my request every time, but he never completely dismissed the subject, and I interpreted his hesitancy as a possibility that he might be inclined to talk about his knowledge with more coaxing.

In this particular session he made it obvious to me that he might consider my request provided I possessed clarity of mind and purpose in reference to what I had asked him. It was impossible for me to fulfill such a condition, for I had asked him to teach me about peyote only as a means of establishing a link of communication with him. I thought his familiarity with the subject might predispose him to be more open and willing to talk, thus allowing me an entrance into his knowledge on the properties of plants. He had interpreted my request literally, however, and was concerned about my purpose in wishing to learn about peyote.

Friday, June 23, 1961

"Would you teach me about peyote, don Juan?"

"Why would you like to undertake such learning?"

"I really would like to know about it. Is not just to want to know a good reason?"

"No! You must search in your heart and find out why a young man like you wants to undertake such a task of learning."

"Why did you learn about it yourself, don Juan?"

"Why do you ask that?"

"Maybe we both have the same reasons."

"I doubt that. I am an Indian. We don't have the same paths."

"The only reason I have is that I *want* to learn about it, just to know. But I assure you, don Juan, my intentions are not bad."

"I believe you. I've smoked you."

"I beg your pardon!"

"It doesn't matter now. I know your intentions."

"Do you mean you saw through me?"

"You could put it that way."

"Will you teach me, then?"

"No!"

"Is it because I'm not an Indian?"

"No. It is because you don't know your heart. What is important is that you know exactly why you want to involve yourself. Learning about 'Mescalito' is a most serious act. If you were an Indian your desire alone would be sufficient. Very few Indians have such a desire."

Sunday, June 25, 1961

I stayed with don Juan all afternoon on Friday. I was going to leave about 7 P.M. We were sitting on the porch in front of his house and I decided to ask him once more about the teaching. It was almost a routine question and I expected him to refuse again. I asked

him if there was a way in which he could accept just
my desire to learn, as if I were an Indian. He took a
long time to answer. I was compelled to stay because
he seemed to be trying to decide something.

Finally he told me that there was a way, and proceeded to delineate a problem. He pointed out that I
was very tired sitting on the floor, and that the proper
thing to do was to find a "spot" *(sitio)* on the floor
where I could sit without fatigue. I had been sitting
with my knees up against my chest and my arms locked
around my calves. When he said I was tired, I realized
that my back ached and that I was quite exhausted.

I waited for him to explain what he meant by a
"spot," but he made no overt attempt to elucidate the
point. I thought that perhaps he meant that I should
change positions, so I got up and sat closer to him.
He protested my movement and clearly emphasized
that a spot meant a place where a man could feel
naturally happy and strong. He patted the place where
he sat and said it was his own spot, adding that he had
posed a riddle I had to solve by myself without any
further deliberation.

What he had posed as a problem to be solved was
certainly a riddle. I had no idea how to begin or even
what he had in mind. Several times I asked for a clue,
or at least a hint, as to how to proceed in locating a
point where I felt happy and strong. I insisted and
argued that I had no idea what he really meant because
I couldn't conceive the problem. He suggested I walk
around the porch until I found the spot.

I got up and began to pace the floor. I felt silly
and sat down in front of him.

He became very annoyed with me and accused me of
not listening, saying that perhaps I did not want to
learn. After a while he calmed down and explained to
me that not every place was good to sit or be on, and
that within the confines of the porch there was one
spot that was unique, a spot where I could be at my
very best. It was my task to distinguish it from all the
other places. The general pattern was that I had to

"feel" all the possible spots that were accessible until I could determine without a doubt which was the right one.

I argued that although the porch was not too large (12 x 8 feet), the number of possible spots was overwhelming, and it would take me a very long time to check all of them, and that since he had not specified the size of the spot, the possibilities might be infinite. My arguments were futile. He got up and very sternly warned me that it might take me days to figure it out, but that if I did not solve the problem, I might as well leave because he would have nothing to say to me. He emphasized that he knew where my spot was, and that therefore I could not lie to him; he said this was the only way he could accept my desire to learn about Mescalito as a valid reason. He added that nothing in this world was a gift, that whatever there was to learn had to be learned the hard way.

He went around the house to the chaparral to urinate. He returned directly into his house through the back.

I thought the assignment to find the alleged spot of happiness was his own way of dismissing me, but I got up and started to pace back and forth. The sky was clear. I could see everything on and near the porch. I must have paced for an hour or more, but nothing happened to reveal the location of the spot. I got tired of walking and sat down; after a few minutes I sat somewhere else, and then at another place, until I had covered the whole floor in a semisystematic fashion. I deliberately tried to "feel" differences between places, but I lacked the criteria for differentiation. I felt I was wasting my time, but I stayed. My rationalization was that I had come a long way just to see don Juan, and I really had nothing else to do.

I lay down on my back and put my hands under my head like a pillow. Then I rolled over and lay on my stomach for a while. I repeated this rolling process over the entire floor. For the first time I thought I had stumbled upon a vague criterion. I felt warmer when I lay on my back.

I rolled again, this time in the opposite direction, and again covered the length of the floor, lying face down on all the places where I had lain face up during my first rolling tour. I experienced the same warm and cold sensations, depending on my position, but there was no difference between spots.

Then an idea occurred to me which I thought to be brilliant: don Juan's spot! I sat there, and then lay, face down at first, and later on my back, but the place was just like all the others. I stood up. I had had enough. I wanted to say good-bye to don Juan, but I was embarrassed to wake him up. I looked at my watch. It was two o'clock in the morning! I had been rolling for six hours.

At that moment don Juan came out and went around the house to the chaparral. He came back and stood at the door. I felt utterly dejected, and I wanted to say something nasty to him and leave. But I realized that it was not his fault; that it was my own choice to go through all that nonsense. I told him I had failed; I had been rolling on his floor like an idiot all night and still couldn't make any sense of his riddle.

He laughed and said that it did not surprise him because I had not proceeded correctly. I had not been using my eyes. That was true, yet I was very sure he had said to feel the difference. I brought that point up, but he argued that one can feel with the eyes, when the eyes are not looking right into things. As far as I was concerned, he said, I had no other means to solve this problem but to use all I had—my eyes.

He went inside. I was certain that he had been watching me. I thought there was no other way for him to know that I had not been using my eyes.

I began to roll again, because that was the most comfortable procedure. This time, however, I rested my chin on my hands and looked at every detail.

After an interval the darkness around me changed. When I focused on the point directly in front of me, the whole peripheral area of my field of vision became brilliantly colored with a homogeneous greenish yellow.

The effect was startling. I kept my eyes fixed on the point in front of me and began to crawl sideways on my stomach, one foot at a time.

Suddenly, at a point near the middle of the floor, I became aware of another change in hue. At a place to my right, still in the periphery of my field of vision, the greenish yellow became intensely purple. I concentrated my attention on it. The purple faded into a pale, but still brilliant, color which remained steady for the time I kept my attention on it.

I marked the place with my jacket, and called don Juan. He came out to the porch. I was truly excited; I had actually seen the change in hues. He seemed unimpressed, but told me to sit on the spot and report to him what kind of feeling I had.

I sat down and then lay on my back. He stood by me and asked me repeatedly how I felt; but I did not feel anything different. For about fifteen minutes I tried to feel or to see a difference, while don Juan stood by me patiently. I felt disgusted. I had a metallic taste in my mouth. Suddenly I had developed a headache. I was about to get sick. The thought of my nonsensical endeavors irritated me to a point of fury. I got up.

Don Juan must have noticed my profound frustration. He did not laugh, but very seriously stated that I had to be inflexible with myself if I wanted to learn. Only two choices were open to me, he said: either to quit and go home, in which case I would never learn, or to solve the riddle.

He went inside again. I wanted to leave immediately, but I was too tired to drive; besides, perceiving the hues had been so startling that I was sure it was a criterion of some sort, and perhaps there were other changes to be detected. Anyway, it was too late to leave. So I sat down, stretched my legs back, and began all over again.

During this round I moved rapidly through each place, passing don Juan's spot, to the end of the floor, and then turned around to cover the outer edge. When I reached the center, I realized that another change in coloration was taking place, again on the edge of my field of vision. The uniform chartreuse I was seeing all over the area turned, at one spot to my right, into a sharp verdigris. It remained for a moment and then abruptly metamorphosed into another steady hue, different from the other one I had detected earlier. I took off one of my shoes and marked the point, and kept on rolling until I had covered the floor in all possible directions. No other change of coloration took place.

I came back to the point marked with my shoe, and examined it. It was located five to six feet away from the spot marked by my jacket, in a southeasterly direction. There was a large rock next to it. I lay down there for quite some time trying to find clues, looking at every detail, but I did not feel anything different.

I decided to try the other spot. I quickly pivoted on my knees and was about to lie down on my jacket when I felt an unusual apprehension. It was more like a physical sensation of something actually pushing on my stomach. I jumped up and retreated in one movement. The hair on my neck pricked up. My legs had arched slightly, my trunk was bent forward, and my arms stuck out in front of me rigidly with my fingers contracted like a claw. I took notice of my strange posture and my fright increased.

I walked back involuntarily and sat down on the rock next to my shoe. From the rock, I slumped to the floor. I tried to figure out what had happened to cause me such a fright. I thought it must have been the fatigue I was experiencing. It was nearly daytime. I felt silly and embarrassed. Yet I had no way to explain what had frightened me, nor had I figured out what don Juan wanted.

I decided to give it one last try. I got up and slowly approached the place marked by my jacket, and again I felt the same apprehension. This time I made a strong effort to control myself. I sat down, and then knelt in order to lie face down, but I could not lie in spite of my will. I put my hands on the floor in front of me. My breathing accelerated; my stomach was upset. I had a clear sensation of panic, and fought not to run away. I thought don Juan was perhaps watching me. Slowly I crawled back to the other spot and propped my back against the rock. I wanted to rest for a while to organize my thoughts, but I fell asleep.

I heard don Juan talking and laughing above my head. I woke up.

"You have found the spot," he said.

I did not understand him at first, but he assured me again that the place where I had fallen asleep was the spot in question. He again asked me how I felt lying there. I told him I really did not notice any difference.

He asked me to compare my feelings at that moment with what I had felt while lying on the other spot. For the first time it occurred to me that I could not possibly explain my apprehension of the preceding night. He urged me in a kind of challenging way to sit on the other spot. For some inexplicable reason I was actually afraid of the other place, and did not sit on it. He asserted that only a fool could fail to see the difference.

I asked him if each of the two spots had a special name. He said that the good one was called the *sitio* and the bad one the enemy; he said these two places were the key to a man's well-being, especially for a man who was pursuing knowledge. The sheer act of sitting on one's spot created superior strength; on the other hand, the enemy weakened a man and could even cause his death. He said I had replenished my energy, which I had spent lavishly the night before, by taking a nap on my spot.

He also said that the colors I had seen in association with each specific spot had the same overall effect of giving strength or of curtailing it.

I asked him if there were other spots for me like the two I had found, and how I should go about finding them. He said that many places in the world would be comparable to those two, and that the best way to find them was by detecting their respective colors.

It was not clear to me whether or not I had solved the problem, and in fact I was not even convinced that there had been a problem; I could not avoid feeling that the whole experience was forced and arbitrary. I was certain that don Juan had watched me all night and then proceeded to humor me by saying that wherever I had fallen asleep *was* the place I was looking for. Yet I failed to see a logical reason for such an act, and when he challenged me to sit on the other spot I could not do it. There was a strange cleavage between my pragmatic experience of fearing the "other spot" and my rational deliberations about the total event.

Don Juan, on the other hand, was very sure I had succeeded, and, acting in accordance with my success, let me know he was going to teach me about peyote.

"You asked me to teach you about Mescalito," he said. "I wanted to find out if you had enough backbone to meet him face to face. Mescalito is not something to make fun of. You must have command over your resources. Now I know I can take your desire alone as a good reason to learn."

"You really are going to teach me about peyote?"

"I prefer to call him Mescalito. Do the same."

"When are you going to start?"

"It is not so simple as that. You must be ready first."

"I think I am ready."

"This is not a joke. You must wait until there is no doubt, and then you will meet him."

"Do I have to prepare myself?"

"No. You simply have to wait. You may give up the whole idea after a while. You get tired easily. Last night you were ready to quit as soon as it got difficult. Mescalito requires a very serious intent."

2

Monday, August 7, 1961

I arrived at don Juan's house in Arizona about seven o'clock on Friday night. Five other Indians were sitting with him on the porch of his house. I greeted him and sat waiting for them to say something. After a formal silence one of the men got up, walked over to me, and said, "Buenas noches." I stood up and answered, "Buenas noches." Then all the other men got up and came to me and we all mumbled "buenas noches" and shook hands either by barely touching one another's fingertips or by holding the hand for an instant and then dropping it quite abruptly.

We all sat down again. They seemed to be rather shy—at a loss for words, although they all spoke Spanish.

It must have been about half past seven when suddenly they all got up and walked toward the back of the house. Nobody had said a word for a long time. Don Juan signaled me to follow and we all got inside an old pickup truck parked there. I sat in the back with don Juan and two younger men. There were no cushions or benches and the metal floor was painfully hard, especially when we left the highway and got onto a dirt road. Don Juan whispered that we were going to the house of one of his friends who had seven mescalitos for me.

I asked him, "Don't you have any of them yourself, don Juan?"

"I do, but I couldn't offer them to you. You see, someone else has to do this."

"Can you tell me why?"

"Perhaps you are not agreeable to 'him' and 'he' won't like you, and then you will never be able to

36

know 'him' with affection, as one should; and our
friendship will be broken."

"Why wouldn't he like me? I have never done anything to him."

"You don't have to *do* anything to be liked or dis-
liked. He either takes you, or throws you away."

"But, if he doesn't take me, isn't there anything I can
do to make him like me?"

The other two men seemed to have overheard my
question and laughed.

"No! I can't think of anything one can do," don
Juan said.

He turned half away from me and I could not talk
to him anymore.

We must have driven for at least an hour before we
stopped in front of a small house. It was quite dark,
and after the driver had turned off the headlights I could
make out only the vague contour of the building.

A young woman, a Mexican, judging by her speech
inflection, was yelling at a dog to make him stop barking. We got out of the truck and walked into the house.
The men mumbled "Buenas noches" as they went by
her. She answered back and went on yelling at the dog.

The room was large and was stacked up with a multitude of objects. A dim light from a very small electric
bulb rendered the scene quite gloomy. There were quite
a few chairs with broken legs and sagging seats leaning
against the walls. Three of the men sat down on a
couch, which was the largest single piece of furniture
in the room. It was very old and had sagged down all
the way to the floor; in the dim light it seemed to be
red and dirty. The rest of us sat in chairs. We sat in
silence for a long time.

One of the men suddenly got up and went into
another room. He was perhaps in his fifties, dark, tall,
and husky. He came back a moment later with a coffee
jar. He opened the lid and handed the jar to me; inside
there were seven odd-looking items. They varied in size
and consistency. Some of them were almost round,
others were elongated. They felt to the touch like the

pulp of walnuts, or the surface of cork. Their brownish color made them look like hard, dry nutshells. I handled them, rubbing their surfaces for quite some time.

"This is to be chewed [*esto se masca*]," don Juan said in a whisper.

I had not realized that he had sat next to me until he spoke. I looked at the other men, but no one was looking at me; they were talking among themselves in very low voices. This was a moment of acute indecision and fear. I felt almost unable to control myself.

"I have to go to the bathroom," I said to him. "I'll go outside and take a walk."

He handed me the coffee jar and I put the peyote buttons in it. I was leaving the room when the man who had given me the jar stood up, came to me, and said he had a toilet bowl in the other room.

The toilet was almost against the door. Next to it, nearly touching the toilet, was a large bed which occupied more than half of the room. The woman was sleeping there. I stood motionless at the door for a while, then I came back to the room where the other men were.

The man who owned the house spoke to me in English: "Don Juan says you're from South America. Is there any mescal there?" I told him that I had never even heard of it.

They seemed to be interested in South America and we talked about the Indians for a while. Then one of the men asked me why I wanted to eat peyote. I told him that I wanted to know what it was like. They all laughed shyly.

Don Juan urged me softly, "Chew it, chew it [*Masca, masca*]."

My hands were wet and my stomach contracted. The jar with the peyote buttons was on the floor by the chair. I bent over, took one at random, and put it in my mouth. It had a stale taste. I bit it in two and started to chew one of the pieces. I felt a strong, pungent bitterness; in a moment my whole mouth was numb. The bitterness increased as I kept on chewing, forcing an incredible flow of saliva. My gums and the inside of my mouth felt as if I had eaten salty, dry meat or fish, which seems to force one to chew more. After a while I chewed the other piece and my mouth was so numb I couldn't feel the bitterness anymore. The peyote button was a bunch of shreds, like the fibrous part of an orange or like sugarcane, and I didn't know whether to swallow it or spit it out. At that moment the owner of the house got up and invited everybody to go out to the porch.

We went out and sat in the darkness. It was quite comfortable outside, and the host brought out a bottle of tequila.

The men were seated in a row with their backs to the wall. I was at the extreme right of the line. Don Juan, who was next to me, placed the jar with the peyote buttons between my legs. Then he handed me the bottle, which was passed down the line, and told me to take some of the tequila to wash away the bitterness.

I spit out the shreds of the first button and took a sip. He told me not to swallow it, but to just rinse out my mouth with it to stop the saliva. It did not help much with the saliva, but it certainly helped to wash away some of the bitterness.

Don Juan gave me a piece of dried apricot, or perhaps it was a dried fig—I couldn't see it in the dark, nor could I taste it—and told me to chew it thoroughly and slowly, without rushing. I had difficulty swallowing it; it felt as if it would not go down.

After a short pause the bottle went around again. Don Juan handed me a piece of crispy dried meat. I told him I did not feel like eating.

"This is not eating," he said firmly.

The pattern was repeated six times. I remember having chewed six peyote buttons when the conversation became very lively; although I could not distinguish what language was spoken, the topic of the conversation, in which everybody participated, was very interesting, and I attempted to listen carefully so that I could take part. But when I tried to speak I realized I couldn't; the words shifted aimlessly about in my mind.

I sat with my back propped against the wall and listened to what the men were saying. They were talking in Italian, and repeated over and over one phrase about the stupidity of sharks. I thought it was a logical coherent topic. I had told don Juan earlier that the Colorado River in Arizona was called by the early Spaniards "el rio de los tizones [the river of charred wood]"; and someone misspelled or misread "tizones," and the river was called "el rio de los tiburones [the river of the sharks]." I was sure they were discussing that story, yet it never occurred to me to think that none of them could speak Italian.

I had a very strong desire to throw up, but I don't recall the actual act. I asked if somebody would get me some water. I was experiencing an unbearable thirst.

Don Juan brought me a large saucepan. He placed it on the ground next to the wall. He also brought a little cup or can. He dipped it into the pan and handed it to me, and said I could not drink but should just freshen my mouth with it.

The water looked strangely shiny, glossy, like a thick varnish. I wanted to ask don Juan about it and laboriously I tried to voice my thoughts in English, but then I realized he did not speak English. I experienced a very confusing moment, and became aware of the fact that although there was a clear thought in my mind, I could not speak. I wanted to comment on the strange quality of the water, but what followed next was not speech; it was the feeling of my unvoiced thoughts coming out of my mouth in a sort of liquid form. It was an effortless sensation of vomiting without the contractions of the diaphragm. It was a pleasant flow of liquid words.

I drank. And the feeling that I was vomiting disappeared. By that time all noises had vanished and I found I had difficulty focusing my eyes. I looked for don Juan and as I turned my head I noticed that my field of vision had diminished to a circular area in front of my eyes. This feeling was neither frightening nor discomforting, but, quite to the contrary, it was a novelty; I could literally sweep the ground by focusing on one spot and then moving my head slowly in any direction. When I had first come out to the porch I had noticed it was all dark except for the distant glare of the city lights. Yet within the circular area of my vision everything was clear. I forgot about my concern with don Juan and the other men, and gave myself entirely to exploring the ground with my pinpoint vision.

I saw the juncture of the porch floor and the wall. I turned my head slowly to the right, following the wall, and saw don Juan sitting against it. I shifted my head to the left in order to focus on the water. I found the bottom of the pan; I raised my head slightly and saw a medium-size black dog approaching. I saw him coming toward the water. The dog began to drink. I raised my hand to push him away from my water; I focused my pinpoint vision on the dog to carry on the movement, and suddenly I saw him become transparent. The water was a shiny, viscous liquid. I saw it going down the dog's throat into his body. I saw it flowing evenly through his entire length and then shooting out through each one of the hairs. I saw the iridescent fluid traveling along the length of each individual hair and then projecting out of the hairs to form a long, white, silky mane.

At that moment I had the sensation of intense convulsions, and in a matter of instants a tunnel formed around me, very low and narrow, hard and strangely cold. It felt to the touch like a wall of solid tinfoil. I found I was sitting on the tunnel floor. I tried to stand up, but hit my head on the metal roof, and the tunnel compressed itself until it was suffocating me. I remember having to crawl toward a sort of round point where the tunnel ended; when I finally arrived, if I did, I had forgotten all about the dog, don Juan, and myself. I was exhausted. My clothes were soaked in a cold, sticky liquid. I rolled back and forth trying to find a position in which to rest, a position where my heart would not pound so hard. In one of those shifts I saw the dog again.

Every memory came back to me at once, and suddenly all was clear in my mind. I turned around to look for don Juan, but I could not distinguish anything or anyone. All I was capable of seeing was the dog becoming iridescent; an intense light radiated from his body. I saw again the water flowing through him, kindling him like a bonfire. I got to the water, sank my face in the pan, and drank with him. My hands were in front of me on the ground, and, as I drank, I saw the fluid running through my veins setting up hues of red and yellow and green. I drank more and more. I drank until I was all afire; I was all aglow. I drank until the fluid went out of my body through each pore, and projected out like fibers of silk, and I too acquired a long, lustrous, iridescent mane. I looked at the dog and his mane was like mine. A supreme happiness filled my whole body, and we ran together toward a sort of yellow warmth that came from some indefinite place. And there we played. We played and wrestled until I knew his wishes and he knew mine. We took turns manipulating each other in the fashion of a puppet show. I could make him move his legs by twisting my toes, and every time he nodded his head I felt an irresistible impulse to jump. But his most impish act was to make me scratch my head with my foot while I sat; he did it by flapping his ears from side to side. The action was to me utterly, unbearably funny. Such a touch of grace and irony; such mastery, I thought. The euphoria that possessed me was indescribable. I laughed until it was almost impossible to breathe.

I had the clear sensation of not being able to open my eyes; I was looking through a tank of water. It was a long and very painful state filled with the anxiety of not being able to wake up and yet being awake. Then slowly the world became clear and in focus. My field of vision became again very round and ample, and with it came an ordinary conscious act, which was to turn around and look for that marvelous being. At this point

I encountered the most difficult transition. The passage
from my normal state had taken place almost without
my realizing it: I was aware; my thoughts and feelings
were a corollary of that awareness; and the passing was
smooth and clear. But this second change, the awakening
to serious, sober consciousness, was genuinely shock-
ing. I had forgotten I was a man! The sadness of such
an irreconcilable situation was so intense that I wept.

Saturday, August 5, 1961

Later that morning, after breakfast, the owner of the
house, don Juan, and I drove back to don Juan's place.
I was very tired, but I couldn't go to sleep in the truck.
Only after the man had left did I fall asleep on the
porch of don Juan's house.

When I woke up it was dark; don Juan had covered
me up with a blanket. I looked for him, but he was
not in the house. He came later with a pot of fried
beans and a stack of tortillas. I was extremely hungry.

After we had finished eating and were resting he
asked me to tell him all that had happened to me the
night before. I related my experience in great detail
and as accurately as possible.

When I finished he nodded his head and said, "I think
you are fine. It is difficult for me to explain now how
and why. But I think it went all right for you. You see,
sometimes he is playful, like a child; at other times he
is terrible, fearsome. He either frolics, or he is dead
serious. It is impossible to know beforehand what he
will be like with another person. Yet, when one knows
him well—sometimes. You played with him tonight.
You are the only person I know who has had such an
encounter."

"In what way does my experience differ from that
of others?"

"You're not an Indian; therefore it is hard for me to
figure out what is what. Yet he either takes people or
rejects them, regardless of whether they are Indians or
not. That I know. I have seen numbers of them. I also

know that he frolics, he makes some people laugh, but never have I seen him play with anyone."

"Can you tell me now, don Juan, how does peyote protect . . ."

He did not let me finish. Vigorously he touched me on the shoulder.

"Don't you ever name him that way. You haven't seen enough of him yet to know him."

"How does Mescalito protect people?"

"He advises. He answers whatever questions you ask."

"Then Mescalito is real? I mean he is something you can see?"

He seemed to be baffled by my question. He looked at me with a sort of blank expression.

"What I meant to say, is that Mescalito . . ."

"I heard what you said. Didn't you see him last night?"

I wanted to say that I saw only a dog, but I noticed his bewildered look.

"Then you think what I saw last night was him?"

He looked at me with contempt. He chuckled, shook his head as though he couldn't believe it, and in a very intelligent tone he added, "A poco crees que era tu—mamá [Don't tell me you believe it was your—mama]?" He paused before saying "mamá" because what he meant to say was "tu chingada madre," an idiom used as a disrespectful allusion to the other party's mother. The word "mamá" was so incongruous that we both laughed for a long time.

Then I realized he had fallen asleep and had not answered my question.

Sunday, August 6, 1961

I drove don Juan to the house where I had taken peyote. On the way he told me that the name of the man who had "offered me to Mescalito" was John. When we got to the house we found John sitting on his porch with two young men. All of them were extremely jovial. They laughed and talked with great ease. The three of them spoke English perfectly. I told John that I had come to thank him for having helped me.

I wanted to get their views on my behavior during the hallucinogenic experience, and told them I had been trying to think of what I had done that night and that I couldn't remember. They laughed and were reluctant to talk about it. They seemed to be holding back on account of don Juan. They all glanced at him as though waiting for an affirmative cue to go on. Don Juan must have cued them, although I did not notice anything, because suddenly John began to tell me what I had done that night.

He said he knew I had been "taken" when he heard me puking. He estimated that I must have puked thirty times. Don Juan corrected him and said it was only ten times.

John continued: "Then we all moved next to you. You were stiff, and were having convulsions. For a very long time, while lying on your back, you moved your mouth as though talking. Then you began to bump your head on the floor, and don Juan put an old hat on your head and you stopped it. You shivered and whined for hours, lying on the floor. I think everybody fell asleep then; but I heard you puffing and groaning in my sleep. Then I heard you scream and I woke up. I saw you leaping up in the air, screaming. You made a dash for the water, knocked the pan over, and began to swim in the puddle.

"Don Juan brought you more water. You sat quietly in front of the pan. Then you jumped up and took off all your clothes. You were kneeling in front of the water, drinking in big gulps. Then you just sat there and stared into space. We thought you were going to be there forever. Nearly everybody was asleep, including don Juan, when suddenly you jumped up again, howling, and took after the dog. The dog got scared and howled too, and ran to the back of the house. Then everybody woke up.

"We all got up. You came back from the other side

still chasing the dog. The dog was running ahead of you barking and howling. I think you must have gone twenty times around the house, running in circles, barking like a dog. I was afraid people were going to be curious. There are no neighbors close, but your howling was so loud it could have been heard for miles."

One of the young men added, "You caught up with the dog and brought it to the porch in your arms."

John continued: "Then you began to play with the dog. You wrestled with him, and the dog and you bit each other and played. That, I thought, was funny. My dog does not play usually. But this time you and the dog were rolling on each other."

"Then you ran to the water and the dog drank with you," the young man said. "You ran five or six times to the water with the dog."

"How long did this go on?" I asked.

"Hours," John said. "At one time we lost sight of you two. I think you must have run to the back. We just heard you barking and groaning. You sounded so much like a dog that we couldn't tell you two apart."

"Maybe it was just the dog alone," I said.

They laughed, and John said, "You were barking there, boy!"

"What happened next?"

The three men looked at one another and seemed to have a hard time deciding what happened next. Finally the young man who had not yet said anything spoke up.

"He choked," he said, looking at John.

"Yes, you certainly choked. You began to cry very strangely, and then you fell to the floor. We thought you were biting your tongue; don Juan opened your jaws and poured water on your face. Then you started shivering and having convulsions all over again. Then you stayed motionless for a long time. Don Juan said it was all over. By then it was morning, so we covered you with a blanket and left you to sleep on the porch."

He stopped there and looked at the other men who were obviously trying not to laugh. He turned to don Juan and asked him something: Don Juan smiled and answered the question. John turned to me and said, "We left you here on the porch because we were afraid you were going to piss all over the rooms."

They all laughed very loudly.

"What was the matter with me?" I asked. "Did I . . ."

"Did you?" John sort of mimicked me. "We were not going to mention it, but don Juan says it is all right. You pissed all over my dog!"

"What did I do?"

"You don't think the dog was running because he was afraid of you, do you? The dog was running because you were pissing on him."

There was general laughter at this point. I tried to question one of the young men, but they were all laughing and he didn't hear me.

John went on: "My dog got even though; he pissed on you too!"

This statement was apparently utterly funny because they all roared with laughter, including don Juan. When they had quieted down, I asked in all earnestness, "Is it really true? This really happened?"

Still laughing, John replied: "I swear my dog really pissed on you."

Driving back to don Juan's place I asked him: "Did all that really happen, don Juan?"

"Yes," he said, "but they don't know what you saw. They don't realize you were playing with 'him.' That is why I did not disturb you."

"But is this business of the dog and me pissing on each other true?"

"It was not a dog! How many times do I have to tell you that? This is the only way to understand it. It's the only way! It was 'he' who played with you."

"Did you know all this was happening before I told you about it?"

He vacillated for an instant before answering.

"No, I remembered, after you told me about it, the strange way you looked. I just suspected you were doing fine because you didn't seem scared."

"Did the dog really play with me as they say?"

"Goddammit! It was not a dog!"

Thursday, August 17, 1961

I told don Juan how I felt about my experience. From the point of view of my intended work it had been a disastrous event. I said I did not care for another similar "encounter" with Mescalito. I agreed that everything that had happened to me had been more than interesting, but added that nothing in it could really move me toward seeking it again. I seriously believed that I was not constructed for that type of endeavor. Peyote had produced in me, as a postreaction, a strange kind of physical discomfort. It was an indefinite fear or unhappiness; a melancholy of some sort, which I could not define exactly. And I did not find that state noble in any way.

Don Juan laughed and said, "You are beginning to learn."

"This type of learning is not for me. I am not made for it, don Juan."

"You always exaggerate."

"This is not exaggeration."

"It is. The only trouble is that you exaggerate the bad points only."

"There are no good points so far as I am concerned. All I know is that it makes me afraid."

"There is nothing wrong with being afraid. When you fear, you see things in a different way."

"But I don't care about seeing things in a different way, don Juan. I think I am going to leave the learning about Mescalito alone. I can't handle it, don Juan. This is really a bad situation for me."

"Of course it is bad—even for me. You are not the only one who is baffled."

"Why should you be baffled, don Juan?"

"I have been thinking about what I saw the other night. Mescalito actually played with you. That baffled me, because it was an indication [omen]."

"What kind of an indication, don Juan?"

"Mescalito was pointing you out to me."

"What for?"

"It wasn't clear to me then, but now it is. He meant you were the 'chosen man' [*escogido*]. Mescalito pointed you out to me and by doing that he told me you were the chosen man."

"Do you mean I was chosen among others for some task, or something of the sort?"

"No. What I mean is, Mescalito told me you could be the man I am looking for."

"When did he tell you that, don Juan?"

"By playing with you, he told me that. This makes you the chosen man for me."

"What does it mean to be the chosen man?"

"There are some secrets I know [*Tengo secretos*]. I have secrets I won't be able to reveal to anyone unless I find my chosen man. The other night when I saw you playing with Mescalito it was clear to me you were that man. But you are not an Indian. How baffling!"

"But what does it mean to me, don Juan? What do I have to do?"

"I've made up my mind and I am going to teach you the secrets that make up the lot of a man of knowledge."

"Do you mean the secrets about Mescalito?"

"Yes, but those are not all the secrets I know. There are others, of a different kind, which I would like to give to someone. I had a teacher myself, my benefactor, and I also became his chosen man upon performing a certain feat. He taught me all I know."

I asked him again what this new role would require of me; he said learning was the only thing involved, learning in the sense of what I had experienced in the two sessions with him.

The way in which the situation had evolved was quite strange. I had made up my mind to tell him I was going to give up the idea of learning about peyote, and then before I could really make my point, he offered to teach me his "knowledge." I did not know what he meant by that, but I felt that this sudden turn was very serious. I argued I had no qualifications for such a task, as it required a rare kind of courage which I did not have. I had told him that my bent of character was to talk about acts others performed. I wanted to hear his views and opinions about everything. I told him I could be happy if I could sit there and listen to him talk for days. To me, *that* would be learning.

He listened without interrupting me. I talked for a long time. Then he said:

"All this is very easy to understand. Fear is the first natural enemy a man must overcome on his path to knowledge. Besides, you are curious. That evens up the score. And you will learn in spite of yourself; that's the rule."

I protested for a while longer, trying to dissuade him. But he seemed to be convinced there was nothing else I could do but learn.

"You are not thinking in the proper order," he said. "Mescalito actually played with you. That's the point to think about. Why don't you dwell on that instead of on your fear?"

"Was it so unusual?"

"You are the only person I have ever seen playing with him. You are not used to this kind of life; therefore the indications [omens] bypass you. Yet you are a serious person, but your seriousness is attached to what you do, not to what goes on outside you. You dwell upon yourself too much. That's the trouble. And that produces a terrible fatigue."

"But what else can anyone do, don Juan?"

"Seek and see the marvels all around you. You will get tired of looking at yourself alone, and that fatigue will make you deaf and blind to everything else."

"You have a point, don Juan, but how can I change?"

"Think about the wonder of Mescalito playing with you. Think about nothing else: The rest will come to you of itself."

Sunday, August 20, 1961

Last night don Juan proceeded to usher me into the
realm of his knowledge. We sat in front of his house
in the dark. Suddenly, after a long silence, we began to
talk. He said he was going to advise me with the same
words his own benefactor had used the first day he took
him as his apprentice. Don Juan had apparently mem-
orized the words, for he repeated them several times, to
make sure I did not miss any:

"A man goes to knowledge as he goes to war, wide-
awake, with fear, with respect, and with absolute assurance. Going to knowledge or going to war in any
other manner is a mistake, and whoever makes it will
live to regret his steps."

I asked him why was it so and he said that when
a man has fulfilled those four requisites there are no
mistakes for which he will have to account; under such
conditions his acts lose the blundering quality of a
fool's acts. If such a man fails, or suffers a defeat, he
will have lost only a battle, and there will be no pitiful
regrets over that.

Then he said he intended to teach me about an "ally"
in the very same way his own benefactor had taught him.
He put strong emphasis on the words "very same way,"
repeating the phrase several times.

An "ally," he said, is a power a man can bring into
his life to help him, advise him, and give him the
strength necessary to perform acts, whether big or
small, right or wrong. This ally is necessary to enhance a
man's life, guide his acts, and further his knowledge.
In fact, an ally is the indispensable aid to knowing.
Don Juan said this with great conviction and force. He
seemed to choose his words carefully. He repeated the
following sentence four times:

"An ally will make you see and understand things
about which no human being could possibly enlighten
you."

"Is an ally something like a guardian spirit?"

"It is neither a guardian nor a spirit. It is an aid."

"Is Mescalito your ally?"

"No! Mescalito is another kind of power. A unique power! A protector, a teacher."

"What makes Mescalito different from an ally?"

"He can't be tamed and used as an ally is tamed and used. Mescalito is outside oneself. He chooses to show himself in many forms to whoever stands in front of him, regardless of whether that person is a brujo or a farm boy."

Don Juan spoke with deep fervor about Mescalito's being the teacher of the proper way to live. I asked him how Mescalito taught the "proper way of life," and don Juan replied that Mescalito *showed* how to live.

"How does he show it?" I asked.

"He has many ways of showing it. Sometimes he shows it on his hand, or on the rocks, or the trees, or just in front of you."

"Is it like a picture in front of you?"

"No. It is a teaching in front of you."

"Does Mescalito talk to the person?"

"Yes. But not in words."

"How does he talk, then?"

"He talks differently to every man."

I felt my questions were annoying him. I did not ask any more. He went on explaining that there were no exact steps to knowing Mescalito; therefore no one could teach about him except Mescalito himself. This quality made him a unique power; he was not the same for every man.

On the other hand, the acquiring of an ally required, don Juan said, the most precise teaching and the following of stages or steps without a single deviation. There are many such ally powers in the world, he said, but he was familiar with only two of them. And he was going to lead me to them and their secrets, but it was up to me to choose *one* of them, for I could have only one. His benefactor's ally was in *la yerba del diablo* (devil's weed), he said, but he personally did not like it, even though his benefactor had taught him its secrets.

His own ally was in the *humito* (the little smoke), he said, but he did not elaborate on the nature of the smoke.

I asked him about it. He remained quiet. After a long pause I asked him:

"What kind of a power is an ally?"

"It is an aid. I have already told you."

"How does it aid?"

"An ally is a power capable of carrying a man beyond the boundaries of himself. This is how an ally can reveal matters no human being could."

"But Mescalito also takes you out of the boundaries of yourself. Doesn't that make him an ally?"

"No. Mescalito takes you out of yourself to teach you. An ally takes you out to give you power."

I asked him to explain this point to me in more detail, or to describe the difference in effect between the two. He looked at me for a long time and laughed. He said that learning through conversation was not only a waste, but stupidity, because learning was the most difficult task a man could undertake. He asked me to remember the time I had tried to find my spot, and how I wanted to find it without doing any work because I had expected him to hand out all the information. If he had done so, he said, I would never have learned. But, knowing how difficult it was to find my spot, and, above all knowing that it existed, would give me a unique sense of confidence. He said that while I remained rooted to my "good spot" nothing could cause me bodily harm, because I had the assurance that at that particular spot I was at my very best. I had the power to shove off anything that might be harmful to me. If, however, he had *told* me where it was, I would never have had the confidence needed to claim it as true knowledge. Thus, knowledge was indeed power.

Don Juan said then that every time a man sets himself to learn he has to labor as hard as I did to find that spot, and the limits of his learning are determined by his own nature. Thus he saw no point in talking about knowledge. He said that certain kinds of knowledge were too powerful for the strength I had, and to talk about them would only bring harm to me. He apparently felt there was nothing else he wanted to say. He got up and walked toward his house. I told him the situation overwhelmed me. It was not what I had conceived or wanted it to be.

He said that fears are natural; that all of us experience them and there is nothing we can do about it. But on the other hand, no matter how frightening learning is, it is more terrible to think of a man without an ally, or without knowledge.

3

In the more than two years that elapsed between the time don Juan decided to teach me about the ally powers and the time he thought I was ready to learn about them in the pragmatic, participatory form he considered as learning, he gradually defined the general features of the two allies in question. He prepared me for the indispensable corollary of all the verbalizations, and the consolidation of all the teachings, the states of nonordinary reality.

At first he talked about the ally powers in a very casual manner. The first references I have in my notes are interjected between other topics of conversation.

Wednesday, August 23, 1961

"The devil's weed [Jimson weed] was my benefactor's ally. It could have been mine also, but I didn't like her."

"Why didn't you like the devil's weed, don Juan?"

"She has a serious drawback."

"Is she inferior to other ally powers?"

"No. Don't get me wrong. She is as powerful as the best of allies, but there is something about her which I personally don't like."

"Can you tell me what it is?"

"She distorts men. She gives them a taste of power too soon without fortifying their hearts and makes them domineering and unpredictable. She makes them weak in the middle of their great power."

"Isn't there any way to avoid that?"

"There is a way to overcome it, but not avoid it. Whoever becomes the weed's ally must pay that price."

"How can one overcome that effect, don Juan?"

"The devil's weed has four heads: the root, the stem and leaves, the flowers, and the seeds. Each one of them is different and whoever becomes her ally must learn about them in that order. The most important head is in the roots. The power of the devil's weed is conquered through the roots. The stem and leaves are the head that cures maladies; properly used, this head is a gift to mankind. The third head is in the flowers, and it is used to turn people crazy, or to make them obedient, or to kill them. The man whose ally is the weed never intakes the flowers, nor does he intake the stem and leaves, for that matter, except in cases of his own illness; but the roots and the seeds are always intaken, especially the seeds; they are the fourth head of the devil's weed and the most powerful of the four.

"My benefactor used to say the seeds are the 'sober head'—the only part that could fortify the heart of man. The devil's weed is hard with her protégés, he used to say, because she aims to kill them fast, a thing she ordinarily accomplishes before they can arrive at the secrets of the 'sober head.' There are, however, tales about men who have unraveled the secrets of the sober head. What a challenge for a man of knowledge!"

"Did your benefactor unravel such secrets?"

"No, he didn't."

"Have you met anyone who has done it?"

"No. But they lived at a time when that knowledge was important."

"Do you know anyone who has met such men?"

"No, I don't."

"Did your benefactor know anyone?"

"He did."

"Why didn't he arrive at the secrets of the sober head?"

"To tame the devil's weed into an ally is one of the most difficult tasks I know. She never became one with me, for example, perhaps because I was never fond of her."

"Can you still use her as an ally in spite of not being fond of her?"

"I can; nevertheless, I prefer not to. Maybe it will be different for you."

"Why is it called the devil's weed?"

Don Juan made a gesture of indifference, shrugged his shoulders, and remained quiet for some time. Finally he said that "devil's weed" was her temporary name [*su nombre de leche*]. He also said there were other names for the devil's weed, but they were not to be used, because the calling of a name was a serious matter, especially if one was learning to tame an ally power. I asked him why the calling of a name was so serious a matter. He said names were reserved to be used only when one was calling for help, in moments of great stress and need, and he assured me that such moments happen sooner or later in the life of whoever seeks knowledge.

Sunday, September 3, 1961

Today, during the afternoon, don Juan collected two *Datura* plants from the field.

Quite unexpectedly he brought the subject of the devil's weed into our conversation, and then asked me to go with him to the hills and look for one.

We drove to the nearby mountains. I got a shovel out of the trunk and walked into one of the canyons. We walked for quite a while, wading through the chaparral, which grew thick in the soft, sandy dirt. He stopped next to a small plant with dark-green leaves, and big, whitish, bell-shaped flowers.

"This one," he said.

Immediately he started to shovel. I tried to help him but he refused with a strong shake of the head, and went on to dig a circular hole around the plant: a hole shaped like a cone, deep toward the outer edge and sloping into a mound in the center of the circle. When he stopped digging he knelt close to the stem and with his fingers cleared the soft dirt around it, uncovering about four inches of a big, tuberous, forked root whose width contrasted markedly with the width of the stem, which was frail in comparison.

Don Juan looked at me and said the plant was a "male" because the root forked out from the exact point where it joined the stem. Then he stood up and started to walk away, looking for something.

"What are you looking for, don Juan?"

"I want to find a stick."

I began to look around, but he stopped me.

"Not you! You sit over there." He pointed to some rocks twenty feet away. "I will find it."

He came back after a while with a long, dry branch. Using it as a digging stick, he loosened the dirt carefully along the two diverging branches of the root. He cleaned around them to a depth of approximately two feet. As he dug deeper the dirt became so hard-packed that it was practically impossible to penetrate it with the stick.

He came to a halt and sat down to catch his breath. I sat next to him. We did not talk for a long time.

"Why don't you dig it out with the shovel?" I asked.

"It could cut and injure the plant. I had to get a stick that belonged to this area so that, if I had struck the root, the injury wouldn't have been as bad as one caused by a shovel or a foreign object."

"What kind of a stick did you get?"

"Any dry branch of the paloverde tree would do. If there are no dry branches you have to cut a fresh one."

"Can you use the branches of any other tree?"

"I told you, only paloverde and not any other."

"Why is that so, don Juan?"

"Because the devil's weed has very few friends, and paloverde is the only tree in this area which agrees with her—the only thing that grabs or hooks onto it [*lo unico que prende*]. If you damage the root with a shovel she will not grow for you when you replant her, but if you injure her with such a stick, chances are the plant will not even feel it."

"What are you going to do with the root now?"

"I'm going to cut it. You must leave me. Go find another plant and wait until I call you."

"Don't you want me to help you?"

"You may help me only if I ask you!"

I walked away and started to look for another plant in order to fight the strong desire to sneak around and watch him. After some time he joined me.

"Let us look for the female now," he said.

"How do you tell them apart?"

"The female is taller and grows above the ground so it really looks like a small tree. The male is large and spreads out near the ground and looks more like a thick bush. Once we dig the female out you will see it has a single root going for quite a way before it becomes a fork. The male, on the other hand, has a forked root joined to the stem."

We looked together through the field of *Daturas*. Then, pointing to a plant, he said, "That's a female." And he proceeded to dig it out as he had done the other. As soon as he had cleared the root I was able to see that the root conformed to his prediction. I left him again when he was about to cut it.

When we got to his house he opened the bundle in which he had put the *Datura* plants. He took the larger one, the male, first and washed it in a big metal tray. Very carefully he scrubbed all the dirt from the root, stem, and leaves. After that meticulous cleaning, he severed the stem from the root by making a superficial incision around the width of their juncture with a short, serrated knife and by cracking them apart. He took the

stem and separated every part of it by making individual
heaps with leaves, flowers, and the prickly seedpods. He
threw away everything that was dry or had been spoiled
by worms, and kept only those parts that were complete. He tied together the two branches of the root with
two pieces of string, cracked them in half after making
a superficial cut at the joint, and got two pieces of root
of equal size.

He then took a piece of rough burlap cloth and placed
in it first the two pieces of root tied together; on top
of them he put the leaves in a neat bunch, then the
flowers, the seedpods, and the stem. He folded the burlap and made a knot with the corners.

He repeated exactly the same steps with the other
plant, the female, except that when he got to the root,
instead of cutting it, he left the fork intact, like an
upside-down letter Y. Then he placed all the parts in
another cloth bundle. When he finished, it was already
dark.

Wednesday, September 6, 1961

Today, late in the afternoon, we returned to the topic
of the devil's weed.

"I think we should start with that weed again," don
Juan said suddenly.

After a polite silence I asked him, "What are you
going to do with the plants?"

"The plants I dug out and cut are mine," he said.
"It is as though they were myself; with them I'm going
to teach you the way to make the devil's weed."

"How will you do that?"

"The devil's weed is divided into portions [*partes*].
Each one of these portions is different; each has its
unique purpose and service."

He opened his left hand and measured on the floor
from the tip of his thumb to the tip of his fourth finger.

"This is my portion. You will measure yours with
your own hand. Now, to establish dominion over the
devil's weed, you must begin by taking the first portion

of the root. But since I have brought you to her, you must take at the beginning."

He went inside the house and brought out one of the burlap bundles. He sat down and opened it. I noticed it was the male plant. I also noticed there was only one piece of root. He took the piece that was left from the original set of two and held it in front of my face.

"This is your first portion," he said. "I give it to you. I have cut it myself for you. I have measured it as my own; now I give it to you."

For an instant, the thought that I would have to chew it like a carrot crossed my mind, but he placed it inside a small, white, cotton bag.

He walked to the back of the house. He sat there on the floor with his legs crossed, and with a round *mano* began to mash the root inside the bag. He worked it over a flat slab which served as a mortar. From time to time he washed the two stones, and kept the water in a small, flat, wooden dugout basin.

As he pounded he sang an unintelligible chant, very softly and monotonously. When he had mashed the root into a soft pulp inside the bag, he placed it in the wooden basin. He again placed the slab mortar and the pestle into the basin, filled it with water, and then carried it to a sort of rectangular pig's trough set against the back fence.

He said the root had to soak all night, and had to be left outside the house so it would catch the night air (*el sereno*). "If tomorrow is a sunny, hot day, it will be an excellent omen," he said.

Sunday, September 10, 1961

Thursday, September 7, was a very clear and hot day. Don Juan seemed very pleased with the good omen and repeated several times that the devil's weed had probably liked me. The root had soaked all night, and about 10:00 A.M. we walked to the back of the house. He took the basin out of the trough, placed it on the ground, and sat next to it. He took the bag and rubbed it on the bottom of the basin. He held it a few inches above the water and squeezed its contents, then dropped the bag into the water. He repeated the same sequence three more times, then discarded the bag, tossing it into the trough, and left the basin in the hot sun.

We came back to it two hours later. He brought with him a medium-size kettle with boiling, yellowish water. He tipped the basin very carefully and emptied the top water, preserving the thick silt that had accumulated on the bottom. He poured the boiling water on the silt and left the basin in the sun again.

This sequence was repeated three times at intervals of more than an hour. Finally he poured out most of the water from the basin, tipped it to an angle to catch the late afternoon sun, and left it.

When we returned hours later, it was dark. On the bottom of the basin there was a layer of gummy substance. It resembled a batch of half-cooked starch, whitish or light gray. There was perhaps a full teaspoon of it. He took the basin inside the house, and while he put some water on to boil, I picked out pieces of dirt the wind had blown into the silt. He laughed at me.

"That little dirt won't hurt anybody."

When the water was boiling he poured about a cup of it into the basin. It was the same yellowish water he had used before. It dissolved the silt, making a sort of milky substance.

"What kind of water is that, don Juan?"

"Water of fruits and flowers from the canyon."

He emptied the contents of the basin into an old clay mug that looked like a flowerpot. It was still very hot, so he blew on it to cool it. He took a sip and handed me the mug.

"Drink now!" he said.

I took it automatically, and without deliberation drank all the water. It tasted somewhat bitter, although the bitterness was hardly noticeable. What was very outstanding was the pungent odor of the water. It smelled like cockroaches.

Almost immediately I began to sweat. I got very

warm, and blood rushed to my ears. I saw a red spot in front of my eyes, and the muscles of my stomach began to contract in painful cramps. After a while, even though I felt no more pain, I began to get cold and perspiration literally soaked me.

Don Juan asked me if I saw blackness or black spots in front of my eyes. I told him I was seeing everything in red.

My teeth were chattering because of an uncontrollable nervousness that came to me in waves, as if radiating out from the middle of my chest.

Then he asked me if I was afraid. His questions seemed meaningless to me. I told him that I was obviously afraid, but he asked me again if I was afraid of her. I did not understand what he meant and I said yes. He laughed and said that I was not really afraid. He asked if I still saw red. All I was seeing was a huge red spot in front of my eyes.

I felt better after a while. Gradually the nervous spasms disappeared, leaving only an aching, pleasant tiredness and an intense desire to sleep. I couldn't keep my eyes open, although I could still hear don Juan's voice. I fell asleep. But the sensation of my being submerged in a deep red persisted all night. I even had dreams in red.

I woke up on Saturday about 3:00 P.M. I had slept almost two days. I had a mild headache and an upset stomach, and very sharp, intermittent pains in my intestines. Except for that, everything else was like an ordinary waking. I found don Juan sitting in front of his house dozing. He smiled at me.

"Everything went fine the other night," he said. "You saw red and that's all that is important."

"What would have happened if I had not seen red?"

"You would have seen black, and that is a bad sign."

"Why is it bad?"

"When a man sees black its means he is not made for the devil's weed, and he vomits his entrails out, all green and black."

"Would he die?"

"I don't think anyone would die, but he would be sick for a long time."

"What happens to those who see red?"

"They do not vomit, and the root gives them an effect of pleasure, which means they are strong and of violent nature—something that the weed likes. That is the way she entices. The only bad point is that men end up as slaves to the devil's weed in return for the power she gives them. But those are matters over which we have no control. Man lives only to learn. And if he learns it is because that is the nature of his lot, for good or bad."

"What shall I do next, don Juan?"

"Next you must plant a shoot [*brote*] that I have cut from the other half of the first portion of root. You took half of it the other night, and now the other half must be put into the ground. It has to grow and seed before you can undertake the real task of taming the plant."

"How will I tame her?"

"The devil's weed is tamed through the *root*. Step by step, you must learn the secrets of each portion of the root. You must intake them in order to learn the secrets and conquer the power."

"Are the different portions prepared in the same way you did the first one?"

"No, each portion is different."

"What are the specific effects of each portion?"

"I already said, each teaches a different form of power. What you took the other night is nothing yet. Anyone can do that. But only the brujo can take the deeper portions. I can't tell you what they do because I don't know yet whether she will take you. We must wait."

"When will you tell me, then?"

"Whenever your plant has grown and seeded."

"If the first portion can be taken by anyone, what is it used for?"

"In a diluted form it is good for all the matters of manhood, old people who have lost their vigor, or young men who are seeking adventures, or even women who want passion."

"You said the root is used for power only, but I see it's used for other matters besides power. Am I correct?"

He looked at me for a very long time, with a steadfast gaze that embarrassed me. I felt my question had made him angry, but I couldn't understand why.

"The weed is used only for power," he finally said in a dry, stern tone. "The man who wants his vigor back, the young people who seek to endure fatigue and hunger, the man who wants to kill another man, a woman who wants to be in heat—they all desire power. And the weed will give it to them! Do you feel you like her?" he asked after a pause.

"I feel a strange vigor," I said, and it was true. I had noticed it on awakening and I felt it then. It was a very peculiar sensation of discomfort, or frustration; my whole body moved and stretched with unusual lightness and strength. My arms and legs itched. My shoulders seemed to swell; the muscles of my back and neck made me feel like pushing, or rubbing, against trees. I felt I could demolish a wall by ramming it.

We did not speak anymore. We sat on the porch for a while. I noticed that don Juan was falling asleep; he nodded a couple of times, then he simply stretched his legs, lay on the floor with his hands behind his head, and went to sleep. I got up and went to the back of the house where I burned up my extra physical energy by clearing away the debris; I remembered his mentioning that he would like me to help him clean up at the back of his house.

Later, when he woke up and came to the back, I was more relaxed.

We sat down to eat, and in the course of the meal he asked me three times how I felt. Since this was a rarity I finally asked, "Why do you worry about how I feel, don Juan? Do you expect me to have a bad reaction from drinking the juice?"

He laughed. I thought he was acting like a mischievous boy who has set up a prank and checks from time to time for the results. Still laughing, he said:

"You don't look sick. A while ago you even talked rough to me."

"I did not, don Juan," I protested. "I don't ever recall talking to you like that." I was very serious on that point because I did not remember that I had ever felt annoyed with him.

"You came out in her defense," he said.

"In whose defense?"

"You were defending the devil's weed. You sounded like a lover already."

I was going to protest even more vigorously about it, but I stopped myself.

"I really did not realize I was defending her."

"Of course you did not. You don't even remember what you said, do you?"

"No, I don't. I must admit it."

"You see. The devil's weed is like that. She sneaks up on you like a woman. You are not even aware of it. All you care about is that she makes you feel good and powerful: the muscles swelling with vigor, the fists itching, the soles of the feet burning to run somebody down. When a man knows her he really becomes full of cravings. My benefactor used to say that the devil's weed keeps men who want power, and gets rid of those who can't handle it. But power was more common then; it was sought more avidly. My benefactor was a powerful man, and according to what he told me, his benefactor, in turn, was even more given to the pursuit of power. But in those days there was good reason to be powerful."

"Do you think there is no reason for power nowadays?"

"Power is alright for you now. You are young. You are not an Indian. Perhaps the devil's weed would be good in your hands. You seem to have liked it. It made you feel strong. I felt all that myself. And yet I didn't like it."

"Can you tell me why, don Juan?"

"I don't like its power! There is no use for it any-more. In other times, like those my benefactor told me about, there was reason to seek power. Men performed phenomenal deeds, were admired for their strength and feared and respected for their knowledge. My benefactor told me stories of truly phenomenal deeds that were performed long, long ago. But now we, the Indians, do not seek that power anymore. Nowadays, the Indians use the weed to rub themselves. They use the leaves and flowers for other matters; they even say it cures their boils. But they do not seek its power, a power that acts like a magnet, more potent and more dangerous to handle as the root goes deeper into the ground. When one arrives to a depth of four yards—and they say some people have—one finds the seat of permanent power, power without end. Very few humans have done this in the past, and nobody has done it today. I'm telling you, the power of the devil's weed is no longer needed by us, the Indians. Little by little, I think we have lost interest, and now power does not matter any-more. I myself do not seek it, and yet at one time, when I was your age, I too felt its swelling inside me. I felt the way you did today, only five hundred times more strong-ly. I killed a man with a single blow of my arm. I could toss boulders, huge boulders not even twenty men could budge. Once I jumped so high I chopped the top leaves off the highest trees. But it was all for nothing! All I did was frighten the Indians—only the Indians. The rest who knew nothing about it did not believe it. They saw either a crazy Indian, or something moving at the top of the trees."

We were silent for a long time. I needed to say some-thing.

"It was different when there were people in the world," he proceeded, "people who knew a man could become a mountain lion, or a bird, or that a man could simply fly. So I don't use the devil's weed anymore. For what? To frighten the Indians? [¿Para que? ¿Para asustar a los indios?]"

And I saw him sad, and a deep empathy filled me.

I wanted to say something to him, even if it was a platitude.

"Perhaps, don Juan, that is the fate of all men who want to know."

"Perhaps," he said quietly.

Thursday, November 23, 1961

I didn't see don Juan sitting on his porch as I drove in. I thought it was strange. I called to him out loud and his daughter-in-law came out of the house.

"He's inside," she said.

I found he had dislocated his ankle several weeks before. He had made his own cast by soaking strips of cloth in a mush made with cactus and powdered bone. The strips, wrapped tightly around his ankle, had dried into a light, streamlined cast. It had the hardness of plaster, but not its bulkiness.

"How did it happen?" I asked.

His daughter-in-law, a Mexican woman from Yucatan, who was tending him, answered me.

"It was an accident! He fell and nearly broke his foot!"

Don Juan laughed and waited until the woman had left the house before answering.

"Accident, my eye! I have an enemy nearby. A woman. 'La Catalina!' She pushed me during a moment of weakness and I fell."

"Why did she do that?"

"She wanted to kill me, that's why."

"Was she here with you?"

"Yes!"

"Why did you let her in?"

"I didn't. She flew in."

"I beg your pardon!"

"She is a blackbird [*chanate*]. And so effective at that. I was caught by surprise. She has been trying to finish me off for a long time. This time she got real close."

"Did you say she is a blackbird? I mean, is she a bird?"

"There you go again with your questions. She is a blackbird! The same way I'm a crow. Am I a man or a bird? I'm a man who knows how to become a bird. But going back to 'la Catalina,' she is a fiendish witch! Her intent to kill me is so strong that I can hardly fight her off. The blackbird came all the way into my house and I couldn't stop it."

"Can you become a bird, don Juan?"

"Yes! But that's something we'll take up later."

"Why does she want to kill you?"

"Oh, there's an old problem between us. I got out of hand and now it looks as if I have to finish her off before she finishes me."

"Are you going to use witchcraft?" I asked with great expectations.

"Don't be silly. No witchcraft would ever work on her. I have other plans! I'll tell you about them someday."

"Can your ally protect you from her?"

"No! The little smoke only tells me what to do. Then I must protect myself."

"How about Mescalito? Can he protect you from her?"

"No! Mescalito is a teacher, not a power to be used for personal reasons."

"How about the devil's weed?"

"I've already said that I must protect myself, following the directions of my ally the smoke. And as far as I know, the smoke can do anything. If you want to know about any point in question, the smoke will tell you. And it will give you not only knowledge, but also the means to proceed. It's the most marvelous ally a man could have."

"Is the smoke the best possible ally for everybody?"

"It's not the same for everybody. Many fear it and won't touch it, or even get close to it. The smoke is like everything else; it wasn't made for all of us."

"What kind of smoke is it, don Juan?"

"The smoke of diviners!"

There was a noticeable reverence in his voice—a mood I had never detected before.

"I will begin by telling you exactly what my benefactor said to me when he began to teach me about it. Although at that time, like yourself now, I couldn't possibly have understood. 'The devil's weed is for those who bid for power. The smoke is for those who want to watch and see.' And in my opinion, the smoke is peerless. Once a man enters into its field, every other power is at his command. It's magnificent! Of course, it takes a lifetime. It takes years alone to become acquainted with its two vital parts: the pipe and the smoke mixture. The pipe was given to me by my benefactor, and after so many years of fondling it, it has become mine. It has grown into my hands. To turn it over to your hands, for instance, will be a real task for me, and a great accomplishment for you—if we succeed! The pipe will feel the strain of being handled by someone else; and if one of us makes a mistake there won't be any way to prevent the pipe from busting open by its own force, or escaping from our hands to shatter, even if it falls on a pile of straw. If that ever happens, it would mean the end of us both. Particularly of me. The smoke would turn against me in unbelievable ways."

"How could it turn against you if it's your ally?"

My question seemed to have altered his flow of thoughts. He didn't speak for a long time.

"The difficulty of the ingredients," he proceeded suddenly, "makes the smoke mixture one of the most dangerous substances I know. No one can prepare it without being coached. It is deadly poisonous to anyone except the smoke's protégé! Pipe and mixture ought to be treated with intimate care. And the man attempting to learn must prepare himself by leading a hard, quiet life. Its effects are so dreadful that only a very strong man can stand the smallest puff. Everything is terrifying and confusing at the outset, but every new puff makes things more precise. And suddenly the world opens up anew! Unimaginable! When this happens the smoke has become one's ally and will resolve any question by allowing one to enter into inconceivable worlds.

"This is the smoke's greatest property, its greatest gift. And it performs its function without hurting in the least. I call the smoke a true ally!"

As usual, we were sitting in front of his house, where the dirt floor is always clean and packed hard; he suddenly got up and went inside the house. After a few moments he returned with a narrow bundle and sat down again.

"This is my pipe," he said.

He leaned over toward me and showed me a pipe he drew out of a sheath made of green canvas. It was perhaps nine or ten inches long. The stem was made of reddish wood; it was plain, without ornamentation. The bowl also seemed to be made of wood, but it was rather bulky in comparison with the thin stem. It had a sleek finish and was dark gray, almost charcoal.

He held the pipe in front of my face. I thought he was handing it over to me. I stretched out my hand to take it, but he quickly drew it back.

"This pipe was given to me by my benefactor," he said. "In turn I will pass it on to you. But first you must get to know it. Every time you come here I will give it to you. Begin by touching it. Hold it very briefly, at first, until you and the pipe get used to each other. Then put it in your pocket, or perhaps inside your shirt. And finally put it to your mouth. All this should be done little by little in a slow, careful way. When the bond has been established [la amistad esta hecha] you will smoke from it. If you follow my advice and don't rush, the smoke may become your preferred ally too."

He handed me the pipe, but without letting go of it. I stretched my right arm toward it.

"With both hands," he said.

I touched the pipe with both hands for a very brief moment. He did not extend it to me all the way so that I could grasp it, but only far enough for me to touch it. Then he pulled it back.

"The first step is to like the pipe. That takes time!"

"Can the pipe dislike me?"

"No. The pipe cannot dislike you, but you must learn to like it so that when the time of smoking comes for you, the pipe will help you to be unafraid."

"What do you smoke, don Juan?"

"This!"

He opened his collar and exposed to view a small bag he kept under his shirt, which hung from his neck like a medallion. He brought it out, untied it, and very carefully poured some of its contents into the palm of his hand.

As far as I could tell, the mixture looked like finely shredded tea leaves, varying in color from dark brown to light green, with a few specks of bright yellow.

He returned the mixture to the bag, closed the bag, tied it with a leather string, and put it under his shirt again.

"What kind of mixture is it?"

"There are lots of things in it. To get all the ingredients is a very difficult undertaking. One must travel afar. The little mushrooms [los honguitos] needed to prepare the mixture grow only at certain times of the year, and only in certain places."

"Do you have a different mixture for each type of aid you need?"

"No! There is only one smoke, and there is no other like it."

He pointed to the bag hanging against his chest, and lifted the pipe which was resting between his legs.

"These two are one! One cannot go without the other. This pipe and the secret of this mixture belonged to my benefactor. They were handed down to him in the same way my benefactor gave them to me. The mixture, although difficult to prepare, is replenishable. Its secret lies in its ingredients, and in the way they are treated and mixed. The pipe, on the other hand, is a lifetime affair. It must be looked after with infinite care. It is hardy and strong, but it should never be struck or knocked about. It should be handled with dry hands, never when the hands are sweaty, and should be used only when one is alone. And no one, absolutely no one, should ever see it, unless you mean to give it to somebody. That is what my benefactor taught me, and that is the way I have dealt with the pipe all my life."

"What would happen if you should lose or break the pipe?"

He shook his head, very slowly, and looked at me.

"I would die!"

"Are all the sorcerers' pipes like yours?"

"Not all of them have pipes like mine. But I know some men who do."

"Can you yourself make a pipe like this one, don Juan?" I insisted. "Suppose you did not have it, how could you give me one if you wanted to do so?"

"If I didn't have the pipe, I could not, nor would I, want to give one. I would give you something else instead."

He seemed to be somehow cross at me. He placed his pipe very carefully inside the sheath, which must have been lined with a soft material because the pipe, which fitted tightly, slid in very smoothly. He went inside the house to put his pipe away.

"Are you angry at me, don Juan?" I asked when he returned. He seemed surprised at my question.

"No! I'm never angry at anybody! No human being can do anything important enough for that. You get angry at people when you feel that their acts are important. I don't feel that way any longer."

Tuesday, December 26, 1961

The specific time to replant the "shoot," as don Juan called the root, was not set, although it was supposed to be the next step in taming the plant-power.

I arrived at don Juan's house on Saturday, December 23, early in the afternoon. We sat in silence for some time, as usual. The day was warm and cloudy. It had been months since he had given me the first portion.

"It is time to return the weed to the earth," he said suddenly. "But first I am going to fix a protection for you. You will keep it and guard it, and it is for you alone to see. Since I am going to fix it I will also see it. That is not good, because, as I told you, I am not fond of the devil's weed. We are not one. But my memory will not live long; I am too old. You must keep it from the eyes of others, however, for so long as their memory of having seen it lasts the power of the protection is harmed."

He went into his room and pulled three burlap bundles out from under an old straw mat. He came back to the porch and sat down.

After a long silence he opened one bundle. It was the female *Datura* he had collected with me; all the leaves, flowers, and seedpods that he had stacked up before were dry. He took the long piece of root shaped like the letter Y and tied the bundle again.

The root had dried and shriveled and the bars of the fork had become more widely separated and more contorted. He put the root on his lap, opened his leather pouch, and pulled out his knife. He held the dry root in front of me.

"This part is for the head," he said, and made the first incision on the tail of the Y, which in an upside-down position resembled the shape of a man with his legs spread out.

"This is for the heart," he said, and cut close to the joint of the Y. Next he chopped the tips of the root, leaving about three inches of wood on each bar of the Y. Then slowly and patiently he carved the shape of a man.

The root was dry and fibrous. In order to carve it, don Juan made two incisions and peeled the fibers between them to the depth of the cuts. Nevertheless, when he came to details, he chiseled the wood, as when he shaped the arms and the hands. The final product was a wiry figurine of a man, arms folded over the chest and hands in a clasping position.

Don Juan got up and walked to a blue agave growing in front of the house, next to the porch. He took the hard thorn of one of the center, pulpy leaves, bent it, and rotated it three or four times. The circular motion almost detached it from the leaf; it hung loose. He bit on it, or rather, he held it between his teeth, and yanked it out. The thorn came out from the pulp, bringing with it a bunch of long threadlike fibers, attached to the woody part like a white tail, two feet long. Still holding the thorn between his teeth, don Juan twisted the fibers together between the palms of his hands and made a string, which he wrapped around the figurine's legs to bring them together. He encircled the lower part of the body until the string was all used up; then very skillfully he worked the thorn like an awl inside the front part of the body under the folded arms, until the sharp tip emerged as though poping out of the figurine's hands. He used his teeth again and, by pulling gently, brought the thorn nearly all the way out. It looked like a long spear protruding from the figure's chest. Without looking at the figure anymore, don Juan placed it inside his leather pouch. He seemed exhausted from the effort. He lay down on the floor and fell asleep.

It was already dark when he woke up. We ate the groceries I had brought him and sat on the porch for a while longer. Then don Juan walked to the back of the house, carrying the three burlap bundles. He cut twigs and dry branches and started a fire. We sat in front of it comfortably, and he opened all three bundles. Besides the one containing the dry pieces of the female plant, there was another with all that was left of the male plant, and a third, bulky one containing green, freshly cut pieces of *Datura*.

Don Juan went to the pig's trough and came back with a stone mortar, a very deep one that looked more like a pot whose bottom ended in a soft curve. He made a shallow hole and set the mortar firmly on the ground. He put more dry twigs on the fire, then took the two bundles with the dry pieces of male and female plants and emptied them into the mortar all at once. He shook the burlap to make sure that all the debris had fallen into the mortar. From the third bundle he extracted two fresh pieces of *Datura* root.

"I am going to prepare them just for you," he said.

"What kind of a preparation is it, don Juan?"

"One of these pieces comes from a male plant, the other from a female plant. This is the only time the two plants should be put together. The pieces come from a depth of one yard."

He mashed them inside the mortar with even strokes of the pestle. As he did so, he chanted in a low voice, which sounded like a rhythmless, monotonous hum. The words were unintelligible to me. He was absorbed in his task.

When the roots were completely mashed he took some *Datura* leaves from the bundle. They were clean and freshly cut, and all were intact and free of wormholes and cuts. He dropped them into the mortar one at a time. He took a handful of *Datura* flowers and dropped them also into the mortar in the same deliberate manner. I counted fourteen of each. Then he got a bunch of fresh, green seedpods which had all their spikes and were not open. I could not count them because he dropped them into the mortar all at once, but I assumed that there were also fourteen of them. He added three stems of *Datura* without any leaves. They were dark red and clean and seemed to have belonged to large plants, judging by their multiple ramifications.

After all these items had been put into the mortar, he mashed them to a pulp with the same even strokes. At a certain moment he tipped the mortar over, and with his hand scooped the mixture into an old pot. He stretched out his hand to me, and I thought he wanted me to dry it. Instead, he took my left hand and with a very fast motion separated the middle and fourth fingers as far as he could. Then, with the point of his knife, he stabbed me right in between the two fingers and ripped downward on the skin of the fourth finger. He acted with so much skill and speed that when I jerked my hand away it was deeply cut, and the blood was flowing abundantly. He grabbed my hand again, placed it over the pot, and squeezed it to force more blood out.

My arm got numb. I was in a state of shock—strangely cold and rigid, with an oppressive sensation in my chest and ears. I felt I was sliding down on my seat. I was fainting! He let go my hand and stirred the contents of the pot. When I recovered from the shock I was really angry with him. It took me quite some time to regain my composure.

He set up three stones around the fire and placed the pot on top of them. To all the ingredients he added something that I took to be a big chunk of carpenter's glue and a pot of water, and let all that boil. *Datura* plants have, by themselves, a very peculiar odor. Combined with the carpenter's glue, which gave off a strong odor when the mixture began to boil, they created so pungent a vapor that I had to fight not to vomit.

The mix boiled for a long time as we sat there motionless in front of it. At times, when the wind blew the vapor in my direction, the stench enveloped me, and I held my breath in an effort to avoid it.

Don Juan opened his leather pouch and took the figurine out; he handed it to me carefully and told me to place it inside the pot without burning my hands. I let it slip gently into the boiling mush. He got out his knife, and for a second I thought he was going to slash me again; instead, he pushed the figurine with the tip of the knife and sank it.

He watched the mush boil for a while longer, and then began to clean the mortar. I helped him. When we had finished he set the mortar and pestle against the fence. We went inside the house, and the pot was left on the stones all night.

The next morning at dawn don Juan instructed me to pull the figurine out of the glue and hang it from the roof facing the east, to dry in the sun. At noon it was stiff as a wire. The heat had sealed the glue, and the green color of the leaves had mixed with it. The figurine had a glossy, eerie finish.

Don Juan asked me to get the figurine down. Then he handed me a leather pouch he had made out of an old suede jacket I had brought for him some time before. The pouch looked like the one he owned himself. The only difference was that his was made of soft, brown leather.

"Put your 'image' inside the pouch and close it," he said.

He did not look at me, and deliberately kept his head turned away. Once I had the figurine inside the pouch he gave me a carrying net, and told me to put the clay pot inside the net.

He walked to my car, took the net from my hands, and fastened it onto the open lid of the glove compartment.

"Come with me," he said.

I followed him. He walked around the house, making a complete clockwise circle. He stopped at the porch and circled the house again, this time going counterclockwise and again returning to the porch. He stood motionless for some time, and then sat down.

I was conditioned to believe that everything he did had some meaning. I was wondering about the significance of circling the house when he said, "Hey! I have forgotten where I put it."

I asked him what he was looking for. He said he had forgotten where he had placed the shoot I was to replant. We walked around the house once more before he remembered where it was.

He showed me a small glass jar on a piece of board nailed to the wall below the roof. The jar contained the other half of the first portion of the *Datura* root. The shoot had an incipient growth of leaves at its top end. The jar contained a small amount of water, but no soil.

"Why doesn't it have any soil?" I asked.

"All soils are not the same, and the devil's weed must know only the soil on which she will live and grow. And now it is time to return her to the ground before the worms damage her."

"Can we plant here here near the house?" I asked.

"No! No! Not around here. She must be returned to a place of your liking."

"But where can I find a place of my liking?"

"I don't know that. You can replant her wherever you want. But she must be cared for and looked after, because she must live so that you will have the power you need. If she dies, it means that she does not want you, and must not disturb her further. It means you won't have power over her. Therefore, you must care for her, and look after her, so that she will grow. You must not pamper her, though."

"Why not?"

"Because if it is not her will to grow, it is of no use to entice her. But, on the other hand, you must prove that you care. Keep the worms away and give her water when you visit her. This must be done regularly until she seeds. After the first seeds bud out, we will be sure that she wants you."

"But, don Juan, it is not possible for me to look after the root the way you wish."

"If you want her power, you must do it! There is no other way!"

"Can you take care of her for me when I am not here, don Juan?"

"No! Not I! I can't do that! Each one must nourish his own shoot. I had my own. Now you must have yours. And not until she has seeded, as I told you, can you consider yourself ready for learning."

"Where do you think I should replant her?"

"That is for you alone to decide! And nobody must know the place, not even I! That is the way the replanting must be done. Nobody, but nobody, can know where your plant is. If a stranger follows you, or sees you, take the shoot and run away to another place. He could cause you unimaginable harm through manipulating the shoot. He could cripple or kill you. That's why not even I must know where your plant is."

He handed me the little jar with the shoot.

"Take it now."

I took it. Then he almost dragged me to my car.

"Now you must leave. Go and pick the spot where you will replant the shoot. Dig a deep hole, in soft dirt, next to a watery place. Remember, she must be near water in order to grow. Dig the hole with your hands only, even if they bleed. Place the shoot in the center of the hole and make a mound [*pilón*] around it. Then soak it with water. When the water sinks, fill the hole with soft dirt. Next, pick a spot two paces away from the shoot, in that direction [pointing to the southeast]. Dig another deep hole there, also with your hands, and dump into it what is in the pot. Then smash the pot and bury it deep in another place, far from the spot where your shoot is. When you have buried the pot go back to your shoot and water it once more. Then take out your image, hold it between the fingers where the flesh wound is, and, standing on the spot where you have buried the glue, touch the shoot lightly with the sharp needle. Circle the shoot four times, stopping each time in the same spot to touch it."

"Do I have to follow a specific direction when I go around the root?"

"Any direction will do. But you must *always remember* in what direction you buried the glue, and what direction you took when you circled the shoot. Touch the shoot lightly with the point every time except the last, when you must thrust it deep. But do it carefully; kneel for a more steady hand because you must not break the point inside the shoot. If you break it, you are finished. The root will be of no use to you."

"Do I have to say any words while I go around the shoot?"

"No, I will do that for you."

Saturday, January 27, 1962

As soon as I got to his house this morning don Juan told me he was going to show me how to prepare the smoke mixture. We walked to the hills and went quite a way into one of the canyons. He stopped next to a tall, slender bush whose color contrasted markedly with that of the surrounding vegetation. The chaparral around the bush was yellowish, but the bush was bright green.

"From this little tree you must take the leaves and the flowers," he said. "The right time to pick them is All Souls' Day [*el día de las ánimas*]."

He took out his knife and chopped off the end of a thin branch. He chose another similar branch and also chopped off its tip. He repeated this operation until he had a handful of branch tips. Then he sat down on the ground.

"Look here," he said. "I have cut all the branches above the fork made by two or more leaves and the stem. Do you see? They are all the same. I have used only the tip of each branch, where the leaves are fresh and tender. Now we must look for a shaded place."

We walked until he seemed to have found what he was looking for. He took a long string from his pocket and tied it to the trunk and the lower branches of two bushes, making a kind of clothesline on which he hung the branch tips upside down. He arranged them along the string in a neat fashion; hooked by the fork between the leaves and the stem, they resembled a long row of green horsemen.

"One must see that the leaves dry in the shade," he said. "The place must be secluded and difficult to get to. That way the leaves are protected. They must be left to dry in a place where it would be almost impossible to find them. After they have dried, they must be put in a bundle and sealed."

He picked up the leaves from the string and threw them into the nearby shrubs. Apparently he had intended only to show me the procedure.

We continued walking and he picked three different flowers, saying they were part of the ingredients and were supposed to be gathered at the same time. But the flowers had to be put in seraparte clay pots and dried in darkness; a lid had to be placed on each pot so the flowers would turn moldy inside the container. He said the function of the leaves and the flowers was to sweeten the smoke mixture.

We came out of the canyon and walked toward the riverbed. After a long detour we returned to his house.

Late in the evening we sat in his own room, a thing he rarely allowed me to do, and he told me about the final ingredient of the mixture, the mushrooms.

"The real secret of the mixture lies in the mushrooms," he said. "They are the most difficult ingredient to collect. The trip to the place where they grow is long and dangerous, and to select the right variety is even more perilous. There are other kinds of mushrooms growing alongside which are of no use; they would spoil the good ones if they were dried together. It takes time to know the mushrooms well in order not to make a mistake. Serious harm will result from using the wrong kind—harm to the man and to the pipe. I know of men who have dropped dead from using the foul smoke.

"As soon as the mushrooms are picked they are put inside a gourd, so there is no way to recheck them. You see, they have to be torn to shreds in order to make them go through the narrow neck of the gourd."

"How can one prevent a mistake?"

"By being careful and knowing how to choose. I told you it is difficult. Not everybody can tame the smoke; most people do not even make the attempt."

"How long do you keep the mushrooms inside the gourd?"

"For a year. All the other ingredients are also sealed for a year. Then equal parts of them are measured and ground separately into a very fine powder. The little mushrooms don't have to be ground because they become a very fine dust by themselves; all one needs to do is to mash the chunks. Four parts of mushrooms are added to one part of all the other ingredients together. Then they are all mixed and put into a bag like mine." He pointed to the little sack hanging under his shirt.

"Then all the ingredients are gathered again, and after they have been put to dry you are ready to smoke the mixture you have just prepared. In your own case, you will smoke next year. And the year after that, the mixture will be all yours because you will have gathered it by yourself. The first time you smoke I will light the pipe for you. You will smoke all the mixture in the bowl and wait. The smoke will come. You will feel it. It will set you free to see anything you want to see. Properly speaking, it is a matchless ally. But whoever seeks it must have an intent and a will beyond reproach. He needs them because he has to intend and will his return, or the smoke will not let him come back. Second, he must intend and will to remember whatever the smoke allowed him to see, otherwise it will be nothing more than a piece of fog in his mind."

Saturday, April 8, 1962

In our conversations, don Juan consistently used or referred to the phrase "man of knowledge," but never explained what he meant by it. I asked him about it.

"A man of knowledge is one who has followed truthfully the hardships of learning," he said. "A man who has, without rushing or without faltering, gone as far as he can in unraveling the secrets of power and knowledge."

"Can anyone be a man of knowledge?"

"No, not anyone."

"Then what must a man do to become a man of knowledge?"

"He must challenge and defeat his four natural enemies."

"Will he be a man of knowledge after defeating these four enemies?"

"Yes. A man can call himself a man of knowledge only if he is capable of defeating all four of them."

"Then, can *anybody* who defeats these enemies be a man of knowledge?"

"Anybody who defeats them becomes a man of knowledge."

"But are there any special requirements a man must fulfill before fighting with these enemies?"

"No. Anyone can try to become a man of knowledge; very few men actually succeed, but that is only natural. The enemies a man encounters on the path of learning to become a man of knowledge are truly formidable; most men succumb to them."

"What kind of enemies are they, don Juan?"

He refused to talk about the enemies. He said it would be a long time before the subject would make any sense to me. I tried to keep the topic alive and asked him if he thought *I* could become a man of knowledge. He said no man could possibly tell that for sure. But I insisted on knowing if there were any clues he could use to determine whether or not I had a chance of becoming a man of knowledge. He said it would depend on my battle against the four enemies—whether I could defeat them or would be defeated by them— but it was impossible to foretell the outcome of that fight.

I asked him if he could use witchcraft or divination to see the outcome of the battle. He flatly stated that the results of the struggle could not be foreseen by any means, because becoming a man of knowledge was a temporary thing. When I asked him to explain this point, he replied:

"To be a man of knowledge has no permanence. One is never a man of knowledge, not really. Rather, one becomes a man of knowledge for a very brief instant, after defeating the four natural enemies."

"You must tell me, don Juan, what kind of enemies they are."

He did not answer. I insisted again, but he dropped the subject and started to talk about something else.

Sunday, April 15, 1962

As I was getting ready to leave, I decided to ask him once more about the enemies of a man of knowledge. I argued that I could not return for some time, and it would be a good idea to write down what he had to say and then think about it while I was away.

He hesitated for a while, but then began to talk.

"When a man starts to learn, he is never clear about his objectives. His purpose is faulty; his intent is vague.

He hopes for rewards that will never materialize for he knows nothing of the hardships of learning.

"He slowly begins to learn—bit by bit at first, then in big chunks. And his thoughts soon clash. What he learns is never what he pictured, or imagined, and so he begins to be afraid. Learning is never what one expects. Every step of learning is a new task, and the fear the man is experiencing begins to mount mercilessly, unyieldingly. His purpose becomes a battlefield.

"And thus he has stumbled upon the first of his natural enemies: Fear! A terrible enemy—treacherous, and difficult to overcome. It remains concealed at every turn of the way, prowling, waiting. And if the man, terrified in its presence, runs away, his enemy will have put an end to his quest."

"What will happen to the man if he runs away in fear?"

"Nothing happens to him except that he will never learn. He will never become a man of knowledge. He will perhaps be a bully, or a harmless, scared man; at any rate, he will be a defeated man. His first enemy will have put an end to his cravings."

"And what can he do to overcome fear?"

"The answer is very simple. He must not run away. He must defy his fear, and in spite of it he must take the next step in learning, and the next, and the next. He must be fully afraid, and yet he must not stop. That is the rule! And a moment will come when his first enemy retreats. The man begins to feel sure of himself. His intent becomes stronger. Learning is no longer a terrifying task.

"When this joyful moment comes, the man can say without hesitation that he has defeated his first natural enemy."

"Does it happen at once, don Juan, or little by little?"

"It happens little by little, and yet the fear is vanquished suddenly and fast."

"But won't the man be afraid again if something new happens to him?"

"No. Once a man has vanquished fear, he is free

from it for the rest of his life because, instead of fear, he has acquired clarity—a clarity of mind which erases fear. By then a man knows his desires; he knows how to satisfy those desires. He can anticipate the new steps of learning, and a sharp clarity surrounds everything. The man feels that nothing is concealed.

"And thus he has encountered his second enemy: Clarity! That clarity of mind, which is so hard to obtain, dispels fear, but also blinds.

"It forces the man never to doubt himself. It gives him the assurance he can do anything he pleases, for he sees clearly into everything. And he is courageous because he is clear, and he stops at nothing because he is clear. But all that is a mistake; it is like something incomplete. If the man yields to this make-believe power, he has succumbed to his second enemy and will be patient when he should rush. And he will fumble with learning until he winds up incapable of learning anything more."

"What becomes of a man who is defeated in that way, don Juan? Does he die as a result?"

"No, he doesn't die. His second enemy has just stopped him cold from trying to become a man of knowledge; instead, the man may turn into a buoyant warrior, or a clown. Yet the clarity for which he has paid so dearly will never change to darkness and fear again. He will be clear as long as he lives, but he will no longer learn, or yearn for, anything."

"But what does he have to do to avoid being defeated?"

"He must do what he did with fear: he must defy his clarity and use it only to see, and wait patiently and measure carefully before taking new steps; he must think, above all, that his clarity is almost a mistake. And a moment will come when he will understand that his clarity was only a point before his eyes. And thus he will have overcome his second enemy, and will arrive at a position where nothing can harm him anymore. This will not be a mistake. It will not be only a point before his eyes. It will be true power.

"He will know at this point that the power he has been pursuing for so long is finally his. He can do with it whatever he pleases. His ally is at his command. His wish is the rule. He sees all that is around him. But he has also come across his third enemy: Power!

"Power is the strongest of all enemies. And naturally the easiest thing to do is to give in; after all, the man is truly invincible. He commands; he begins by taking calculated risks, and ends in making rules, because he is a master.

"A man at this stage hardly notices his third enemy closing in on him. And suddenly, without knowing, he will certainly have lost the battle. His enemy will have turned him into a cruel, capricious man."

"Will he lose his power?"

"No, he will never lose his clarity or his power."

"What then will distinguish him from a man of knowledge?"

"A man who is defeated by power dies without really knowing how to handle it. Power is only a burden upon his fate. Such a man has no command over himself, and cannot tell when or how to use his power."

"Is the defeat by any of these enemies a final defeat?"

"Of course it is final. Once one of these enemies overpowers a man there is nothing he can do."

"Is it possible, for instance, that the man who is defeated by power may see his error and mend his ways?"

"No. Once a man gives in he is through."

"But what if he is temporarily blinded by power, and then refuses it?"

"That means his battle is still on. That means he is still trying to become a man of knowledge. A man is defeated only when he is no longer tries, and abandons himself."

"But then, don Juan, it is possible that a man may abandon himself to fear for years, but finally conquer it."

"No, that is not true. If he gives in to fear he will never conquer it, because he will shy away from learning and never try again. But if he tries to learn for years in the midst of his fear, he will eventually conquer it because he will never have really abandoned himself to it."

"How can he defeat his third enemy, don Juan?"

"He has to defy it, deliberately. He has to come to realize the power he has seemingly conquered is in reality never his. He must keep himself in line at all times, handling carefully and faithfully all that he has learned. If he can see that clarity and power, without his control over himself, are worse than mistakes, he will reach a point where everything is held in check. He will know then when and how to use his power. And thus he will have defeated his third enemy.

"The man will be, by then, at the end of his journey of learning, and almost without warning he will come upon the last of his enemies: Old age! This enemy is the cruelest of all, the one he won't be able to defeat completely, but only fight away.

"This is the time when a man has no more fears, no more impatient clarity of mind—a time when all his power is in check, but also the time when he has an unyielding desire to rest. If he gives in totally to his desire to lie down and forget, if he soothes himself in tiredness, he will have lost his last round, and his enemy will cut him down into a feeble old creature. His desire to retreat will overrule all his clarity, his power, and his knowledge.

"But if the man sloughs off his tiredness, and lives his fate through, he can then be called a man of knowledge, if only for the brief moment when he succeeds in fighting off his last, invincible enemy. That moment of clarity, power, and knowledge is enough."

4

Don Juan seldom spoke openly about Mescalito. Every time I questioned him on the subject he refused to talk, but he always said enough to create an impression of Mescalito, an impression that was always anthropomorphic. Mescalito was a male, not only because of the mandatory grammatical rule that gives the word a masculine gender, but also because of his constant qualities of being a protector and a teacher. Don Juan reaffirmed these characteristics in various forms every time we talked.

Sunday, December 24, 1961

"The devil's weed has never protected anyone. She serves only to give power. Mescalito, on the other hand, is gentle, like a baby."

"But you said Mescalito is terrifying at times."

"Of course he is terrifying, but once you get to know him, he is gentle and kind."

"How does he show his kindness?"

"He is a protector and a teacher."

"How does he protect?"

"You can keep him with you at all times and he will see that nothing bad happens to you."

"How can you keep him with you at all times?"

"In a little bag, fastened under your arm or around your neck with a string."

"Do you have him with you?"

"No, because I have an ally. But other people do."

"What does he teach?"

"He teaches you to live properly."

"How does he teach?"

"He shows things and tells what is what [*enzeña las cosas y te dice lo que son*]."

"How?"

"You will have to see for yourself."

Tuesday, January 30, 1962

"What do you see when Mescalito takes you with him, don Juan?"

"Such things are not for ordinary conversation. I can't tell you that."

"Would something bad happen to you if you told?"

"Mescalito is a protector, a kind, gentle protector; but that does not mean you can make fun of him. Because he is a kind protector he can also be horror itself with those he does not like."

"I do not intend to make fun of him. I just want to know what he makes other people do or see. I described to you all that Mescalito made me see, don Juan."

"With you it is different, perhaps because you don't know his ways. You have to be taught his ways as a child is taught how to walk."

"How long do I still have to be taught?"

"Until he himself begins to make sense to you."

"And then?"

"Then you will understand by yourself. You won't have to tell me anything anymore."

"Can you just tell me where Mescalito takes you?"

"I can't talk about it."

"All I want to know is if there is another world to which he takes people."

"There is."

"Is it heaven?" (The Spanish word for heaven is *cielo,* but that also means "sky.")

"He takes you through the sky [*cielo*]."

"I mean, is it heaven [*cielo*] where God is?"

"You are being stupid now. I don't know where God is."

"Is Mescalito God—the only God? Or is he one of the gods?"

"He is just a protector and a teacher. He is a power."

"Is he a power within ourselves?"

"No. Mescalito has nothing to do with ourselves. He is outside us."

"Then everyone who takes Mescalito must see him in the same form."

"No, not at all. He is not the same for everybody."

Thursday, April 12, 1962

"Why don't you tell me more about Mescalito, don Juan?"

"There is nothing to tell."

"There must be thousands of things I should know before I encounter him again."

"No. Perhaps for you there is nothing you have to know. As I have already told you, he is not the same for everyone."

"I know, but still I'd like to know how others feel about him."

"The opinion of those who care to talk about him is not worth much. You will see. You will probably talk about him up to a certain point, and from then on you will never discuss him."

"Can you tell me about your own first experiences?"

"What for?"

"Then I'll know how to behave with Mescalito."

"You already know more than I do. You actually played with him. Someday you will see how kind the protector was with you. That first time I am sure he told you many, many things, but you were deaf and blind."

Sunday, April 14, 1962

"Does Mescalito take *any* form when he shows himself?"

"Yes, any form."

"Then, which are the most common forms you know?"

"There are no common forms."

"Do you mean, don Juan, that he appears in any form, even to men who know him well?"

"No. He appears in any form to those who know him only a little, but to those who know him well, he is always constant."

"How is he constant?"

"He appears to them sometimes as a man, like us, or as a light. Just a light."

"Does Mescalito ever change his permanent form with those who know him well?"

"Not to my knowledge."

Friday, July 6, 1962

Don Juan and I started on a trip late in the afternoon of Saturday, June 23. He said we were going to look for *honguitos* (mushrooms) in the state of Chihuahua. He said it was going to be a long, hard trip. He was right. We arrived in a little mining town in northern Chihuahua at 10:00 P.M. on Wednesday, June 27. We walked from the place I had parked the car at the outskirts of town, to the house of his friends, a Tarahumara Indian and his wife. We slept there.

The next morning the man woke us up around five. He brought us gruel and beans. He sat and talked to don Juan while we ate, but he said nothing concerning our trip.

After breakfast the man put water into my canteen, and two sweet rolls into my knapsack. Don Juan handed me the canteen, fixed the knapsack with a cord over his shoulders, thanked the man for his courtesies, and turning to me, said, "It is time to go."

We walked on the dirt road for about a mile. From there we cut through the fields and in two hours we were at the foot of the hills south of town. We climbed the gentle slopes in a southwesterly direction. When we reached the steeper inclines, don Juan changed directions and we followed a high valley to the east. Despite his advanced age, don Juan kept up a pace so incredibly fast that by midday I was completely exhausted. We sat down and he opened the bread sack.

"You can eat all of it, if you want," he said.

"How about you?"

"I am not hungry, and we won't need this food later on."

I was very tired and hungry and took him up on his offer. I felt this was a good time to talk about the purpose of our trip, and quite casually I asked, "Do you think we are going to stay here for a long time?"

"We are here to gather some Mescalito. We will stay until tomorrow."

"Where is Mescalito"

"All around us."

Cacti of many species were growing in profusion all through the area, but I could not distinguish peyote among them.

We started to hike again and by three o'clock we came to a long, narrow valley with steep side hills. I felt strangely excited at the idea of finding peyote, which I had never seen in its natural environment. We entered the valley and must have walked about four hundred feet when suddenly I spotted three unmistakable peyote plants. They were in a cluster a few inches above the ground in front of me, to the left of the path. They looked like round, pulpy, green roses. I ran toward them, pointing them out to don Juan.

He ignored me and deliberately kept his back turned as he walked away. I knew I had done the wrong thing, and for the rest of the afternoon we walked in silence, moving slowly on the flat valley floor, which was covered with small, sharp-edged rocks. We moved among the cacti, disturbing crowds of lizards and at times a solitary bird. And I passed scores of peyote plants without saying a word.

At six o'clock we were at the bottom of the mountains that marked the end of the valley. We climbed to a ledge. Don Juan dropped his sack and sat down.

I was hungry again, but we had no food left; I suggested that we pick up the Mescalito and head back for town. He looked annoyed and made a smacking sound with his lips. He said we were going to spend the night there.

We sat quietly. There was a rock wall to the left, and to the right was the valley we had just crossed. It extended for quite a distance and seemed to be wider than, and not so flat as, I had thought. Viewed from the spot where I sat, it was full of small hills and protuberances.

"Tomorrow we will start walking back," don Juan said without looking at me, and pointing to the valley. "We will work our way back and pick him as we cross the field. That is, we will pick him only when he is in our way. *He* will find us and not the other way around. *He* will find us—if he wants to."

Don Juan rested his back against the rock wall and, with his head turned to his side, continued talking as though another person were there besides myself. "One more thing. Only *I* can pick him. You will perhaps carry the bag, or walk ahead of me—I don't know yet. But tomorrow you will not point at him as you did today!"

"I am sorry, don Juan."

"It is alright. You didn't know."

"Did your benefactor teach you all this about Mescalito?"

"No! Nobody has taught me about him. It was the protector himself who was my teacher."

"Then Mescalito is like a person to whom you can talk?"

"No, he isn't."

"How does he teach, then?"

He remained silent for a while.

"Remember the time when you played with him? You understood what he meant, didn't you?"

"I did!"

"That is the way he teaches. You did not know it then, but if you had paid attention to him, he would have talked to you."

"When?"

"When you saw him for the first time."

He seemed to be very annoyed by my questioning. I told him I had to ask all these questions because I wanted to find out all I could.

"Don't ask *me!*" He smiled maliciously. "Ask *him.* The next time you see him, ask him everything you want to know."

"Then Mescalito *is* like a person you can talk . . ."

He did not let me finish. He turned away, picked up the canteen, stepped down from the ledge, and disappeared around the rock. I did not want to be alone there, and even though he had not asked me to go along, I followed him. We walked for about five hundred feet to a small creek. He washed his hands and face and filled up the canteen. He swished water around in his mouth, but did not drink it. I scooped up some water in my hands and drank, but he stopped me and said it was unnecessary to drink.

He handed me the canteen and started to walk back to the ledge. When we got there we sat again facing the valley with our backs to the rock wall. I asked if we could build a fire. He reacted as if it was inconceivable to ask such a thing. He said that for that night we were Mescalito's guests and he was going to keep us warm.

It was already dusk. Don Juan pulled two thin, cotton blankets from his sacks, threw one into my lap, and sat cross-legged with the other one over his shoulders. Below us the valley was dark, with its edges already diffused in the evening mist.

Don Juan sat motionless facing the peyote field. A steady wind blew on my face.

"The twilight is the crack between the worlds," he said softly, without turning to me.

I didn't ask what he meant. My eyes became tired. Suddenly I felt elated; I had a strange, overpowering desire to weep!

I lay on my stomach; the rock floor was hard and uncomfortable, and I had to change my position every few minutes. Finally I sat up and crossed my legs, putting the blanket over my shoulders. To my amazement this position was supremely comfortable, and I fell asleep.

When I woke up, I heard don Juan talking to me. It was very dark. I could not see him well. I did not understand what he said, but I followed him when he started to go down from the ledge. We moved carefully, or at least I did, because of the darkness. We stopped at the bottom of the rock wall. Don Juan sat down and signaled me to sit at his left. He opened up his shirt and took out a leather sack, which he opened and placed on the ground in front of him. It contained a number of dried peyote buttons.

After a long pause he picked up one of the buttons. He held it in his right hand, rubbing it several times between the thumb and the first finger as he chanted softly. Suddenly he let out a tremendous cry.

"Ahiiii!"

It was weird, unexpected. It terrified me. Vaguely I saw him place the peyote button in his mouth and begin to chew it. After a moment he picked up the whole sack, leaned toward me, and told me in a whisper to take the sack, pick out one mescalito, put the sack in front of us again, and then do exactly as he did.

I picked a peyote button and rubbed it as he had done. Meanwhile he chanted, swaying back and forth. I tried to put the button into my mouth several times, but I felt embarrassed to cry out. Then, as in a dream, an unbelievable shriek came out of me: Ahiiii! For a moment I thought it was someone else. Again I felt the effects of nervous shock in my stomach. I was falling backward. I was fainting. I put the peyote button into my mouth and chewed it. After a while Don Juan picked up another from the sack. I was relieved to see that he put it into his mouth after a short chant. He passed the sack to me, and I placed it in front of us again after taking one button. This cycle went on five times before I noticed any thirst. I picked up the canteen to drink, but don Juan told me just to wash my mouth, and not to drink or I would vomit.

I swished the water around in my mouth repeatedly.

At a certain moment drinking was a formidable tempta-
tion, and I swallowed a bit of water. Immediately my
stomach began to convulse. I expected to have painless
and effortless flowing of liquid from my mouth, as had
happened during my first experience with peyote, but to
my surprise I had only the ordinary sensation of vomiting. It did not last long, however.

Don Juan picked up another button and handed me
the sack, and the cycle was renewed and repeated until
I had chewed fourteen buttons. By this time all my
early sensations of thirst, cold, and discomfort had
disappeared. In their place I felt an unfamiliar sense of
warmth and excitation. I took the canteen to freshen
my mouth, but it was empty.

"Can we go to the creek, don Juan?"

The sound of my voice did not project out, but hit
the roof of my palate, bounced back in to my throat,
and echoed to and fro between them. The echo was soft
and musical, and seemed to have wings that flapped inside my throat. Its touch soothed me. I followed its
back-and-forth movements until it had vanished.

I repeated the question. My voice sounded as though
I was talking inside a vault.

Don Juan did not answer. I got up and turned in
the direction of the creek. I looked at him to see if he
was coming, but he seemed to be listening attentively
to something.

He made an imperative sign with his hand to be
quiet.

"Abuhtol[?] is already here!" he said.

I had never heard that word before, and I was wondering whether to ask him about it when I detected a
noise that seemed to be a buzzing inside my ears. The
sound became louder by degrees until it was like the
vibration caused by an enormous bull-roarer. It blasted
for a brief moment and subsided gradually until everything was quiet again. The violence and the intensity
of the noise terrified me. I was shaking so much that
I could hardly remain standing, yet I was perfectly
rational. If I had been drowsy a few minutes before,

this feeling had totally vanished, giving way to a state of extreme lucidity. The noise reminded me of a science fiction movie in which a gigantic bee buzzed its wings coming out of an atomic radiation area. I laughed at the thought. I saw don Juan slumping back into his relaxed position. And suddenly the image of a gigantic bee accosted me again. It was more real than ordinary thoughts. It stood alone surrounded by an extraordinary clarity. Everything else was driven from my mind. This state of mental clearness, which had no precedents in my life, produced another moment of terror.

I began to perspire. I leaned toward don Juan to tell him I was afraid. His face was a few inches from mine. He was looking at me, but his eyes were the eyes of a bee. They looked like round glasses that had a light of their own in the darkness. His lips were pushed out, and from them came a pattering noise: "Pehtuh-peh-tuh-pet-tuh." I jumped backward, nearly crashing into the rock wall. For a seemingly endless time I experienced an unbearable fear. I was panting and whining. The perspiration had frozen on my skin, giving me an awkward rigidity. Then I heard don Juan's voice saying, "Get up! Move around! Get up!"

The image vanished and again I could see his familiar face.

"I'll get some water," I said after another endless moment. My voice cracked. I could hardly articulate the words. Don Juan nodded yes. As I walked away I realized that my fear had gone as fast and as mysteriously as it had come.

Upon approaching the creek I noticed that I could see every object in the way. I remembered I had just seen don Juan clearly, whereas earlier I could hardly distinguish the outlines of his figure. I stopped and looked into the distance, and I could even see across the valley. Some boulders on the other side became perfectly visible. I thought it must be early morning, but it occurred to me that I might have lost track of time. I looked at my watch. It was ten of twelve! I checked the watch to see if it was working. It couldn't be midday; it had to be midnight! I intended to make a dash for the water and come back to the rocks, but I saw don Juan coming down and I waited for him. I told him I could see in the dark.

He stared at me for a long time without saying a word; if he did speak, perhaps I did not hear him, for I was concentrating on my new, unique ability to see in the dark. I could distinguish the very minute pebbles in the sand. At moments everything was so clear it seemed to be early morning, or dusk. Then it would get dark; then it would clear again. Soon I realized that the brightness corresponded to my heart's diastole, and the darkness to its systole. The world changed from bright to dark to bright again with every beat of my heart.

I was absorbed in this discovery when the same strange sound that I had heard before became audible again. My muscles stiffened.

"Anuhctal [as I heard the word this time] is here," don Juan said. I fancied the roar so thunderous, so overwhelming, that nothing else mattered. When it had subsided, I perceived a sudden increase in the volume of water. The creek, which a minute before had been less than a foot wide, expanded until it was an enormous lake. Light that seemed to come from above it touched the surface as though shining through thick foliage. From time to time the water would glitter for a second —gold and black. Then it would remain dark, lightless, almost out of sight, and yet strangely present.

I don't recall how long I stayed there just watching, squatting on the shore of the black lake. The roar must have subsided in the meantime, because what jolted me back (to reality?) was again a terrifying buzzing. I turned around to look for don Juan. I saw him climbing up and disappearing behind the rock ledge. Yet the feeling of being alone did not bother me at all; I squatted there in a state of absolute confidence and abandonment. The roar again became audible; it was very intense, like the noise made by a high wind. Listening to it as carefully as I could, I was able to detect a definite melody. It was a composite of high-pitched sounds like human voices, accompanied by a deep bass drum. I focused all my attention on the melody, and again noticed that the systole and diastole of my heart coincided with the sound of the bass drum, and with the pattern of the music.

I stood up and the melody stopped. I tried to listen to my heartbeat, but it was not detectable. I squatted again, thinking that perhaps the position of my body had caused or induced the sounds! But nothing happened! Not a sound! Not even my heart! I thought I had had enough, but as I stood up to leave, I felt a tremor of the earth. The ground under my feet was shaking. I was losing my balance. I fell backward and remained on my back while the earth shook violently. I tried to grab a rock or a plant, but something was sliding under me. I jumped up, stood for a moment, and fell down again. The ground on which I sat was moving, sliding into the water like a raft. I remained motionless, stunned by a terror that was, like everything else, unique, uninterrupted, and absolute.

I moved through the water of the black lake perched on a piece of soil that looked like an earthen log. I had the feeling I was going in a southerly direction, transported by the current. I could see the water moving and swirling around. It felt cold, and oddly heavy, to the touch. I fancied it alive.

There were no distinguishable shores or landmarks, and I can't recall the thoughts or the feelings that must have come to me during this trip. After what seemed like hours of drifting, my raft made a right-angle turn to the left, the east. It continued to slide on the water for a very short distance, and unexpectedly rammed against something. The impact threw me forward. I closed my eyes and felt a sharp pain as my knees and my outstretched arms hit the ground. After a moment I looked up. I was lying on the dirt. It was as though my earthen log had merged with the land. I sat up and turned around. The water was receding! It moved backward, like a wave in reverse, until it disappeared.

I sat there for a long time, trying to collect my

thoughts and resolve all that had happened into a coherent unit. My entire body ached. My throat felt like an open sore; I had bitten my lips when I "landed." I stood up. The wind made me realize I was cold. My clothes were wet. My hands and jaws and knees shook so violently that I had to lie down again. Drops of perspiration slid into my eyes and burned them until I yelled with pain.

After a while I regained a measure of stability and stood up. In the dark twilight, the scene was very clear. I took a couple of steps. A distinct sound of many human voices came to me. They seemed to be talking loudly. I followed the sound; I walked for about fifty yards and came to a sudden stop. I had reached a dead end. The place where I stood was a corral formed by enormous boulders. I could distinguish another row, and then another, and another, until they merged into the sheer mountain. From among them came the most exquisite music. It was a fluid, uninterrupted, eerie flow of sounds.

At the foot of one boulder I saw a man sitting on the ground, his face turned almost in profile. I approached him until I was perhaps ten feet away; then he turned his head and looked at me. I stopped—his eyes were the water I had just seen! They had the same enormous volume, the sparkling of gold and black. His head was pointed like a strawberry; his skin was green, dotted with innumerable warts. Except for the pointed shape, his head was exactly like the surface of the peyote plant. I stood in front of him, staring; I couldn't take my eyes away from him. I felt he was deliberately pressing on my chest with the weight of his eyes. I was choking. I lost my balance and fell to the ground. His eyes turned away. I heard him talking to me. At first his voice was like the soft rustle of a light breeze. Then I heard it as music—as a melody of voices—and I "knew" it was saying, "What do you want?"

I knelt before him and talked about my life, then wept. He looked at me again. I felt his eyes pulling me away, and I thought that moment would be the moment

of my death. He signaled me to come closer. I vacillated
for an instant before I took a step forward. As I
came closer he turned his eyes away from me and
showed me the back of his hand. The melody said,
"Look!" There was a round hole in the middle of his
hand. "Look!" said the melody again. I looked into the
hole and I saw myself. I was very old and feeble and
was running stooped over, with bright sparks flying
all around me. Then three of the sparks hit me, two in
the head and one in the left shoulder. My figure, in the
hole, stood up for a moment until it was fully vertical,
and then disappeared together with the hole.

Mescalito turned his eyes to me again. They were
so close to me that I "heard" them rumble softly with
that peculiar sound I had heard many times that night.
They became peaceful by degrees until they were like
a quiet pond rippled by gold and black flashes.

He turned his eyes away once more and hopped like
a cricket for perhaps fifty yards. He hopped again and
again, and was gone.

The next thing I remember is that I began to walk.
Very rationally I tried to recognize landmarks, such as
mountains in the distance, in order to orient myself. I
had been obsessed by cardinal points throughout the
whole experience, and I believed that north had to be to
my left. I walked in that direction for quite a while
before I realized that it was daytime, and that I was no
longer using my "night vision." I remembered I had a
watch and looked at the time. It was eight o'clock.

It was about ten o'clock when I got to the ledge
where I had been the night before. Don Juan was lying
on the ground asleep.

"Where have you been?" he asked.

I sat down to catch my breath.

After a long silence he asked, "Did you see him?"

I began to narrate to him the sequence of my experiences from the beginning, but he interrupted me saying
that all that mattered was whether I had seen him or
not. He asked how close to me Mescalito was. I told
him I had nearly touched him.

The part of my story interested him. He listened attentively to every detail without comment, interrupting only to ask questions about the form of the entity I had seen, its disposition, and other details about it. It was about noon when don Juan seemed to have had enough of my story. He stood up and strapped a canvas bag to my chest; he told me to walk behind him and said he was going to cut Mescalito loose and I had to receive him in my hands and place him inside the bag gently.

We drank some water and started to walk. When we reached the edge of the valley he seemed to hesitate for a moment before deciding which direction to take. Once he had made his choice we walked in a straight line.

Every time we came to a peyote plant, he squatted in front of it and very gently cut off the top with his short, serrated knife. He made an incision level with the ground, and sprinkled the "wound," as he called it, with pure sulphur powder which he carried in a leather sack. He held the fresh button in his left hand and spread the powder with his right hand. Then he stood up and handed me the button, which I received with both hands, as he had prescribed, and placed inside the bag. "Stand erect and don't let the bag touch the ground or the bushes or anything else," he said repeatedly, as though he thought I would forget.

We collected sixty-five buttons. When the bag was completely filled, he put it on my back and strapped a new one to my chest. By the time we had crossed the plateau we had two full sacks, containing one hundred and ten peyote buttons. The bags were so heavy and bulky that I could hardly walk under the weight and volume.

Don Juan whispered to me that the bags were heavy because Mescalito wanted to return to the ground. He said it was the sadness of leaving his abode which made Mescalito heavy; my real chore was not to let the bags touch the ground, because if I did Mescalito would never allow me to take him again.

At one particular moment the pressure of the straps on my shoulders became unbearable. Something was exerting tremendous force in order to pull me down. I felt very apprehensive. I noticed that I had started to walk faster, almost at a run; I was in a way trotting behind don Juan.

Suddenly the weight on my back and chest diminished. The load became spongy and light. I ran freely to catch up with don Juan, who was ahead of me. I told him I did not feel the weight any longer. He explained that we had already left Mescalito's abode.

Tuesday, July 3, 1962

"I think Mescalito has almost accepted you," don Juan said.

"Why do you say he has *almost* accepted me, don Juan?"

"He did not kill you, or even harm you. He gave you a good fright, but not a really bad one. If he had not accepted you at all, he would have appeared to you as monstrous and full of wrath. Some people have learned the meaning of horror upon encountering him and not being accepted by him."

"If he is so terrible, why didn't you tell me about it before you took me to the field?"

"You do not have the courage to seek him deliberately. I thought it would be better if you did not know."

"But I might have died, don Juan!"

"Yes, you might have. But I was certain it was going to be alright for you. He played with you once. He did not harm you. I thought he would also have compassion for you this time."

I asked him if he really thought Mescalito had had compassion for me. The experience had been terrifying; I felt that I had already died of fright.

He said Mescalito had been most kind to me; he had showed me a scene that was an answer to a question. Don Juan said Mescalito had given me a lesson. I asked him what the lesson was and what it meant.

He said it would be impossible to answer that question because I had been too afraid to know *exactly* what I asked Mescalito.

Don Juan probed my memory as to what I had said to Mescalito before he showed me the scene on his hand. But I could not remember. All I remembered was my falling on my knees and "confessing my sins" to him.

Don Juan seemed uninterested in talking about it anymore. I asked him, "Can you teach me the words to the songs you chanted?"

"No, I can't. Those words are my own, the words the protector himself taught me. The songs are *my* songs. I can't tell you what they are."

"Why can't you tell me, don Juan?"

"Because these songs are a link between the protector and myself. I am sure someday he will teach you your own songs. Wait until then; and never, absolutely never, copy or ask about the songs that belong to another man."

"What was the name you called out? Can you tell me that, don Juan?"

"No. His name can never be voiced, except to call him."

"What if I want to call him myself?"

"If someday he accepts you, he will tell you his name. That name will be for you alone to use, either to call him loudly or to say quietly to yourself. Perhaps he will tell you his name is José. Who knows?"

"Why is it wrong to use his name when talking about him?"

"You have seen his eyes, haven't you? You can't fool around with the protector. That is why I can't get over the fact that he chose to play with you!"

"How can he be a protector when he hurts some people?"

"The answer is very simple. Mescalito is a protector because he is available to anyone who seeks him."

"But isn't it true that everything in the world is available to anyone who seeks it?"

"No, that is not true. The ally powers are available, only to the brujos, but anyone can partake of Mescalito."

"But why then does he hurt some people?"

"Not everybody likes Mescalito; yet they all seek him with the idea of profiting without doing any work. Naturally their encounter with him is always horrifying."

"What happens when he accepts a man completely?"

"He appears to him as a man, or as a light. When a man has won this kind of acceptance, Mescalito is constant. He never changes after that. Perhaps when you meet him again he will be light, and someday he may even take you flying and reveal all his secrets to you."

"What do I have to do to arrive at that point, don Juan?"

"You have to be a strong man, and your life has to be truthful."

"What is a truthful life?"

"A life lived with deliberateness, a good, strong life."

5

Don Juan inquired periodically, in a casual way, about the state of my *Datura* plant. In the year that had elapsed from the time I replanted the root, the plant had grown into a large bush. It had seeded and the seedpods had dried. And don Juan judged it was time for me to learn more about the devil's weed.

Sunday, January 27, 1963

Today don Juan gave me the preliminary information on the "second portion" of the *Datura* root, the second step in learning the tradition. He said the second portion of the root was the real beginning of learning; in comparison with it, the first portion was like child's play. The second portion had to be mastered; it had to be intaken at least twenty times, he said, before one could go on to the third step.

I asked, "What does the second portion do?"

"The second portion of the devil's weed is used for seeing. With it, a man can soar through the air to see what is going on at any place he chooses."

"Can a man actually fly through the air, don Juan?"

"Why not? As I have already told you, the devil's weed is for those who seek power. The man who masters the second portion can use the devil's weed to do unimaginable things to gain more power."

"What kind of things, don Juan?"

"I can't tell you that. Every man is different."

Monday, January 28, 1963

Don Juan said: "If you complete the second step successfully, I can show you only one more step. In the course of learning about the devil's weed, I realized she was not for me, and I did not pursue her path any further."

"What made you decide against it, don Juan?"

"The devil's weed nearly killed me every time I tried to use her. Once it was so bad I thought I was finished. And yet, I could have avoided all that pain."

"How? Is there a special way to avoid pain?"

"Yes, there is a way."

"Is it a formula, a procedure, or what?"

"It is a way of grabbing onto things. For instance, when I was learning about the devil's weed I was too eager. I grabbed onto things the way kids grab onto candy. The devil's weed is only one of a million paths. Anything is one of a million paths [*un camino entre cantidades de caminos*]. Therefore you must always keep in mind that a path is only a path; if you feel you should not follow it, you must not stay with it under any conditions. To have such clarity you must lead a disciplined life. Only then will you know that any path is only a path, and there is no affront, to oneself or to others, in dropping it if that is what your heart tells you to do. But your decision to keep on the path or to leave it must be free of fear or ambition. I warn you. Look at every path closely and deliberately. Try it as many times as you think necessary. This question is one that only a very old man asks. My benefactor told me about it once when I was young, and my blood was too vigorous for me to understand it. Now I do understand it. I will tell you what it is: Does this path have a heart? All paths are the same: they lead nowhere. They are paths going through the bush, or into the bush. In my own life I could say I have traversed long, long paths, but I am not anywhere. My benefactor's question has meaning now. Does this path have a heart? If it does, the path is good; if it doesn't, it is of no use. Both paths lead nowhere; but one has a heart, the other doesn't. One makes for a joyful journey; as long as you follow it, you are one with it. The other will make you curse your life. One makes you strong; the other weakens you."

Sunday, April 21, 1963

On Tuesday afternoon, April 16, don Juan and I went to the hills where his *Datura* plants are. He asked me to leave him alone there, and wait for him in the car. He returned nearly three hours later carrying a package wrapped in a red cloth. As we started to drive back to his house he pointed to the bundle and said it was his last gift for me.

I asked if he meant he was not going to teach me anymore. He explained that he was referring to the fact that I had a plant fully mature and would no longer need his plants.

Late in the afternoon we sat in his room; he brought out a smoothly finished mortar and pestle. The bowl of the mortar was about six inches in diameter. He untied a large package full of small bundles, selected two of them, and placed them on a straw mat by my side; then he added four more bundles of the same size from the pack he had carried home. He said they were seeds, and I had to grind them into a fine powder. He opened the first bundle and poured some of its contents into the mortar. The seeds were dried, round and caramel yellow in color.

I began working with the pestle; after a while he corrected me. He told me to push the pestle against one side of the mortar first, and then slide it across the bottom and up against the other side. I asked what he was going to do with the powder. He did not want to talk about it.

The first batch of seeds was extremely hard to grind. It took me four hours to finish the job. My back ached because of the position in which I had been sitting. I lay down and wanted to go to sleep right there, but don Juan opened the next bag and poured some of the contents into the mortar. The seeds this time were slightly darker than the first ones, and were lumped together. The rest of the bag's contents was a sort of powder, made of very small, round, dark granules.

I wanted something to eat, but don Juan said that if I wished to learn I had to follow the rule, and the rule was that I could only drink a little water while learning the secrets of the second portion.

The third bag contained a handful of live, black, grain weevils. And in the last bag were some fresh white seeds, almost mushy soft, but fibrous and difficult to grind into a fine paste, as he expected me to do. After I had finished grinding the contents of the four bags, don Juan measured two cups of greenish water, poured it into a clay pot, and put the pot on the fire. When the water was boiling he added the first batch of powdered seeds. He stirred it with a long, pointed piece of wood or bone which he carried in his leather pouch. As soon as the water boiled again he added the other substances one by one, following the same procedure. Then he added one more cup of the same water, and let the mixture simmer over a low fire.

Then he told me it was time to mash the root. He

carefully extracted a long piece of *Datura* root from the bundle he had carried home. The root was about sixteen inches long. It was thick, perhaps an inch and a half in diameter. He said it was the second portion, and again he had measured the second portion himself, because it was still *his* root. He said the next time I tried the devil's weed I would have to measure my own root.

He pushed the big mortar toward me, and I proceeded to pound the root in exactly the same way he had mashed the first portion. He directed me through the same steps, and again we left the mashed root soaking in water, exposed to the night air. By that time the boiling mixture had solidified in the clay pot. Don Juan took the pot from the fire, placed it inside a hanging net, and hooked it to a beam in the middle of the room.

About eight o'clock in the morning of April 17, don Juan and I began to leach the root extract with water. It was a clear, sunny day, and don Juan interpreted the fine weather as an omen that the devil's weed liked me; he said that with me around he could remember only how bad she had been with him.

The procedure we followed in leaching the root extract was the same I had observed for the first portion. By late afternoon, after pouring out the top water for the eighth time, there was a spoonful of a yellowish substance in the bottom of the bowl.

We returned to his room where there were still two little sacks he had not touched. He opened one, slid his hand inside, and wrinkled the open end around his wrist with the other hand. He seemed to be holding something, judging by the way his hand moved inside the bag. Suddenly, with a swift movement, he peeled the bag off his hand like a glove, turning it inside out, and shoved his hand close to my face. He was holding a lizard. Its head was a few inches from my eyes. There was something strange about the lizard's mouth. I gazed at it for a moment, and then recoiled involuntarily. The lizard's mouth was sewed up with rude stitches. Don

Juan ordered me to hold the lizard in my left hand. I clutched it; it wriggled against my palm. I felt nauseated. My hands began to perspire.

He took the last bag, and, repeating the same motions, he extracted another lizard. He also held it close to my face. I saw that its eyelids were sewed together. He ordered me to hold this lizard in my right hand.

By the time I had both lizards in my hands I was almost sick. I had an overpowering desire to drop them and get out of there.

"Don't squeeze them!" he said, and his voice brought me a sense of relief and direction. He asked what was wrong with me. He tried to be serious, but couldn't keep a straight face and laughed. I tried to ease my grip, but my hands were sweating so profusely that the lizards began to wriggle out of them. Their sharp little claws scratched my hands, producing an incredible feeling of disgust and nausea. I closed my eyes and clenched my teeth. One of the lizards was already sliding onto my wrist; all it needed was to yank its head from between my fingers to be free. I had a peculiar sensation of physical despair, of supreme discomfort. I growled at don Juan, between my teeth, to take the damn things off me. My head shook involuntarily. He looked at me curiously. I growled like a bear, shaking my body. He dropped the lizards into their bags and began to laugh. I wanted to laugh also, but my stomach was upset. I lay down.

I explained to him that what had affected me was the sensation of their claws on my palms; he said there were lots of things that could drive a man mad, especially if he did not have the resolution, the purpose, required for learning; but when a man had a clear, unbending intent, feelings were in no way a hindrance, for he was capable of controlling them.

Don Juan waited awhile and then, going through the same motions, handed me the lizards again. He told me to hold their heads up and rub them softly against my temples, as I asked them anything I wanted to know.

I did not understand at first what he wanted me to

do. He told me again to ask the lizards about anything I could not find out for myself. He gave me a whole series of examples: I could find out about persons I did not see ordinarily, or about objects that were lost, or about places I had not seen. Then I realized he was talking about *divination*. I got very excited. My heart began to pound. I felt that I was losing my breath.

He warned me not to ask about personal matters this first time; he said I should think rather of something that had nothing to do with me. I had to think fast and clearly because there would be no way of reversing my thoughts.

I tried frantically to think of something I wanted to know. Don Juan urged me on imperiously, and I was astonished to realize I could think of nothing I wanted to "ask" the lizards.

After a painfully long wait I thought of something. Some time earlier a large number of books had been stolen from a reading room. It was not a personal matter, and yet I was interested in it. I had no preconceived ideas about the identity of the person, or persons, who had taken the books. I rubbed the lizards against my temples, asking them who the thief was.

After a while don Juan put the lizards inside their bags, and said that there were no deep secrets about the root and the paste. The paste was made to give direction; the root made things clear. But the real mystery was the lizards. They were the secret of the whole sorcery of the second portion, he said. I asked whether they were a special kind of lizard. He said they were. They had to come from the area of one's own plant; they had to be one's friends. And to have lizards as friends, he said, required a long period of grooming. One had to develop a strong friendship with them by giving them food and speaking kind words to them.

I asked why their friendship was so important. He said the lizards would allow themselves to be caught only if they knew the man, and whoever took the devil's weed seriously had to treat the lizards seriously. He said that, as a rule, the lizards should be caught after the paste and the root had been prepared. They should be caught in the late afternoon. If one was not on intimate terms with the lizards, he said, days could be spent trying to catch them without success; and the paste lasts only one day. He then gave me a long series of instructions concerning the procedure to follow after the lizards had been caught.

"Once you have caught the lizards, put them in separate bags. Then take the first one and talk to her. Apologize for hurting her, and beg her to help you. And with a wooden needle sew up her mouth. Use the fibers of agave and one of the thorns of a choya to do the sewing. Draw the stitches tight. Then tell the other lizard the same things and sew her eyelids together. By the time night begins to fall you will be ready. Take the lizard with the sewed-up mouth and explain to her the matter you want to know about. Ask her to go and see for you; tell her you had to sew up her mouth so she would hurry back to you and not talk to anyone else. Let her scramble in the paste after you have rubbed it on her head; then put her on the ground. If she goes in the direction of your good fortune, the sorcery will be successful and easy. If she goes in the opposite direction, it will be unsuccessful. If the lizard moves toward you (south), you can expect more than ordinary good luck; but if she moves away from you (north), the sorcery will be terribly difficult. You may even die! So if she moves away from you, that is a good time to quit. At this point you can make the decision to quit. If you do, you will lose your capacity to command the lizards, but that is better than losing your life. On the other hand, you may decide to go ahead with the sorcery in spite of my warning. If you do, the next step is to take the other lizard and tell her to listen to her sister's story, and then describe it to you."

"But how can the lizard with the sewed-up mouth tell me what she sees? Wasn't her mouth closed to prevent her from talking?"

"Sewing up her mouth prevents her from telling her

story to strangers. People say lizards are talkative; they will stop anywhere to talk. Anyway, the next step is to smear the paste on the back of her head, and then rub her head against your right temple, keeping the paste away from the center of your forehead. At the beginning of your learning it is a good idea to tie the lizard by its middle to your right shoulder with a string. Then you won't lose her or injure her. But as you progress and become more familiar with the power of the devil's weed, the lizards learn to obey your commands and will stay perched on your shoulder. After you have smeared the paste on your right temple with the lizard, dip the fingers of both hands into the gruel; first rub it on both temples and then spread it all over both sides of your head. The paste dries very fast, and can be applied as many times as necessary. Begin every time by using the lizard's head first and then your fingers. Sooner or later the lizard that went to see comes back and tells her sister all about her journey, and the blind lizard describes it to you as though you were her kind. When the sorcery is finished, put the lizard down and let her go, but don't watch where she goes. Dig a deep hole with your bare hands and bury everything you used in it."

About 6:00 P.M. don Juan scooped the root extract out of the bowl onto a flat piece of shale; there was less than a teaspoon of a yellowish starch. He put half of it into a cup and added some yellowish water. He rotated the cup in his hand to dissolve the substance. He handed me the cup and told me to drink the mixture. It was tasteless, but it left a slightly bitter flavor in my mouth. The water was too hot and that annoyed me. My heart began pounding fast, but soon I was relaxed again.

Don Juan got the other bowl with the paste. The paste looked solid, and had a glossy surface. I tried to poke the crust with my finger, but don Juan jumped toward me and pushed my hand away from the bowl. He became very annoyed; he said it was very thoughtless of me to try that, and if I really wanted to learn there was no need to be careless. This was power, he said, pointing to the paste, and nobody could tell what kind of power it really was. It was bad enough that we had to tamper with it for our own purposes—a thing we cannot help doing because we are men, he said—but we should at least treat it with the proper respect. The mixture looked like oatmeal. Apparently it had enough starch to give it that consistency. He asked me to get the bags with the lizards. He took the lizard with the sewed-up mouth and carefully handed it over to me. He made me take it with my left hand and told me to get some of the paste with my finger and rub it on the lizard's head and then put the lizard into the pot and hold it there until the paste covered its entire body.

Then he told me to remove the lizard from the pot. He picked up the pot and led me to a rocky area not too far from his house. He pointed to a large rock and told me to sit in front of it, as if it were my *Datura* plant, and, holding the lizard in front of my face, to explain to her again what I wanted to know, and beg her to go and find the answer for me. He advised me to tell the lizard I was sorry I had to cause her discomfort, and to promise her I would be kind to all lizards in return. And then he told me to hold her between the third and fourth fingers of my left hand, where he had once made a cut, and to dance around the rock doing exactly what I had done when I replanted the root of the devil's weed; he asked me if I remembered all I had done at that time. I said I did. He emphasized that everything had to be just the same, and if I did not remember I had to wait until everything was clear in my mind. He warned me with great urgency that if I acted too quickly, without deliberation, I was going to get hurt. His last instruction was that I was to place the lizard with the sewed-up mouth on the ground and watch where she went, so that I could determine the outcome of the experience. He said I was not to take my eyes away from the lizard, even for an instant, because it was a common trick of lizards to distract one and then dash away.

It was not quite dark yet. Don Juan looked at the sky. "I will leave you alone," he said, and walked away.

I followed all his instructions and then placed the lizard on the ground. The lizard stood motionless where I had put it. Then it looked at me, and ran to the rocks toward the east and disappeared among them.

I sat on the ground in front of the rock, as though I were facing my plant. A profound sadness overtook me. I wondered about the lizard with its sewed-up mouth. I thought of its strange journey and of how it looked at me before it ran away. It was a weird thought, an annoying projection. In my own way I too was a lizard, undergoing another strange journey. My fate was, perhaps, only to see; at that moment I felt that I would never be able to tell what I had seen. It was very dark by then. I could hardly see the rocks in front of me. I thought of don Juan's words: "The twilight—there's the crack between the worlds!"

After long hesitation I began to follow the steps prescribed. The paste, though it looked like oatmeal, did not feel like oatmeal. It was very smooth and cold. It had a peculiar, pungent smell. It produced a sensation of coolness on the skin and dried quickly. I rubbed my temples eleven times, without noticing any effect. I tried very carefully to take account of any change in perception or mood, for I did not even know what to anticipate. As a matter of fact, I could not conceive the nature of the experience, and kept on searching for clues.

The paste had dried up and scaled off my temples. I was about to rub some more of it on when I realized I was sitting on my heels in Japanese fashion. I had been sitting cross-legged and did not recall changing positions. It took some time to realize fully that I was sitting on the floor in a sort of cloister with high arches. I thought they were brick arches, but upon examining them I saw they were stone.

This transition was very difficult. It came so suddenly that I was not ready to follow. My perception of the elements of the vision was diffused, as if I were dreaming. Yet the components did not change. They remained steady, and I could stop alongside any of them and actually examine it. The vision was not so clear or so real as one induced by peyote. It had a misty character, an intensely pleasing pastel quality.

I wondered whether I could get up or not, and the next thing I noticed was that I had moved. I was at the top of a stairway and H., a friend of mine, was standing at the bottom. Her eyes were feverish. There was a mad glare in them. She laughed aloud and with such intensity that she was terrifying. She began coming up the stairs. I wanted to run away or take cover, because "she'd been off her rocker once." That was the thought that came to my mind. I hid behind a column and she went by me without looking. "She's going on a long trip now," was another thought that occurred to me then; and finally the last thought I remembered was, "She laughs every time she's ready to crack up."

Suddenly the scene became very clear; it was no longer like a dream. It was like an ordinary scene, but I seemed to be looking at it through window glass. I tried to touch a column but all I sensed was that I couldn't move; yet I knew I could stay as long as I wanted, viewing the scene. I was in it and yet I was not part of it.

I experienced a barrage of rational thoughts and arguments. I was, so far as I could judge, in any ordinary state of sober consciousness. Every element belonged to the realm of my normal processes. And yet I knew it was not an ordinary state.

The scene changed abruptly. It was nighttime. I was in the hall of a building. The darkness inside the building made me aware that in the earlier scene the sunlight had been beautifully clear. Yet it had been so commonplace that I did not notice it at the time. As I looked further into the new vision I saw a young man coming out of a room carrying a large knapsack on his shoulders. I didn't know who he was, although I had seen him once or twice. He walked by me and went down the stairs. By then I had forgotten my apprehension, my rational dilemmas. "Who's that guy?" I thought. "Why did I see him?"

The scene changed again and I was watching the young man deface books; he glued some of the pages together, erased markings, and so on. Then I saw him arranging the books neatly in a wooden crate. There was a pile of crates. They were not in his room, but in a storage place. Other images came to my mind, but they were not clear. The scene became foggy. I had a sensation of spinning.

Don Juan shook me by the shoulders and I woke up. He helped me to stand and we walked back to his house. It had been three and a half hours from the moment I began rubbing the paste on my temples to the time I woke up, but the visionary state could not have lasted more than ten minutes. I had no ill effects whatsoever. I was just hungry and sleepy.

Thursday, April 18, 1963

Don Juan asked me last night to describe my recent experience, but I was too sleepy to talk about it. I could not concentrate. Today, as soon as I woke up, he asked me again.

"Who told you this girl H. had been off her rocker?" he asked when I finished my story.

"Nobody. It was just one of the thoughts I had."

"Do you think they were your thoughts?"

I told him they were my thoughts, although I had no reason to think that H. had been sick. They were strange thoughts. They seemed to pop up in my mind from nowhere. He looked at me inquisitively. I asked him if he did not believe me; he laughed and said that it was my routine to be careless with my acts.

"What did I do wrong, don Juan?"

"You should have listened to the lizards."

"How should I have listened?"

"The little lizard on your shoulder was describing to you everything her sister was seeing. She was talking to you. She was telling you everything, and you paid no attention. Instead, you believed the lizard's words were your own thoughts."

"But they *were* my own thoughts, don Juan."

"They were not. That is the nature of this sorcery. Actually, the vision is to be listened to, rather than looked at. The same thing happened to me. I was about to warn you when I remembered my benefactor had not warned me."

"Was your experience like mine, don Juan?"

"No. Mine was a hellish journey. I nearly died."

"Why was it hellish?"

"Maybe because the devil's weed did not like me, or because I was not clear about what I wanted to ask. Like you yesterday. You must have had that girl in mind when you asked the question about the books."

"I can't remember it."

"The lizards are never wrong; they take every thought as a question. The lizard came back and told you things about H. no one will ever be able to understand, because not even you know what your thoughts were."

"How about the other vision I had?"

"Your thoughts must have been steady when you asked that question. And that is the way this sorcery should be conducted, with clarity."

"Do you mean the vision of the girl is not to be taken seriously?"

"How can it be taken seriously if you don't know what questions the little lizards were answering?"

"Would it be more clear to the lizard if one asked only one question?"

"Yes, that would be clearer. If you could hold one thought steadily."

"But what would happen, don Juan, if the one question was not a simple one?"

"As long as your thought is steady, and does not go into other things, it is clear to the little lizards, and then their answer is clear to you."

"Can one ask more questions of the lizards as one goes along in the vision?"

"No. The vision is to look at whatever the lizards are

telling you. That is why I said it is a vision to hear more than a vision to see. That is why I asked you to deal with impersonal matters. Usually, when the question is about people, your longing to touch them or talk to them is too strong, and the lizard will stop talking and the sorcery will be dispelled. You should know much more than you do now before trying to see things that concern you personally. Next time you must listen carefully. I am sure the lizards told you many, many things, but you were not listening."

Friday, April 19, 1963

"What were all the things I ground for the paste, don Juan?"

"Seeds of devil's weed and the weevils that live off the seeds. The measure is one handful of each." He cupped his right hand to show me how much.

I asked him what would happen if one element was used by itself, without the others. He said that such a procedure would only antagonize the devil's weed and the lizards. "You must not antagonize the lizards," he said, "for the next day, during the late afternoon, you must return to the site of your plant. Speak to all lizards and ask the two that helped you in the sorcery to come out again. Search all over until it is quite dark. If you can't find them, you must try it once more the next day. If you are strong you will find both of them, and then you have to eat them, right there. And you will be endowed forever with the capacity to see the unknown. You will never need to catch lizards again to practice this sorcery. They will live inside you from then on."

"What do I do if I find only one of them?"

"If you find only one of them you must let her go at the end of your search. If you find her the first day, don't keep her, hoping you will catch the other one the next day. That will only spoil your friendship with them."

"What happens if I can't find them at all?"

"I think that would be the best thing for you. It implies that you must catch two lizards every time you want their help, but it also implies that you are free."

"What do you mean, free?"

"Free from being the slave of the devil's weed. If the lizards are to live inside you, the devil's weed will never let you go."

"Is that bad?"

"Of course it is bad. She will cut you off from everything else. You will have to spend your life grooming her as an ally. She is possessive. Once she dominates you, there is only one way to go—her way."

"What if I find that the lizards are dead?"

"If you find one or both of them dead, you must not attempt to do this sorcery for some time. Lay off for a while.

"I think this is all I need to tell you; what I have told you is the rule. Whenever you practice this sorcery by yourself, you must follow all the steps I have described while you sit in front of your plant. One more thing. You must not eat or drink until the sorcery is finished."

6

The next step in don Juan's teachings was a new aspect of mastering the second portion of the *Datura* root. In the time that elapsed between the two stages of learning don Juan inquired only about the development of my plant.

Thursday, June 27, 1963

"It is a good practice to test the devil's weed before embarking fully on her path," don Juan said.

"How do you test her, don Juan?"

"You must try another sorcery with the lizards. You have all the elements that are needed to ask one more question of the lizards, this time without my help."

"Is it very necessary that I do this sorcery, don Juan?"

"It is the best way to test the feelings of the devil's weed toward you. She tests you all the time, so it is only fair that you test her too, and if you feel anywhere along her path that for some reason you should not go on, then you must simply stop."

Saturday, June 29, 1963

I brought up the subject of the devil's weed. I wanted don Juan to tell me more about it, and yet I did not want to be committed to participate.

"The second portion is used only to divine, isn't that so, don Juan?" I asked to start the conversation.

"Not only to divine. One learns the sorcery of the lizards with the aid of the second portion, and at the same time one tests the devil's weed; but in reality the second portion is used for other purposes. The sorcery of the lizards is only the beginning."

"Then what is it used for, don Juan?"

He did not answer. He abruptly changed the subject and asked me how big were the *Datura* plants growing around my own plant. I made a gesture of size.

Don Juan said, "I have taught you how to tell a male from a female. Now, go to your plants and bring me both. Go first to your old plant and watch carefully the watercourse made by the rain. By now the rain must have carried the seeds far away. Watch the crevices [*zanjitas*] made by the runoff, and from them determine the direction of the flow. Then find the plant that is growing at the farthest point from your plant. All the devil's weed plants that are growing in between are yours. Later, as they seed, you can extend the size of your territory by following the watercourse from each plant along the way."

He gave me meticulous instructions on how to pro-

cure a cutting tool. The cutting of the root, he said, had
to be done in the following way. First, I had to select
the plant I was to cut and clear away the dirt around
the place where the root joined the stem. Second, I had
to repeat exactly the same dance I had performed when
I replanted the root. Third, I had to cut the stem off,
and leave the root in the ground. The final step was to
dig out sixteen inches of root. He admonished me not
to talk or to betray any feeling during this act.

"You should carry two pieces of cloth," he said.
"Spread them on the ground and place the plants on
them. Then cut the plants into parts and stack them
up. The order is up to you; but you must always remember what order you used, because that is the way
you must always do it. Bring the plants to me as soon
as you have them."

Saturday, July 6, 1963

On Monday, July 1, I cut the *Datura* plants don Juan
had asked for. I waited until it was fairly dark to do
the dancing around the plants because I did not want
anybody to see me. I felt quite apprehensive. I was sure
someone was going to witness my strange acts. I had
previously chosen the plants I thought were a male and
a female. I had to cut off sixteen inches of the root of
each one, and digging to that depth with a wooden stick
was not an easy task. It took me hours. I had to finish
the job in complete darkness, and when I was ready
to cut them I had to use a flashlight. My original apprehension that somebody would watch me was minimal
compared with the fear that someone would spot the
light in the bushes.

I took the plants to don Juan's house on Tuesday,
July 2. He opened the bundles and examined the pieces.
He said he still had to give me the seeds of his plants.
He pushed a mortar in front of me. He took a glass
jar and emptied its contents—dried seeds lumped to-
gether—into the mortar.

I asked him what they were, and he said they were

seeds eaten by weevils. There were quite a few bugs among the seeds—little black grain weevils. He said they were special bugs, and that we had to take them out and put them into a separate jar. He handed me another jar, one-third full of the same kind of weevils. A piece of paper was stuffed into the jar to keep the weevils from escaping.

"Next time you will have to use the bugs from your own plants," don Juan said. "What you do is to cut the seedpods that have tiny holes; they are full of bugs. Open the pod and scrape everything into a jar. Collect one handful of bugs and put them into another container. Treat them rough. Don't be considerate or delicate with them. Measure one handful of the lumped seeds that the bugs have eaten and one handful of the bugs' powder, and bury the rest any place in that direction [here he pointed southeast] from your plant. Then gather good, dry seeds and store them separately. You can gather all you want. You can always use them. It is a good idea to get the seeds out of the pods there so that you can bury everything at once."

Next don Juan told me to grind the lumped seeds first, then the weevil eggs, then the bugs, and last the good, dry seeds.

When all of them were mashed into a fine powder don Juan took the pieces of *Datura* I had cut and stacked up. He separated the male root and wrapped it gently in a piece of cloth. He handed me the rest, and told me to cut everything into little pieces, mash them well, and then put every bit of the juice into a pot. He said I had to mash them in the same order in which I had stacked them up.

After I had finished he told me to measure one cup of boiling water and stir it with everything in the pot, and then to add two more cups. He handed me a smoothly finished bone stick. I stirred the mush with it and put the pot on the fire. Then he said we had to prepare the root, and for that we had to use the larger mortar because the male root could not be cut at all. We went to the back of the house. He had the mortar ready, and I proceeded to pound the root as I had done before. We left the root soaking in water, exposed to the night air, and went inside the house.

He told me to watch the mixture in the pot. I was to let it boil until it had some body—until it was hard to stir. Then he lay down on his mat and went to sleep. The mush had boiled for at least an hour when I noticed that it was getting harder and harder to stir. I judged it must be ready, and pulled it off the fire. I put it in the net under the eaves, and went to sleep.

I woke up when don Juan got up. The sun was shining in a clear sky. It was a hot, dry day. Don Juan commented again that he was sure the devil's weed liked me.

We proceeded to treat the root, and at the end of the day we had quite a bit of yellowish substance in the bottom of the bowl. Don Juan poured off the top water. I thought that was the end of the procedure, but he filled the bowl with boiling water again.

He brought down the pot with the mush from under the roof. The mush seemed to be almost dry. He took the pot inside the house, placed it carefully on the floor, and sat down. Then he began to talk.

"My benefactor told me it was permissible to mix the plant with lard. And that is what you are going to do. My benefactor mixed it with lard for me, but, as I have already said, I never was very fond of the plant and never really tried to become one with her. My benefactor told me that for best results, for those who really want to master the power, the proper thing is to mix the plant with the lard of a wild boar. The fat of the intestines is the best. But it is for you to choose. Perhaps the turn of the wheel will decide that you take the devil's weed as an ally, in which case I will advise you, as my benefactor advised me, to hunt a wild boar and get the fat from the intestines [*sebo de tripa*]. In other times, when the devil's weed was tops, brujos used to go on special hunting trips to get fat from wild boars. They sought the biggest and strongest males. They had a special magic for wild boars; they took from them a special power, so special that it was hard to believe, even in those days. But that power is lost. I don't know anything about it. And I don't know any man who knows about it. Perhaps the weed herself will teach you all that."

Don Juan measured a handful of lard, dumped it into the bowl containing the dry gruel, and scraped the lard left on his hand onto the edge of the pot. He told me to stir the contents until they were smooth and thoroughly mixed.

I whipped the mixture for nearly three hours. Don Juan looked at it from time to time and thought it was not done yet. Finally he seemed satisfied. The air whipped into the paste had given it a light-gray color and the consistency of jelly. He hung the bowl from the roof next to the other bowl. He said he was going to leave it there until the next day because it would take two days to prepare this second portion. He told me not to eat anything in the meantime. I could have water, but no food at all.

The next day, Thursday, July 4, don Juan directed me to leach the root four times. By the last time I poured the water out of the bowl it had already become dark. We sat on the porch. He put both bowls in front of him. The root extract measured a teaspoon of a whitish starch. He put it into a cup and added water. He rotated the cup in his hand to dissolve the substance and then handed the cup to me. He told me to drink all that was in the cup. I drank it fast and then put the cup on the floor and slumped back. My heart began pounding; I felt I could not breathe. Don Juan ordered me, matter-of-factly, to take off all of my clothes. I asked him why, and he said I had to rub myself with the paste. I hesitated. I did not know whether to undress. Don Juan urged me to hurry up. He said there was very little time to fool around. I removed all my clothes.

He took his bone stick and cut two horizontal lines on the surface of the paste, thus dividing the contents of the bowl into three equal parts. Then, starting at the center of the top line, he cut a vertical line perpendicular to the other two, dividing the paste into five parts. He pointed to the bottom right area, and said that was for my left foot. The area above it was for my left leg. The top and largest part was for my genitals. The next one below, on the left side, was for my right leg, and the area at the bottom left was for my right foot. He told me to apply the part of the paste designated for my left foot to the sole of my foot and rub it thoroughly. Then he guided me in applying the paste on the inside part of my whole left leg, on my genitals, down the inside of my whole right leg, and finally on the sole of my right foot.

I followed his directions. The paste was cold and had a particularly strong odor. When I had finished applying it I straightened up. The smell from the mixture entered my nostrils. It was suffocating me. The pungent odor was actually choking me. It was like a gas of some sort. I tried to breathe through my mouth and tried to talk to don Juan, but I couldn't.

Don Juan kept staring at me. I took a step toward him. My legs were rubbery and long, extremely long. I took another step. My knee joints felt springy, like a vault pole; they shook and vibrated and contracted elastically. I moved forward. The motion of my body was slow and shaky; it was more like a tremor forward and up. I looked down and saw don Juan sitting below me, way below me. The momentum carried me forward one more step, which was even more elastic and longer than the preceding one. And from there I soared. I remember coming down once; then I pushed up with both feet, sprang backward, and glided on my back. I saw the dark sky above me, and the clouds going by me. I jerked my body so I could look down. I saw the dark mass of the mountains. My speed was extraordinary. My arms were fixed, folded against my sides. My head was the directional unit. If I kept it bent backward I made vertical circles. I changed directions by turning my head to the side. I enjoyed such freedom and swiftness as I had never known before. The marvelous darkness gave me a feeling of sadness, of longing, perhaps. It was as if I had found a place where I belonged—the darkness of the night. I tried to look around, but all I sensed was that the night was serene, and yet it held so much power.

Suddenly I knew it was time to come down; it was as if I had been given an order I had to obey. And I began descending like a feather with lateral motions. That type of movement made me very ill. It was slow and jerky, as though I were being lowered by pulleys. I got sick. My head was bursting with the most excruciating pain. A kind of blackness enveloped me. I was very aware of the feeling of being suspended in it.

The next thing I remember is the feeling of waking up. I was in my bed in my own room. I sat up. And the image of my room dissolved. I stood up. I was naked! The motion of standing made me sick again.

I recognized some of the landmarks. I was about half a mile from don Juan's house, near the place of his *Datura* plants. Suddenly everything fitted into place, and I realized that I would have to walk all the way back to his house, naked. To be deprived of clothes was a profound psychological disadvantage, but there was nothing I could do to solve the problem. I thought of making myself a skirt with branches, but the thought seemed ludicrous and, besides, it was soon going to be dawn, for the morning twilight was already clear. I forgot about my discomfort and my nausea and started to walk toward the house. I was obsessed with the fear of being discovered. I watched for people and dogs. I tried to run, but I hurt my feet on the small, sharp stones. I walked slowly. It was already very clear. Then I saw somebody coming up the road, and I quickly jumped behind the bushes. My situation seemed so incongruous to me. A moment before I had been enjoying the unbelievable pleasure of flying; the next minute I found myself hiding, embarrassed by my own nakedness. I thought of jumping out on the road again and running with all my might past the person who was coming. I thought he would be so startled that by the time he realized it was a naked man I would have left him far behind. I thought all that, but I did not dare to move.

The person coming up the road was just upon me and stopped walking. I heard him calling my name. It was don Juan, and he had my clothes. As I put them on he looked at me and laughed; he laughed so hard that I wound up laughing too.

The same day, Friday, July 5, late in the afternoon, don Juan asked me to narrate the details of my experience. As carefully as I could, I related the whole episode.

"The second portion of the devil's weed is used to fly," he said when I had finished. "The unguent by itself is not enough. My benefactor said that it is the root that gives direction and wisdom, and it is the cause of flying. As you learn more, and take it often in order to fly, you will begin to see everything with great clarity. You can soar through the air for hundreds of miles to see what is happening at any place you want, or to deliver a fatal blow to your enemies far away. As you become familiar with the devil's weed, she will teach you how to do such things. For instance, she has taught you already how to change directions. In the same manner, she will teach you unimaginable things."

"Like what, don Juan?"

"That I can't tell you. Every man is different. My benefactor never told me what he had learned. He told me how to proceed, but never what he saw. That is only for oneself."

"But I tell you all I see, don Juan."

"Now you do. Later you will not. The next time you take the devil's weed you will do it by yourself, around your own plants, because that is where you will land, around your plants. Remember that. That is why I came down here to my plants to look for you."

He said nothing more, and I fell asleep. When I woke up in the evening, I felt invigorated. For some reason I exuded a sort of physical contentment. I was happy, satisfied.

Don Juan asked me, "Did you like the night? Or was it frightful?"

I told him that the night was truly magnificent.

"How about your headache? Was it very bad?" he asked.

"The headache was as strong as all the other feelings. It was the worst pain I have ever had," I said.

"Would that keep you from wanting to taste the power of the devil's weed again?"

"I don't know. I don't want it now, but later I might. I really don't know, don Juan."

There was a question I wanted to ask him. I knew he was going to evade it, so I waited for him to mention the subject; I waited all day. Finally, before I left that evening, I had to ask him, "Did I really fly, don Juan?"

"That is what you told me. Didn't you?"

"I know, don Juan. I mean, did my body fly? Did I take off like a bird?"

"You always ask me questions I cannot answer. You flew. That is what the second portion of the devil's weed is for. As you take more of it, you will learn how to fly perfectly. It is not a simple matter. A man *flies* with the help of the second portion of the devil's weed. That is all I can tell you. What you want to know makes no sense. Birds fly like birds and a man who has taken the devil's weed flies as such [*el enyerbado vuela así*]."

"As birds do? [*¿Así como los pájaros?*]."

"No, he flies as a man who has taken the weed [*No, así como los enyerbados*]."

"Then I didn't really fly, don Juan. I flew in imagination, in my mind alone. Where was my body?"

"In the bushes," he replied cuttingly, but immediately broke into laughter again. "The trouble with you is that you understand things in only one way. You don't think a man flies; and yet a brujo can move a thousand miles in one second to see what is going on. He can deliver a blow to his enemies long distances away. So, does he or doesn't he fly?"

"You see, don Juan, you and I are differently oriented. Suppose, for the sake of argument, one of my fellow students had been here with me when I took the devil's weed. Would he have been able to see me flying?"

"There you go again with your questions about what would happen if . . . It is useless to talk that way. If your friend, or anybody else, takes the second portion of the weed all he can do is fly. Now, if he had simply watched you, he might have seen you flying, or he might not. That depends on the man."

"But what I mean, don Juan, is that if you and I look at a bird and see it fly, we agree that it is flying. But if two of my friends had seen me flying as I did last night, would they have agreed that I was flying?"

"Well, they might have. You agree that birds fly because you have seen them flying. Flying is a common thing with birds. But you will not agree on other things birds do, because you have never seen birds doing them. If your friends knew about men flying with the devil's weed, then they would agree."

"Let's put it another way, don Juan. What I meant to say is that if I had tied myself to a rock with a heavy chain I would have flown just the same, because my body had nothing to do with my flying."

Don Juan looked at me incredulously. "If you tie yourself to a rock," he said, "I'm afraid you will have to fly holding the rock with its heavy chain."

7

Collecting the ingredients and preparing them for the smoke mixture formed a yearly cycle. The first year don Juan taught me the procedure. In December of 1962, the second year, when the cycle was renewed, don Juan merely directed me; I collected the ingredients myself, prepared them, and put them away until the next year.

In December, 1963, a new cycle started for the third time. Don Juan then showed me how to combine the dried ingredients I had collected and prepared the year before. He put the smoking mixture into a small leather bag, and we set out once again to collect the different components for the following year.

Don Juan seldom mentioned the "little smoke" during the year that elapsed between the two gatherings. Every time I went to see him, however, he gave me his pipe to hold, and the procedure of "getting familiar" with the pipe developed in the way he had described. He put the pipe in my hands very gradually. He demanded absolute and careful concentration on that action, and gave me very explicit directions. Any fumbling with the pipe would inevitably result in his or my death, he said.

As soon as we had finished the third collecting and preparing cycle, don Juan began to talk about the smoke as an ally for the first time in more than a year.

Monday, December 23, 1963

We were driving back to his house after collecting some yellow flowers for the mixture. They were one of the necessary ingredients. I made the remark that this year we did not follow the same order in collecting the ingredients as we had the year before. He laughed and said the smoke was not moody or petty, as the devil's weed was. For the smoke, the order of collecting was unimportant; all that was required was that the man using the mixture had to be accurate and exact.

I asked don Juan what we were going to do with the mixture he had prepared and given me to keep. He replied that it was mine, and added that I had to use it as soon as possible. I asked how much of it was needed each time. The small bag he had given me contained approximately three times the amount a small tobacco bag would hold. He told me I would have to use all the contents of my bag in one year, and how much I needed each time I smoked was a personal matter.

I wanted to know what would happen if I never finished the bag. Don Juan said that nothing would happen; the smoke did not require anything. He himself did not need to smoke anymore, and yet he made a new mixture each year. He then corrected himself and said that he *rarely* had to smoke. I asked what he did with the unused mixture, but he did not answer. He said the mixture was no longer good if not used in one year.

At this point we got into a long argument. I did not phrase my questions correctly and his answers seemed confusing. I wanted to know if the mixture would lose its hallucinogenic properties, or power, after a year, thus making the yearly cycle necessary; but he insisted that the mixture would not lose its power at any time. The only thing that happened, he said, was that a man did not need it anymore because he had made a new supply; he had to dispose of the remaining old mixture in a specific way, which don Juan did not want to reveal to me at that point.

Tuesday, December 24, 1963

"You said, don Juan, you don't have to smoke anymore."

"Yes, because the smoke is my ally I don't need to smoke anymore. I can call him anytime, anyplace."

"Do you mean he comes to you even if you do not smoke?"

"I mean I go to him freely."

"Will I be able to do that, too?"

"If you succeed in getting him as your ally, you will."

Tuesday, December 31, 1963

On Thursday, December 26, I had my first experience with don Juan's ally, the smoke. All day I drove him around and did chores for him. We returned to his house in the later afternoon. I mentioned that we had

had nothing to eat all day. He was completely unconcerned over that; instead he began to tell me it was imperative for me to become familiar with the smoke. He said I had to experience it myself to realize how important it was as an ally.

Without giving me an opportunity to say anything, don Juan told me he was going to light his pipe for me, right then. I tried to dissuade him, arguing that I did not believe I was ready. I told him I felt I had not handled the pipe for a long enough time. But he said there was not much time left for me to learn, and I had to use the pipe very soon. He brought the pipe out of its sack and fondled it. I sat on the floor next to him and frantically tried to get sick and pass out—to do anything to put off this unavoidable step.

The room was almost dark. Don Juan had lighted the kerosene lamp and placed it in a corner. Usually the lamp kept the room in a relaxing semidarkness, its yellowish light always soothing. This time, however, the light seemed dim and unusually red; it was unnerving. He untied his small bag of mixture without removing it from the cord fastened around his neck. He brought the pipe close to him, put it inside his shirt, and poured some of the mixture into the bowl. He made me watch the procedure, pointing out that if some of the mixture spilled it would fall inside his shirt.

Don Juan filled three-fourths of the bowl, then tied the bag with one hand while holding the pipe in the other. He picked up a small clay dish, handed it to me, and asked me to get some small charcoals from the fire outside. I went to the back of the house and scooped a bunch of charcoals from the adobe stove. I hurried back to his room. I felt deep anxiety. It was like a premonition.

I sat next to don Juan and gave him the dish. He looked at it and calmly said the charcoals were too big. He wanted smaller ones that would fit inside the pipe bowl. I went back to the stove and got some. He took the new dish of charcoals and put it before him. He was sitting with his legs crossed and tucked under him. He glanced at me out of the corner of his eye and leaned forward until his chin nearly touched the charcoals. He held the pipe in his left hand, and with an extremely swift movement of his right hand picked up a burning piece of charcoal and put it into the bowl of the pipe; then he sat up straight and, holding the pipe with both hands, put it to his mouth and puffed three times. He stretched his arms to me and told me in a forceful whisper to take the pipe with both hands and smoke.

The thought of refusing the pipe and running away crossed my mind for an instant; but don Juan demanded again—still in a whisper—that I take the pipe and smoke. I looked at him. His eyes were fixed on me. But his stare was friendly, concerned. It was clear that I had made the choice a long time before; there was no alternative but to do what he said.

I took the pipe and nearly dropped it. It was hot! I put it to my mouth with extreme care because I imagined its heat would be intolerable on my lips. But I felt no heat at all.

Don Juan told me to inhale. The smoke flowed into my mouth, and seemed to circulate there. It was heavy! I felt as though I had a mouthful of dough. The simile occurred to me although I had never had a mouthful of dough. The smoke was also like menthol, and the inside of my mouth suddenly became cold. It was a refreshing sensation. "Again! Again!" I heard don Juan whispering. I felt the smoke seep inside my body freely, almost without my control. I needed no more urging from don Juan. Mechanically I kept inhaling.

Suddenly don Juan leaned over and took the pipe from my hands. He tapped the ashes gently on the dish with the charcoals, then he wet his finger with saliva and rotated it inside the bowl to clean its sides. He blew through the stem repeatedly. I saw him put the pipe back into its sheath. His actions held my interest.

When he had finished cleaning the pipe and putting it away, he stared at me, and I realized for the first time that my whole body was numb, mentholated. My face felt heavy and my jaws hurt. I could not keep my mouth closed, but there was no saliva flow. My mouth was burning dry, and yet I was not thirsty. I began to sense an unusual heat all over my head. A cold heat! My breath seemed to cut my nostrils and upper lip every time I exhaled. But it didn't burn; it hurt like a piece of ice.

Don Juan sat next to me, to my right, and without moving held the pipe sheath against the floor as though keeping it down by force. My hands were heavy. My arms sagged, pulling my shoulders down. My nose was running. I wiped it with the back of my hand, and my upper lip was rubbed off! I wiped my face, and all the flesh was wiped off! I was melting! I felt as if my flesh was actually melting. I jumped to my feet and tried to grab hold of something—anything—with which to support myself. I was experiencing a terror I had never felt before. I held onto a pole that don Juan keeps stuck on the floor in the center of his room. I stood there for a moment, then I turned to look at him. He was still sitting motionless, holding his pipe, staring at me.

My breath was painfully hot (or cold?). It was choking me. I bent my head forward to rest it on the pole, but apparently I missed it, and my head kept on moving downward beyond the point where the pole was. I stopped when I was nearly down to the floor. I pulled myself up. The pole was there in front of my eyes! I tried again to rest my head on it. I tried to control myself and to be aware, and kept my eyes open as I leaned forward to touch the pole with my forehead. It was a few inches from my eyes, but as I put my head against it I had the queerest feeling that I was going right through it.

In a desperate search for a rational explanation I concluded that my eyes were distorting depth, and that the pole must have been ten feet away, even though I saw it directly in front of my face. I then conceived a logical, rational way to check the position of the pole. I began moving sideways around it, one little step at a time. My argument was that in walking around the pole in that way I couldn't possibly make a circle more than five feet in diameter; if the pole was really ten feet away from me, or beyond my reach, a moment would come when I would have my back to it. I trusted that at that moment the pole would vanish, because in reality it would be behind me.

I then proceeded to circle the pole, but it remained in front of my eyes as I went around it. In a fit of frustration I grabbed it with both hands, but my hands went through it. I was grabbing the air. I carefully calculated the distance between the pole and myself. I figured it must be three feet. That is, my eyes perceived it as three feet. I played for a moment with the perception of depth by moving my head from one side to the other, focusing each eye in turn on the pole and then on the background. According to my way of judging depth, the pole was unmistakably before me, possibly three feet away. Stretching out my arms to protect my head, I charged with all my strength. The sensation was the same—I went through the pole. This time I went all the way to the floor. I stood up again. And standing up was perhaps the most unusual of all the acts I performed that night. I thought myself up! In order to get up I did not use my muscles and skeletal frame in the way I am accustomed to doing, because I no longer had control over them. I knew it the instant I hit the ground. But my curiosity about the pole was so strong I "thought myself up" in a kind of reflex action. And before I fully realized I could not move, I was up.

I called to don Juan for help. At one moment I yelled frantically at the top of my voice, but don Juan did not move. He kept on looking at me, sideways, as though he didn't want to turn his head to face me fully. I took a step toward him, but instead of moving forward I staggered backward and fell against the wall. I knew I had rammed against it with my back, yet it did not feel hard; I was completely suspended in a soft, spongy substance—it was the wall. My arms were stretched out laterally, and slowly my whole body seemed to sink into the wall. I could only look forward

into the room. Don Juan was still watching me, but he
made no move to help me. I made a supreme effort to
jerk my body out of the wall, but it only sank deeper
and deeper. In the midst of indescribable terror, I felt
that the spongy wall was closing in on my face. I tried
to shut my eyes but they were fixed open.

I don't remember what else happened. Suddenly don
Juan was in front of me, a short distance away. We
were in the other room. I saw his table and the dirt
stove with the fire burning, and with the corner of my
eye I distinguished the fence outside the house. I could
see everything very clearly. Don Juan had brought the
kerosene lantern and hung it from the beam in the
middle of the room. I tried to look in a different direction, but my eyes were set to see only straight forward.
I couldn't distinguish, or feel, any part of my body. My
breathing was undetectable. But my thoughts were extremely lucid. I was clearly aware of whatever was taking place in front of me. Don Juan walked toward me,
and my clarity of mind ended. Something seemed to stop
inside me. There were no more thoughts. I saw don
Juan coming and I hated him. I wanted to tear him
apart. I could have killed him then, but I could not
move. At first I vaguely sensed a pressure on my head,
but it also disappeared. There was only one thing
left—an overwhelming anger at don Juan. I saw him
only a few inches from me. I wanted to claw him apart.
I felt I was groaning. Something in me began to convulse. I heard don Juan talking to me. His voice was
soft and soothing, and, I felt, infinitely pleasing. He
came even closer and started to recite a Spanish lullaby.

"Lady Saint Ana, why does the baby cry? For an
apple he has lost. I will give you one. I will give you
two. One for the boy and one for you [¿Señora Santa
Ana, porque llora el niño? Por una manzana que se le
ha perdido. Yo le daré una. Yo le daré dos. Una para
el niño y otra para vos]." A warmth pervaded me. It
was a warmth of heart and feelings. Don Juan's words
were a distant echo. They recalled the forgotten mem-
ories of childhood.

The violence I had felt before disappeared. The resentment changed into a longing—a joyous affection for don Juan. He said I must struggle not to fall asleep; that I no longer had a body and was free to turn into anything I wanted. He stepped back. My eyes were at a normal level as though I were standing in front of him. He extended both his arms toward me and told me to come inside them.

Either I moved forward, or he came closer to me. His hands were almost on my face—on my eyes, although I did not feel them. "Get inside my chest," I heard him say. I felt I was engulfing him. It was the same sensation of the sponginess of the wall.

Then I could hear only his voice commanding me to look and see. I could not distinguish him anymore. My eyes were apparently open for I saw flashes of light on a red field; it was as though I was looking at a light through my closed eyelids. Then my thoughts were turned on again. They came back in a fast barrage of images—faces, scenery. Scenes without any coherence popped up and disappeared. It was like a fast dream in which images overlap and change. Then the thoughts began to diminish in number and intensity, and soon they were gone again. There was only an awareness of affection, of being happy. I couldn't distinguish any shapes or light. All of a sudden I was pulled up. I distinctly felt I was being lifted. And I was free, moving with tremendous lightness and speed in water or air. I swam like an eel; I contorted and twisted and soared up and down at will. I felt a cold wind blowing all around me, and I began to float like a feather back and forth, down, and down, and down.

Saturday, December 28, 1963

I woke up yesterday late in the afternoon. Don Juan told me I had slept peacefully for nearly two days. I had a splitting headache. I drank some water and got sick. I felt tired, extremely tired, and after eating I went back to sleep.

Today I felt perfectly relaxed again. Don Juan and I talked about my experience with the little smoke. Thinking that he wanted me to tell the whole story the way I always did, I began to describe my impressions, but he stopped me and said it was not necessary. He told me I had really not done anything, and that I had fallen asleep right away, so there was nothing to talk about.

"How about the way I felt? Isn't that important at all?" I insisted.

"No, not with the smoke. Later on, when you learn how to travel, we will talk; when you learn how to get into things."

"Does one really 'get into' things?"

"Don't you remember? You went *into* and *through* that wall."

"I think I really went *out* of my mind."

"No, you didn't."

"Did you behave the same way I did when you smoked for the first time, don Juan?"

"No, it wasn't the same. We have different characters."

"How did you behave?"

Don Juan did not answer. I rephrased the question and asked it again. But he said he did not remember his experiences, and that my question was comparable to asking a fisherman how he felt the first time he fished.

He said the smoke as an ally was unique, and I reminded him that he had also said Mescalito was unique. He argued that each was unique, but that they differed in quality.

"Mescalito is a protector because he talks to you and can guide your acts," he said. "Mescalito teaches the right way to live. And you can see him because he is outside you. The smoke, on the other hand, is an ally. It transforms you and gives you power without ever showing its presence. You can't talk to it. But you know it exists because it takes your body away and makes you as light as air. Yet you never see it. But it is there giving you power to accomplish unimaginable things, such as when it takes your body away."

"I really felt I had lost my body, don Juan."

"You did."

"You mean, I really didn't have a body?"

"What do *you* think yourself?"

"Well, I don't know. All I can tell you is what I felt."

"That is all there is in reality—what you felt."

"But how did you see me, don Juan? How did I appear to you?"

"How I saw you does not matter. It is like the time when you grabbed the pole. You felt it was not there and you went around it to make sure it was there. But when you jumped at it you felt again that it was not really there."

"But you saw me as I am now, didn't you?"

"No! You were NOT as you are now!"

"True! I admit that. But I had my body, didn't I, although *I* couldn't feel it?"

"No! Goddammit! You did not have a body like the body you have today!"

"What happened to my body then?"

"I thought you understood. The little smoke took your body."

"But where did it go?"

"How in hell do you expect me to know that?"

It was useless to persist in trying to get a "rational" explanation. I told him I did not want to argue or to ask stupid questions, but if I accepted the idea that it was possible to lose my body I would lose all my rationality.

He said that I was exaggerating, as usual, and that I did not, nor was I going to, lose anything because of the little smoke.

Tuesday, January 28, 1964

I asked don Juan what he thought of the idea of giving the smoke to anyone who wanted the experience.

He indignantly replied that to give the smoke to any-one would be just the same as killing him, for he would have no one to guide him. I asked don Juan to explain what he meant. He said I was *there,* alive and talking to him, because he had brought me back. He had restored my body. Without him I would never have awakened.

"How did you restore my body, don Juan?"

"You will learn that later, but you will have to learn to do it all by yourself. That is the reason I want you to learn as much as you can while I am still around. You have wasted enough time asking stupid questions about nonsense. But perhaps it is not in your destiny to learn all about the little smoke."

"Well, what shall I do, then?"

"Let the smoke teach you as much as you can learn."

"Does the smoke also teach?"

"Of course it teaches."

"Does it teach as Mescalito does?"

"No, it is not a teacher as Mescalito is. It does not show the same things."

"But what does the smoke teach, then?"

"It shows you how to handle its power, and to learn that you must take it as many times as you can."

"Your ally is very frightening, don Juan. It was unlike anything I ever experienced before. I thought I had lost my mind."

For some reason this was the most poignant image that came to my mind. I viewed the total event from the peculiar stand of having had other hallucinogenic experiences from which to draw a comparison, and the only thing that occurred to me, over and over again, was that with the smoke one loses one's mind.

Don Juan discarded my simile, saying that what I felt was its unimaginable power. And to handle that power, he said, one has to live a strong life. The idea of the strong life not only pertains to the preparation period, but also entails the attitude of the man after the experience. He said that smoke is so strong one can match it only with strength; otherwise, one's life would be shattered to bits.

I asked him if the smoke had the same effect on everyone. He said it produced a transformation, but not in everyone.

"Then, what is the special reason the smoke produced the transformation in me?" I asked.

"That, I think, is a very silly question. You have followed obediently every step required. It is no mystery that the smoke transformed you."

I asked him again to tell me about my appearance. I wanted to know how I looked, for the image of a bodiless being he had planted in my mind was understandably unbearable.

He said that to tell the truth he was afraid to look at me; he felt the same way his benefactor must have felt when he saw don Juan smoking for the first time.

"Why were you afraid? Was I that frightening?" I asked.

"I had never seen anyone smoking before."

"Didn't you see your benefactor smoke?"

"No."

"You have never seen even yourself?"

"How could I?"

"You could smoke in front of a mirror."

He did not answer, but stared at me and shook his head. I asked him again if it was possible to look into a mirror. He said it would be possible, although it would be useless because one would probably die of fright, if of nothing else.

I said, "Then one must look frightful."

"I have wondered all my life about the same thing," he said. "Yet I did not ask, nor did I look into a mirror. I did not even think of that."

"How can I find out then?"

"You will have to wait, the same way I did, until you give the smoke to someone else—if you ever master it, of course. Then you will see how a man looks. That is the rule."

"What would happen if I smoked in front of a camera and took a picture of myself?"

"I don't know. The smoke would probably turn against you. But I suppose you find it so harmless you feel you can play with it."

I told him I did not mean to play, but that he had told me before that the smoke did not require steps, and I thought there would be no harm in wanting to know how one looked. He corrected me, saying that he had meant there was no necessity to follow a specific order, as there is with the devil's weed; all that was needed with the smoke was the proper attitude, he said. From that point of view one had to be exact in following the rule. He gave me an example, explaining that it did not matter what ingredient for the mixture was picked first, so long as the amount was correct.

I asked if there would be any harm in my telling others about my experience. He replied that the only secrets never to be revealed were how to make the mixture, how to move around, and how to return; other matters concerning the subject were of no importance.

8

My last encounter with Mescalito was a cluster of four sessions which took place within four consecutive days. Don Juan called this long session a *mitote*. It was a peyote ceremony for *peyoteros* and apprentices. There were two older men, about don Juan's age, one of whom was the leader, and five younger men including myself.

The ceremony took place in the state of Chihuahua, Mexico, near the Texas border. It consisted of singing and of ingesting peyote during the night. In the daytime women attendants, who stayed outside the confines of the ceremony site, supplied each man with water, and only a token of ritual food was consumed each day.

Saturday, September 12, 1964

During the first night of the ceremony, Thursday, September 3, I took eight peyote buttons. They had no effect on me, or if they did, it was a very slight one. I kept my eyes closed most of the night. I felt much better that way. I did not fall asleep, nor was I tired. At the very end of the session the singing became extraordinary. For a brief moment I felt uplifted and wanted to weep, but as the song ended the feeling vanished.

We all got up and went outside. The women gave us water. Some of the men gargled it; others drank it. The men did not talk at all, but the women chatted and giggled all day long. The ritual food was served at midday. It was cooked corn.

At sundown on Friday, September 4, the second session began. The leader sang his peyote song, and the cycle of songs and intake of peyote buttons began once again. It ended in the morning with each man singing his own song, in unison with the others.

When I went out I did not see as many women as had been there the day before. Someone gave me water, but I was no longer concerned with my surroundings. I had ingested eight buttons again, but the effect had been different.

It must have been toward the end of the session that the singing was greatly accelerated, with everybody singing at once. I perceived that something or somebody outside the house wanted to come in. I couldn't tell whether the singing was done to prevent "it" from bursting in, or to lure it inside.

I was the only one who did not have a song. They all seemed to look at me questioningly, especially the young men. I grew embarrassed and closed my eyes.

Then I realized I could perceive what was going on much better if I kept my eyes closed. This idea held my undivided attention. I closed my eyes, and saw the men in front of me. I opened my eyes, and the image was unchanged. The surroundings were exactly the same for me, whether my eyes were open or closed.

Suddenly everything vanished, or crumbled, and there emerged in its place the manlike figure of Mescalito I had seen two years before. He was sitting some distance away with his profile toward me. I stared fixedly at him, but he did not look at me; not once did he turn.

I believed I was doing something wrong, something that kept him away. I got up and walked toward him to ask him about it. But the act of moving dispelled the image. It began to fade, and the figures of the men I was with were superimposed upon it. Again I heard the loud, frantic singing.

I went into the nearby bushes and walked for a while. Everything stood out very clearly. I noticed I was seeing in the darkness, but it mattered very little this time. The important point was, why did Mescalito avoid me?

I returned to join the group, and as I was about to enter the house I heard a heavy rumbling and felt a tremor. The ground shook. It was the same noise I had heard in the peyote valley two years before.

I ran into the bushes again. I knew that Mescalito was there, and that I was going to find him. But he was not there. I waited until morning, and joined the others just before the session ended.

The usual procedure was repeated on the third day. I was not tired, but I slept during the afternoon.

In the evening of Saturday, September 5, the old man sang his peyote song to start the cycle once more. During this session I chewed only one button and did not listen to any of the songs, nor did I pay attention to anything that went on. From the first moment my whole being was uniquely concentrated on one point. I knew something terribly important for my well-being was missing.

While the men sang I asked Mescalito, in a loud voice, to teach me a song. My pleading mingled with the men's loud singing. Immediately I heard a song in my ears. I turned around and sat with my back to the group and listened. I heard the words and the tune over and over, and I repeated them until I had learned the whole song. It was a long song in Spanish. Then I sang it to the group several times. And soon afterward a new song came to my ears. By morning I had sung both songs countless times. I felt I had been renewed, fortified.

After the water was given to us, don Juan gave me a bag, and we all went into the hills. It was a long, strenuous walk to a low mesa. There I saw several peyote plants. But for some reason I did not want to look at them. After we had crossed the mesa, the group broke up. Don Juan and I walked back, collecting peyote buttons just as we had done the first time I helped him.

We returned in the late afternoon of Sunday, September 6. In the evening the leader opened the cycle again. Nobody had said a word but I knew perfectly well it was the last gathering. This time the old man sang a new song. A sack with fresh peyote buttons was passed around. This was the first time I had tasted a fresh button. It was pulpy but hard to chew. It resembled a hard, green fruit, and was sharper and more bitter than the dried buttons. Personally, I found the fresh peyote infinitely more alive.

I chewed fourteen buttons. I counted them carefully. I did not finish the last one, for I heard the familiar rumble that marked the presence of Mescalito. Everybody sang frantically, and I knew that don Juan, and everybody else, had actually heard the noise. I refused to think that their reaction was a response to a cue given by one of them merely to deceive me.

At that moment I felt a great surge of wisdom engulfing me. A conjecture I had played with for three years turned into a certainty. It had taken me three years to realize, or rather to find out, that whatever is contained in the cactus *Lophophora williamsii* had nothing to do with me in order to exist as an entity; it existed by itself out there, at large. I knew it then.

I sang feverishly until I could no longer voice the words. I felt as if my songs were inside my body, shaking me uncontrollably. I needed to go out and find Mescalito, or I would explode. I walked toward the peyote field. I kept on singing my songs. I knew they were individually mine—the unquestionable proof of my singleness. I sensed each one of my steps. They resounded on the ground; their echo produced the indescribable euphoria of being a man.

Each one of the peyote plants on the field shone with a bluish, scintillating light. One plant had a very bright light. I sat in front of it and sang my songs to it. As I sang Mescalito came out of the plant—the same manlike figure I had seen before. He looked at me. With great audacity, for a person of my temperament, I sang to him. There was a sound of flutes, or of wind, a familiar musical vibration. He seemed to have said, as he had two years before, "What do you want?"

I spoke very loudly. I said that I knew there was something amiss in my life and in my actions, but I could not find out what it was. I begged him to tell me what was wrong with me, and also to tell me his name so that I could call him when I needed him. He looked at me, elongated his mouth like a trumpet until it reached my ear, and then told me his name.

Suddenly I saw my own father standing in the middle of the peyote field; but the field had vanished and the scene was my old home, the home of my childhood. My father and I were standing by a fig tree. I embraced my father and hurriedly began to tell him things I had never before been able to say. Every one of my thoughts was concise and to the point. It was as if we had no time, really, and I had to say everything at once. I said staggering things about my feelings toward him, things I would never have been able to voice under ordinary circumstances.

My father did not speak. He just listened and then

was pulled, or sucked, away. I was alone again. I wept with remorse and sadness.

I walked through the peyote field calling the name Mescalito had taught me. Something emerged from a strange, starlike light on a peyote plant. It was a long shiny object—a stick of light the size of a man. For a moment it illuminated the whole field with an intense yellowish or amber light; then it lit up the whole sky above, creating a portentous, marvelous sight. I thought I would go blind if I kept on looking; I covered my eyes and buried my head in my arms.

I had a clear notion that Mescalito told me to eat one more peyote button. I thought, "I can't do that because I have no knife to cut it."

"Eat one from the ground," he said to me in the same strange way.

I lay on my stomach and chewed the top of a plant. It kindled me. It filled every corner of my body with warmth and directness. Everything was alive. Everything had exquisite and intricate detail, and yet everything was so simple. I was everywhere; I could see up and down and around, all at the same time.

This particular feeling lasted long enough for me to become aware of it. Then it changed into an oppressive terror, terror that did not come upon me abruptly, but somehow swiftly. At first my marvelous world of silence was jolted by sharp noises, but I was not concerned. Then the noises became louder and were uninterrupted, as if they were closing in on me. And gradually I lost the feeling of floating in a world undifferentiated, indifferent, and beautiful. The noises became gigantic steps. Something enormous was breathing and moving around me. I believed it was hunting for me.

I ran and hid under a boulder, and tried to determine from there what was following me. At one moment I crept out of my hiding place to look, and whoever was my pursuer came upon me. It was like sea kelp. It threw itself on me. I thought its weight was going to crush me, but I found myself inside a pipe or a cavity. I clearly saw that the kelp had not covered all the ground surface around me. There remained a bit of free ground underneath the boulder. I began to crawl underneath it. I saw huge drops of liquid falling from the kelp. I "knew" it was secreting digestive acid in order to dissolve me. A drop fell on my arms. I tried to rub off the acid with dirt, and applied saliva to it as I kept on digging. At one point I was almost vaporous. I was being pushed up toward a light. I thought the kelp had dissolved me. I vaguely detected a light which grew brighter; it was pushing from under the ground until finally it erupted into what I recognized as the sun coming out from behind the mountains.

Slowly I began to regain my usual sensorial processes. I lay on my stomach with my chin on my folded arm. The peyote plant in front of me began to light up again, and before I could move my eyes the long light emerged again. It hovered over me. I sat up. The light touched my whole body with quiet strength, and then rolled away out of sight.

I ran all the way to the place where the other men were. We all returned to town. Don Juan and I stayed one more day with don Roberto, the peyote leader. I slept all the time we were there. When we were about to leave, the young men who had taken part in the peyote sessions came up to me. They embraced me one by one, and laughed shyly. Each one of them introduced himself. I talked with them for hours about everything except the peyote meetings.

Don Juan said it was time to leave. The young men embraced me again. "Come back," one of them said. "We are already waiting for you," another one added. I drove away slowly, trying to see the older men, but none of them was there.

Thursday, September 10, 1964

To tell don Juan about an experience always forced me to recall it step by step, to the best of my ability. This seemed to be the only way to remember everything.

Today I told him the details of my last encounter

with Mescalito. He listened to my story attentively up to the point when Mescalito told me his name. Don Juan interrupted me there.

"You are on your own now," he said. "The protector has accepted you. I will be of very little help to you from now on. You don't have to tell me anything more about your relationship with him. You know his name now; and neither his name, nor his dealings with you, should ever be mentioned to a living being."

I insisted that I wanted to tell him all the details of the experience, because it made no sense to me. I told him I needed his assistance to interpret what I have seen. He said I could do that by myself, that it was better for me to start thinking on my own. I argued that I was interested in hearing his opinions because it would take me too long to arrive at my own, and I did not know how to proceed.

I said, "Take the songs for instance. What do they mean?"

"Only you can decide that," he said. "How could I know what they mean? The protector alone can tell you that, just as he alone can teach you his songs. If I were to tell you what they mean, it would be the same as if you learned someone else's songs."

"What do you mean by that, don Juan?"

"You can tell who are the phonies by listening to people singing the protector's songs. Only the songs with soul are his and were taught by him. The others are copies of other men's songs. People are sometimes as deceitful as that. They sing someone else's songs without even knowing what the songs say."

I said that I had meant to ask for what purpose the songs were used. He answered that the songs I had learned were for calling the protector, and that I should always use them in conjunction with his name to call him. Later Mescalito would probably teach me other songs for other purposes, don Juan said.

I asked him then if he thought the protector had accepted me fully. He laughed as if my question were foolish. He said the protector had accepted me and had made sure I knew that he had accepted me by showing himself to me as a light, twice. Don Juan seemed to be very impressed by the fact that I had seen the light twice. He emphasized that aspect of my encounter with Mescalito.

I told him I could not understand how it was possible to be accepted by the protector, yet terrified by him at the same time.

He did not answer for a very long time. He seemed bewildered. Finally he said, "It is so clear. What he wanted is so clear that I don't see how you can misunderstand."

"Everything is still incomprehensible to me, don Juan."

"It takes time really to see and understand what Mescalito means; you should think about his lessons until they become clear."

Friday, September 11, 1964

Again I insisted upon having don Juan interpret my visionary experiences. He stalled for a while. Then he spoke as if we had already been carrying on a conversation about Mescalito.

"Do you see how stupid it is to ask if he is like a person you can talk to?" don Juan said. "He is like nothing you have ever seen. He is like a man, but at the same time he is not at all like one. It is difficult to explain that to people who know nothing about him and want to know everything about him all at once. And then, his lessons are as mysterious as he is himself. No man, to my knowledge, can predict his acts. You ask him a question and he shows you the way, but he does not tell you about it in the same manner you and I talk to each other. Do you understand now what he does?"

"I don't think I have trouble understanding that. What I can't figure out is his meaning."

"You asked him to tell you what's wrong with you, and he gave you the full picture. There can be no mistake! You can't claim you did not understand. It was not conversation—and yet it was. Then you asked him another question, and he answered you in exactly the same manner. As to what he meant I am not sure I understand it, because you chose not to tell me what your question was."

I repeated very carefully the questions I remembered having asked; I put them in the order in which I had voiced them: "Am I doing the right thing? Am I on the right path? What should I do with my life?" Don Juan said the questions I had asked were only words; it was better not to voice the questions, but to ask them from within. He told me the protector meant to give me a lesson; and to prove that he meant to give me a lesson and not to scare me away, he showed himself as a light twice.

I said I still could not understand why Mescalito terrorized me if he had accepted me. I reminded don Juan that, according to his statements, to be accepted by Mescalito implied that his form was constant and did not shift from bliss to nightmare. Don Juan laughed at me again and said that if I would think about the question I had had in my heart when I talked to Mescalito, then I myself would understand the lesson.

To think about the question I had had in my "heart" was a difficult problem. I told don Juan I had had many things in mind. When I asked if I was on the right path, I meant: Do I have one foot in each of two worlds? Which world is the right one? What course should my life take?

Don Juan listened to my explanations and concluded that I did not have a clear view of the world, and that the protector had given me a beautifully clear lesson. He said, "You think there are two worlds for you —two paths. But there is only one. The protector showed you this with unbelievable clarity. The only world available to you is the world of men, and that world you cannot choose to leave. You are a man! The protector showed you the world of happiness where there is no difference between things because there is no one there to ask about the difference. But that is not the world of men. The protector shook you out of it and showed you how a man thinks and fights. *That* is the world of man! And to be a man is to be condemned to that world. You have the vanity to believe you live in two worlds, but that is only your vanity. There is but one single world for us. We are men, and must follow the world of men contentedly.

"I believe that was the lesson."

9

Don Juan seemed to want me to work with the devil's weed as much as possible. This stand was incongruous with his alleged dislike of the power. He explained himself by saying that the time when I had to smoke again was near, and by then I ought to have developed a better knowledge of the power of the devil's weed.

He suggested repeatedly that I should at least test the devil's weed with one more sorcery with the lizards. I played with the idea for a long time. Don Juan's urgency increased dramatically until I felt obliged to heed his demand. And one day I made up my mind to divine about some stolen objects.

Monday, December 28, 1964

On Saturday, December 19, I cut the *Datura* root. I waited until it was fairly dark to do my dancing around the plant. I prepared the root extract during the night and on Sunday, about 6:00 A.M., I went to the site of my *Datura*. I sat in front of the plant. I had taken careful notes on don Juan's teachings about the procedure. I read my notes gain, and realized I did not have to grind the seeds there. Somehow just being in front of the plant gave me a rare kind of emotional stability, a clarity of thought or a power to concentrate on my actions which I ordinarily lacked.

I followed all the instructions meticulously, calculating my time so that the paste and the root were ready by late afternoon. About five o'clock I was busy trying to catch a pair of lizards. For an hour and a half I tried every method I could think of, but I failed in every attempt.

I was sitting in front of the *Datura* plant trying to figure out an expedient way of accomplishing my purpose when I suddenly remembered that don Juan had said the lizards had to be talked to. At first I felt ludicrous talking to the lizards. It was like being embarrassed by talking in front of an audience. The feeling soon vanished and I went on talking. It was almost dark. I lifted a rock. A lizard was under it. It had the appearance of being numb. I picked it up. And then I saw that there was another stiff lizard under another rock. They did not even wriggle.

The sewing of the mouth and eyes was the most difficult task. I noticed that don Juan had imparted a sense of irrevocability to my acts. His stand was that when a man begins an act there is no way to stop. If I had wanted to stop, however, there was nothing to prevent me. Perhaps I did not want to stop.

I set one lizard free and it went in a northeasterly direction—the omen of a good, but difficult, experience. I tied the other lizard to my shoulder and smeared my temples as prescribed. The lizard was stiff; for a moment I thought it had died, and don Juan had never told me what to do if that happened. But the lizard was only numb.

I drank the potion and waited awhile. I felt nothing out of the ordinary. I began rubbing the paste on my temples. I applied it twenty-five times. Then quite mechanically, as if I were absent-minded, I spread it repeatedly all over my forehead. I realized my mistake and hurriedly wiped the paste off. My forehead was sweaty; I became feverish. Intense anxiety gripped me, for don Juan had strongly advised me not to rub the paste on my forehead. The fear changed into a feeling of absolute loneliness, a feeling of being doomed. I was there by myself. If something harmful was going to happen to me, there was no one there to help me. I wanted to run away. I had an alarming sensation of indecision, of not knowing what to do. A flood of thoughts rushed into my mind, flashing with extraordinary speed. I noticed that they were rather strange thoughts; that is, they were strange in the sense that they seemed to come in a different way from ordinary thoughts. I am familiar with the way I think. My thoughts have a definite order that is my own, and any deviation is noticeable.

One of the alien thoughts was about a statement made by an author. It was, I vaguely remember, more like a voice, or something said somewhere in the background. It happened so fast that it startled me. I paused to consider it but it changed into an ordinary thought. I was certain I had read the statement, but I could not think of the author's name. I suddenly remembered that it was Alfred Kroeber. Then another alien thought popped up and "said" that it was not Kroeber, but Georg Simmel, who had made the statement. I insisted that it was Kroeber, and the next thing I knew I was in the midst of an argument with myself. And had forgotten about my feeling of being doomed.

My eyelids were heavy, as though I had taken sleeping pills. Although I have never taken any, it was the image that came to my mind. I was falling asleep. I wanted to go to my car and crawl in, but I couldn't move.

Then, quite suddenly, I woke up, or rather, I clearly felt that I had. My first thought was about the time of day. I looked around. I was not in front of the *Datura* plant. Nonchalantly I accepted the fact that I was undergoing another divinatory experience. It was 12:35 by a clock above my head. I knew it was afternoon.

I saw a young man carrying a stack of papers. I was nearly touching him. I saw the veins of his neck pulsating and heard the fast beating of his heart. I had become absorbed in what I was seeing and had not been aware, so far, of the quality of my thoughts. Then I heard a "voice" in my ear describing the scene, and I realized that the "voice" was the alien thought in my mind.

I became so engrossed in listening that the scene lost its visual interest for me. I heard the voice at my right ear above my shoulder. It actually created the scene by describing it. But it obeyed my will, because I could stop it at any time and examine the details of what it said at my leisure. I "heard-saw" the entire sequence of the young man's action. The voice went on explaining them in minute detail, but somehow the action was not important. The little voice was the extraordinary issue. Three times during the course of the experience I tried to turn around to see who was talking. I tried to turn my head all the way to the right, or just whirl around unexpectedly to see if somebody was there. But every time I did it, my vision became blurry. I thought: "The reason I cannot turn around is because the scene is not in the realm of ordinary reality." And that thought was my own.

From then on I concentrated my attention on the voice alone. It seemed to come from my shoulder. It was perfectly clear, although it was a small voice. It was, however, not a child's voice or a falsetto voice, but a miniature man's voice. It wasn't my voice either. I presumed it was English that I heard. Whenever I tried deliberately to trap the voice, it subsided altogether or became vague and the scene faded. I thought of a simile. The voice was like the image created by dust particles in the eyelashes, or the blood vessels in the cornea of the eye, a wormlike shape that can be seen as long as one is not looking at it directly; but the moment one tries to look at it, it shifts out of sight with the movement of the eyeball.

I became totally disinterested in the action. As I listened the voice became more complex. What I thought to be a voice was more like something whispering thoughts into my ear. But that was not accurate. Something was *thinking* for me. The thoughts were outside myself. I knew that was so, because I could hold my own thoughts and the thoughts of the "other" at the same time.

At one point the voice created scenes acted out by the young man, which had nothing to do with my original question about the lost objects. The young man performed very complex acts. The action had become important again and I paid no more attention to the voice. I began to lose patience; I wanted to stop. "How can I end this?" I thought. The voice in my ear said I should go back to the canyon. I asked how, and the voice answered that I should think of my plant.

I thought of my plant. Usually I sat in front of it. I had done it so many times that it was quite easy for me to visualize it. I believed that seeing it, as I did at that moment, was another hallucination, but the voice said I was "back"! I strained to listen. There was only silence. The *Datura* plant in front of me seemed as real as everything else I had seen, but I could touch it, I could move around.

I stood up and walked toward my car. The effort exhausted me, and I sat down and closed my eyes. I felt dizzy and wanted to vomit. There was a buzzing in my ears.

Something slid on my chest. It was the lizard. I remembered don Juan's admonition about setting it free. I went back to the plant and untied the lizard. I did not want to see whether it was dead or alive. I broke the clay pot with the paste and kicked some dirt over it. I got into my car and fell asleep.

Thursday, December 24, 1964

Today I narrated the whole experience to don Juan. As usual, he listened without interrupting me. At the end we had the following dialogue.

"You did something very wrong."

"I know it. It was a very stupid error, an accident."

"There are no accidents when you deal with the devil's weed. I told you she would test you all the way. As I see it, either you are very strong or the weed really likes you. The center of the forehead is only for the great brujos who know how to handle her power."

"What usually happens when a man rubs his forehead with the paste, don Juan?"

"If the man is not a great brujo he will never come back from the journey."

"Have you ever rubbed the paste on your forehead, don Juan?"

"Never! My benefactor told me very few people return from such a journey. A man could be gone for months, and would have to be tended by others. My benefactor said the lizards could take a man to the end of the world and show him the most marvelous secrets upon request."

"Do you know anybody who has ever taken that journey?"

"Yes, my benefactor. But he never taught me how to return."

"Is it so very difficult to return, don Juan?"

"Yes. That is why your act is truly astonishing to me. You had no steps to follow, and we must follow certain steps, because it is in the steps where man finds strength. Without them we are nothing."

We remained silent for hours. He seemed to be immersed in very deep deliberation.

Saturday, December 26, 1964

Don Juan asked me if I had looked for the lizards. I told him I had, but that I couldn't find them. I asked him what would have happened if one of the lizards had died while I was holding it. He said the death of a lizard would be an unfortunate event. If the lizard with the sewed-up mouth had died at any time there would have been no sense in pursuing the sorcery, he said. It would also have meant that the lizards had withdrawn their friendship, and I would have had to give up learning about the devil's weed for a long time.

"How long, don Juan?" I asked.

"Two years or more."

"What would have happened if the other lizard had died?"

"If the second lizard had died, you would have been in real danger. You would have been alone, without a guide. If she died before you started the sorcery, you could have stopped it; but if you had stopped it, you would also have to give up the devil's weed for good. If the lizard had died while she was on your shoulder, after you had begun the sorcery, you would have had to go ahead with it, and that would truly have been madness."

"Why would it have been madness?"

"Because under such conditions nothing makes sense. You are alone without a guide, seeing terrifying, nonsensical things."

"What do you mean by 'nonsensical things'?"

"Things we see by ourselves. Things we see when we have no direction. It means the devil's weed is trying to get rid of you, finally pushing you away."

"Do you know anyone who ever experienced that?"

"Yes. *I* did. Without the wisdom of the lizards I went mad."

"What did you see, don Juan?"

"A bunch of nonsense. What else could I have seen without direction?"

Monday, December 28, 1964

"You told me, don Juan, that the devil's weed tests men. What did you mean by that?"

"The devil's weed is like a woman, and like a woman she flatters men. She sets traps for them at every turn. She did it to you when she forced you to rub the paste on your forehead. She will try it again, and you will probably fall for it. I warn you against it. Don't take her with passion; the devil's weed is only one path to the secrets of a man of knowledge. There are other paths. But her trap is to make you believe that hers is the only way. I say it is useless to waste your life on one path, especially if that path has no heart."

"But how do you know when a path has no heart, don Juan?"

"Before you embark on it you ask the question: Does this path have a heart? If the answer is no, you will know it, and then you must choose another path."

"But how will I know for sure whether a path has a heart or not?"

"Anybody would know that. The trouble is nobody asks the question; and when a man finally realizes that he has taken a path without a heart, the path is ready to kill him. At that point very few men can stop to deliberate, and leave the path."

"How should I proceed to ask the question properly, don Juan?"

"Just ask it."

"I mean, is there a proper method, so I would not lie to myself and believe the answer is yes when it really is no?"

"Why would you lie?"

"Perhaps because at the moment the path is pleasant and enjoyable."

"That is nonsense. A path without a heart is never enjoyable. You have to work hard even to take it. On the other hand, a path with heart is easy; it does not make you work at liking it."

Don Juan suddenly changed the direction of the conversation and bluntly confronted me with the idea that I liked the devil's weed. I had to admit that I had at least a preference for it. He asked me how I felt about his ally, the smoke, and I had to tell him that just the idea of it frightened me out of my senses.

"I have told you that to choose a path you must be free from fear and ambition. But the smoke blinds you with fear, and the devil's weed blinds you with ambition."

I argued that one needs ambition even to embark on any path, and that his statement that one had to be free from ambition did not make sense. A person has to have ambition in order to learn.

"The desire to learn is not ambition," he said. "It is our lot as men to want to know, but to seek the devil's weed is to bid for power, and that is ambition, because you are not bidding to know. Don't let the devil's weed blind you. She has hooked you already. She entices men and gives them a sense of power; she makes them feel they can do things that no ordinary man can. But that is her trap. And, the next thing, the path without a heart will turn against men and destroy them. It does not take much to die, and to seek death is to seek nothing."

10

In the month of December, 1964, don Juan and I went to collect the different plants needed to make the smoking mixture. It was the fourth cycle. Don Juan merely supervised my actions. He urged me to take time, to watch, and to deliberate before I picked any of the plants. As soon as the ingredients had been gathered and stored, he prompted me to meet with his ally again.

Thursday, December 31, 1964

"Now that you know a bit more about the devil's weed and the smoke, you can tell more clearly which of the two you like better," don Juan said.

"The smoke really terrifies me, don Juan. I don't know exactly why, but I don't have a good feeling about it."

"You like flattery, and the devil's weed flatters you. Like a woman, she makes you feel good. The smoke, on the other hand, is the most noble power; he has the purest heart. He does not entice men or make them prisoners, nor does he love or hate. All he requires is strength. The devil's weed also requires strength, but of a different kind. It is closer to being virile with women. On the other hand, the strength required by the smoke is strength of the heart. You don't have that! But very few men have it. That is why I recommend that you learn more about the smoke. He reinforces the heart. He is not like the devil's weed, full of passions, jealousies, and violence. The smoke is constant. You don't have to worry about forgetting something along the line."

Wednesday, January 27, 1965

On Tuesday, January 19, I smoked again the hallucinogenic mixture. I had told don Juan I felt very apprehensive about the smoke, and that it frightened me. He said I had to try it again to evaluate it with justice.

We walked into his room. It was almost two o'clock in the afternoon. He brought out the pipe. I got the charcoals, then we sat facing each other. He said he was going to warm up the pipe and awaken her, and if I watched carefully I would see how she glowed. He put the pipe to his lips three or four times, and sucked through it. He rubbed it tenderly. Suddenly he nodded, almost imperceptibly, to signal me to look at the pipe's awakening. I looked, but I couldn't see it.

He handed the pipe to me. I filled the bowl with my own mixture, and then picked a burning charcoal with a pair of tweezers I had made from a wooden clothespin and had been saving for this occasion. Don Juan looked at my tweezers and began to laugh. I vacillated for a moment, and the charcoal stuck to the tweezers. I was afraid to tap them against the pipe bowl, and I had to spit on the charcoal to put it out.

Don Juan turned his head away and covered his face with his arm. His body shook. For a moment I thought he was crying, but he was laughing silently.

The action was interrupted for a long time; then he swiftly picked up a charcoal himself, put it in the bowl, and ordered me to smoke. It required quite an effort to suck through the mixture; it seemed to be very compact. After the first try I felt I had sucked the fine powder into my mouth. It numbed my mouth immediately. I saw the glow in the bowl, but I never felt the smoke as the smoke of a cigarette is felt. Yet I had the sensation of inhaling something, something that filled my lungs first and then pushed itself down to fill the rest of my body.

I counted twenty inhalations, and then the count did not matter any longer. I began to sweat; don Juan looked at me fixedly and told me not to be afraid and to do exactly as he said. I tried to say "alright," but instead I made a weird, howling sound. It went on resounding after I had closed my mouth. The sound startled don Juan, who had another attack of laughter. I wanted to say "yes" with my head, but I couldn't move.

Don Juan opened my hands gently and took the pipe away. He ordered me to lie down on the floor, but not to fall asleep. I wondered if he was going to help me lie down but he did not. He just stared at me uninterruptedly. All of a sudden I saw the room tumbling, and I was looking at don Juan from a position on my side. From that point on the images became strangely blurry, as in a dream. I can vaguely recall hearing don Juan talk to me a great deal during the time I was immobilized.

I did not experience fear, or unpleasantness, during the state itself, nor was I sick upon awakening the next day. The only thing out of the ordinary was that I could not think clearly for some time after waking up. Then gradually, in a period of four or five hours, I became myself again.

Wednesday, January 20, 1965

Don Juan did not talk about my experience, nor did
he ask me to relate it to him. His sole comment was
that I had fallen asleep too soon.

"The only way to stay awake is to become a bird,
or a cricket, or something of the sort," he said.

"How do you do that, don Juan?"

"That is what I am teaching you. Do you remember
what I said to you yesterday while you were without
your body?"

"I can't recall clearly."

"I am a crow. I am teaching you how to become a
crow. When you learn that, you will stay awake, and
you will move freely; otherwise you will always be
glued to the ground, wherever you fall."

Sunday, February 7, 1965

My second attempt with the smoke took place about
midday on Sunday, January 31. I woke up the following day in the early evening. I had the sensation of
possessing an unusual power to recollect whatever don
Juan had said to me during the experience. His words
were imprinted on my mind. I kept on hearing them
with extraordinary clarity and persistence. During this
attempt another fact became obvious to me: my entire
body had become numb soon after I began to swallow
the fine powder, which got into my mouth every time I
sucked the pipe. Thus I not only inhaled the smoke,
but also ingested the mixture.

I tried to narrate my experience to don Juan; he said
I had done nothing important. I mentioned that I could
remember everything that had happened, but he did not
want to hear about it. Every memory was precise and
unmistakable. The smoking procedure had been the
same as in the previous attempt. It was almost as if
the two experiences were perfectly juxtaposable, and
I could start my recollection from the time the first

experience ended. I clearly remembered that from the time I fell to the ground on my side I was completely devoid of feeling or thought. Yet my clarity was not impaired in any way. I remember thinking my last thought at about the time the room became a vertical plane: "I must have clunked my head on the floor, yet I don't feel any pain."

From that point on I could only see and hear. I could repeat every word don Juan had said. I followed each one of his directions. They seemed clear, logical, and easy. He said that my body was disappearing and only my head was going to remain, and in such a condition the only way to stay awake and move around was by becoming a crow. He commanded me to make an effort to wink, adding that whenever I was capable of winking I would be ready to proceed. Then he told me that my body had vanished completely and all I had was my head; he said the head never disappears because the head is what turns into a crow.

He ordered me to wink. He must have repeated this command, and all his other commands, countless times, because I could remember all of them with extraordinary clarity. I must have winked, because he said I was ready and ordered me to straighten up my head and put it on my chin. He said that in the chin were the crow's legs. He commanded me to feel the legs and observe that they were coming out slowly. He then said that I was not solid yet, that I had to grow a tail, and that the tail would come out of my neck. He ordered me to extend the tail like a fan, and to feel how it swept the floor.

Then he talked about the crow's wings, and said they would come out of my cheekbones. He said it was hard and painful. He commanded me to unfold them. He said they had to be extremely long, as long as I could stretch them, otherwise I would not be able to fly. He told me the wings were coming out and were long and beautiful, and that I had to flap them until they were real wings.

He talked about the top of my head next and said it was still very large and heavy, and its bulk would

prevent my flying. He told me that the way to reduce
its size was by winking; with every wink my head
would become smaller. He ordered me to wink until the
top weight was gone and I could jump freely. Then
he told me I had reduced my head to the size of a
crow, and that I had to walk around and hop until I
had lost my stiffness.

There was one last thing I had to change, he said,
before I could fly. It was the most difficult change, and
to accomplish it I had to be docile and do exactly as he
told me. I had to learn to see like a crow. He said that
my mouth and nose were going to grow between my
eyes until I had a strong beak. He said that crows see
straight to the side, and commanded me to turn my
head and look at him with one eye. He said that if I
wanted to change and look with the other eye I had to
shake my beak down, and that that movement would
make me look through the other eye. He ordered me
to shift from one eye to the other. And then he said
I was ready to fly, and that the only way to fly was to
have him toss me into the air.

I had no difficulty whatsoever eliciting the corre-
sponding sensation to each one of his commands. I had
the perception of growing bird's legs, which were weak
and wobbly at first. I felt a tail coming out of the back
of my neck and wings out of my cheekbones. The
wings were folded deeply. I felt them coming out by
degrees. The process was hard but not painful. Then
I winked my head down to the size of a crow. But the
most astonishing effect was accomplished with my eyes.
My bird's sight!

When don Juan directed me to grow a beak, I had
an annoying sensation of lack of air. Then something
bulged out and created a block in front of me. But it
was not until don Juan directed me to see laterally that
my eyes actually were capable of having a full view
to the side. I could wink one eye at a time and shift
the focusing from one eye to the other. But the sight
of the room and all the things in it was not like an
ordinary sight. Yet it was impossible to tell in what way

it was different. Perhaps it was lopsided, or perhaps things were out of focus. Don Juan became very big and glowy. Something about him was comforting and safe. Then the images blurred; they lost their outlines, and became sharp abstract patterns that flickered for a while.

Sunday, March 28, 1965

On Thursday, March 18, I smoked again the hallucinogenic mixture. The initial procedure was different in small details. I had to refill the pipe bowl once. After I had finished the first batch, don Juan directed me to clean the bowl, but he poured the mixture into the bowl himself because I lacked muscular coordination. It took a great deal of effort to move my arms. There was enough mixture in my bag for one refill. Don Juan looked at the bag and said this was my last attempt with the smoke until the next year because I had used up all my provisions.

He turned the little bag inside out and shook the dust into the dish that held the charcoals. It burned with an orange glow, as if he had placed a sheet of transparent material over the charcoals. The sheet burst into flame, and then it cracked into an intricate pattern of lines. Something zigzagged inside the lines at high speed. Don Juan told me to look at the movement in the lines. I saw something that looked like a small marble rolling back and forth in the glowing area. He leaned over, put his hand into the glow, picked out the marble, and placed it in the pipe bowl. He ordered me to take a puff. I had a clear impression that he had put the small ball into the pipe so that I would inhale it. In a moment the room lost its horizontal position. I felt a profound numbness, a sensation of heaviness.

When I awakened, I was lying on my back at the bottom of a shallow irrigation ditch, immersed in water up to my chin. Someone was holding my head up. It was don Juan. The first thought I had was that the water in the channel had an unusual quality; it was cold and heavy. It slapped lightly against me, and my thoughts cleared with every movement it made. At first the water had a bright green halo, or fluorescence, which soon dissolved, leaving only a stream of ordinary water.

I asked don Juan about the time of the day. He said it was early morning. After awhile I was completely awake, and got out of the water.

"You must tell me all you saw," don Juan said when we got to his house. He also said he had been trying to "bring me back" for three days, and had had a very difficult time doing it. I made numerous attempts to describe what I had seen, but I could not concentrate. Later on, during the early evening, I felt I was ready to talk with don Juan, and I began to tell him what I remembered from the time I had fallen on my side, but he did not want to hear about it. He said the only interesting part was what I saw and did after he "tossed me into the air and I flew away."

All I could remember was a series of dreamlike images or scenes. They had no sequential order. I had the impression that each one of them was like an isolated bubble, floating into focus and then moving away. They were not, however, merely scenes to look at. I was inside them. I took part in them. When I tried to recollect them at first, I had the sensation that they were vague, diffused flashes, but as I thought about them I realized that each one of them was extremely clear although totally unrelated to ordinary seeing— hence, the sensation of vagueness. The images were few and simple.

As soon as don Juan mentioned that he had "tossed me into the air" I had a faint recollection of an absolutely clear scene in which I was looking straight at him from some distance away. I was looking at his face only. It was monumental in size. It was flat and had an intense glow. His hair was yellowish, and it moved. Each part of his face moved by itself, projecting a sort of amber light.

The next image was one in which don Juan had actually tossed me up, or hurled me, in a straight onward direction. I remember I "extended my wings and flew." I felt alone, cutting through the air, painfully moving straight ahead. It was more like walking than like flying. It tired my body. There was no feeling of flowing free, no exuberance.

Then I remembered an instant in which I was motionless, looking at a mass of sharp, dark edges set in an area that had a dull, painful light; next I saw a field with an infinite variety of lights. The lights moved and flickered and changed their luminosity. They were almost like colors. Their intensity dazzled me.

At another moment, an object was almost against my eye. It was a thick, pointed object; it had a definite pinkish glow. I felt a sudden tremor somewhere in my body and saw a multitude of similar pink forms coming toward me. They all moved on me. I jumped away.

The last scene I remembered was three silvery birds. They radiated a shiny, metallic light, almost like stainless steel, but intense and moving and alive. I liked them. We flew together.

Don Juan did not make any comments on my recounting.

Tuesday, March 23, 1965

The following conversation took place the next day, after the recounting of my experience.

Don Juan said: "It does not take much to become a crow. You did it and now you will always be one."

"What happened after I became a crow, don Juan? Did I fly for three days?"

"No, you come back at nightfall as I had told you to."

"But how did I come back?"

"You were very tired and went to sleep. That is all."

"I mean did I fly back?"

"I have already told you. You obeyed me and came

back to the house. But don't concern yourself with that matter. It is of no importance."

"What is important, then?"

"In your whole trip there was only one thing of great value—the silvery birds!"

"What was so special about them? They were just birds."

"Not just birds—they were crows."

"Were they white crows, don Juan?"

"The black feathers of a crow are really silvery. The crows shine so intensely that they are not bothered by other birds."

"Why did their feathers look silvery?"

"Because you were seeing as a crow sees. A bird that looks dark to us looks white to a crow. The white pigeons, for instance, are pink or bluish to a crow; sea gulls are yellow. Now, try to remember how you joined them."

I thought about it, but the birds were a dim, disassociated image which had no continuity. I told him I could remember only that I felt I had flown with them. He asked me whether I had joined them in the air or on the ground, but I could not possibly answer that. He became almost angry with me. He demanded that I think about it. He said: "All this will not mean a damn; it will be only a mad dream unless you remember correctly." I strained myself to recollect, but I could not.

Saturday, April 3, 1965

Today I thought of another image in my "dream" about the silvery birds. I remembered seeing a dark mass with myriads of pinholes. In fact, the mass was a dark cluster of little holes. I don't know why I thought it was soft. As I was looking at it, three birds flew straight at me. One of them made a noise; then all three of them were next to me on the ground.

I described the image to don Juan. He asked me from what direction the birds had come. I said I couldn't pos-

sibly determine that. He became quite impatient and
accused me of being inflexible in my thinking. He said
I could very well remember if I tried to, and that I
was afraid to let myself become less rigid. He said that
I was thinking in terms of men and crows, and that I
was neither a man nor a crow at the time that I wanted
to recollect.

He asked me to remember what the crow had said
to me. I tried to think about it, but my mind played
on scores of other things instead. I couldn't concentrate.

Sunday, April 4, 1965

I took a long hike today. It got quite dark before I
reached don Juan's house. I was thinking about the
crows when suddenly a very strange "thought" crossed
my mind. It was more like an impression or a feeling
than a thought. The bird that had made the noise said
they were coming from the north and were going south,
and when we met again they would be coming the same
way.

I told don Juan what I had thought up, or maybe
remembered. He said, "Don't think about whether you
remembered it or made it up. Such thoughts fit men
only. They do not fit crows, especially those you saw,
for they are the emissaries of your fate. You are already
a crow. You will never change that. From now on the
crows will tell you with their flight about every turn
of your fate. In which direction did you fly with them?"

"I couldn't know that, don Juan!"

"If you think properly you will remember. Sit on
the floor and tell me the position in which you were
when the birds flew to you. Close your eyes and make
a line on the floor."

I followed his suggestion and determined the point.

"Don't open your eyes yet!" He proceeded, "In which
direction did you all fly in relation to that point?"

I made another mark on the ground.

Taking these points of orientation as a reference,
don Juan interpreted the different patterns of flight the

crows would observe to foretell my personal future or
fate. He set up the four points of the compass as the
axis of the crows' flight.

I asked him whether the crows always followed the
cardinal points to tell a man's fate. He said that the
orientation was mine alone; whatever the crows did in
my first meeting with them was of crucial importance.
He insisted on my recalling every detail, for the message
and the pattern of the "emissaries" were an individual,
personalized matter.

There was one more thing he insisted I should remember, and that was the time of day when the
emissaries left me. He asked me to think of the difference in the light around me between the time when I
"began to fly" and the time when the silvery birds
"flew with me." When I first had the sensation of painful flight, it was dark. But when I saw the birds, everything was reddish—light red, or perhaps orange.

He said: "That means it was late in the day; the
sun was not down yet. When it is completely dark a
crow is blind with whiteness and not with darkness, the
way we are at night. This indication of the time places
your last emissaries at the end of the day. They will
call you, and as they fly above your head, they will become silvery white; you will see them shining against
the sky, and it will mean your time is up. It will mean
you are going to die and become a crow yourself."

"What if I see them during the morning?"

"You won't see them in the morning!"

"But crows fly all day."

"Not your emissaries, you fool!"

"How about *your* emissaries, don Juan?"

"Mine will come in the morning. There will also be
three of them. My benefactor told me that one could
shout them back to black if one does not want to die.
But now I know it can't be done. My benefactor was
given to shouting, and to all the clatter and violence of
the devil's weed. I know the smoke is different because he has no passion. He is fair. When your silvery
emissaries come for you, there is no need to shout at

them. Just fly with them as you have already done. After they have collected you they will reverse directions, and there will be four of them flying away."

Saturday, April 10, 1965

I had been experiencing brief flashes of disassociation, or shallow states of nonordinary reality.

One element from the hallucinogenic experience with the mushrooms kept recurring in my thoughts: the soft, dark mass of pinholes. I continued to visualize it as a grease or an oil bubble which began to draw me to its center. It was almost as if the center would open up and swallow me, and for very brief moments I experienced something resembling a state of nonordinary reality. As a result I suffered moments of profound agitation, anxiety, and discomfort, and I willfully strove to end the experiences as soon as they began.

Today I discussed this condition with don Juan. I asked for advice. He seemed to be unconcerned and told me to disregard the experiences because they were meaningless, or rather valueless. He said the only experiences worth my effort and concern would be those in which I saw a crow; any other kind of "vision" would be merely the product of my fears. He reminded me again that in order to partake of the smoke it was necessary to lead a strong, quiet life. Personally I seemed to have reached a dangerous threshold. I told him felt I could not go on; there was something truly frightening about the mushrooms.

In going over the images I recalled from my hallucinogenic experience, I had come to the unavoidable conclusion that I had seen the world in a way that was structurally different from ordinary vision. In other states of nonordinary reality I had undergone, the forms and the patterns I had visualized were always within the confines of my visual conception of the world. But the sensation of seeing under the influence of the hallucinogenic smoke mixture was not the same.

Everything I saw was in front of me in a direct line of vision; nothing was above or below that line of vision.

Every image had an irritating flatness, and yet, disconcertingly, a profound depth. Perhaps it would be more accurate to say that the images were a conglomerate of unbelievably sharp details set inside fields of different light; the light in the fields moved, creating an effect of rotation.

After probing and exerting myself to remember, I was forced to make a series of analogies or similes in order to "understand" what I had "seen." Don Juan's face, for instance, looked as if he had been submerged in water. The water seemed to move in a continuous flow over his face and hair. It so magnified them that I could see every pore in his skin or every hair on his head whenever I focused my vision. On the other hand, I saw masses of matter that were flat and full of edges, but did not move because there was no fluctuation in the light that came from them.

I asked don Juan what were the things that I had seen. He said that because this was the first time I was seeing as a crow the images were not clear or important, and that later on with practice I would be able to recognize everything.

I brought up the issue of the difference I had detected in the movement of light. "Things that are alive," he said, "move inside, and a crow can easily see when something is dead, or about to die, because the movement has stopped or is slowing down to a stop. A crow can also tell when something is moving too fast, and by the same token a crow can tell when something is moving just right."

"What does it mean when something is moving too fast, or just right?"

"It means a crow can actually tell what to avoid and what to seek. When something is moving too fast inside, it means it is about to explode violently, or to leap forward, and a crow will avoid it. When it moves inside just right, it is a pleasing sight and a crow will seek it."

"Do rocks move inside?"

"No, not rocks or dead animals or dead trees. But they are beautiful to look at. That is why crows hang around dead bodies. They like to look at them. No light moves inside them."

"But when the flesh rots, doesn't it change or move?"

"Yes, but that is a different movement. What a crow sees then is millions of things moving inside the flesh with a light of their own, and that is what a crow likes to see. It is truly an unforgettable sight."

"Have you seen it yourself, don Juan?"

"Anybody who learns to become a crow can see it. You will see it yourself."

At this point I asked don Juan the unavoidable question.

"Did I really become a crow? I mean would anyone seeing me have thought I was an ordinary crow?"

"No. You can't think that way when dealing with the power of the allies. Such questions make no sense, and yet to become a crow is the simplest of all matters. It is almost like frolicking; it has little usefulness. As I have already told you, the smoke is not for those who seek power. It is only for those who crave to see. I learned to become a crow because these birds are the most effective of all. No other birds bother them, except perhaps larger, hungry eagles, but crows fly in groups and can defend themselves. Men don't bother crows either, and that is an important point. Any man can distinguish a large eagle, especially an unusual eagle, or any other large, unusual bird, but who cares about a crow? A crow is safe. It is ideal in size and nature. It can go safely into any place without attracting attention. On the other hand, it is possible to become a lion or a bear, but that is rather dangerous. Such a creature is too large; it takes too much energy to become one. One can also become a cricket, or a lizard, or even an ant, but that is even more dangerous, because large animals prey on small creatures."

I argued that what he was saying meant that one really changed into a crow, or a cricket, or anything else. But he insisted I was misunderstanding.

"It takes a very long time to learn to be a proper crow," he said. "But you did not change, nor did you stop being a man. There is something else."

"Can you tell me what the something else is, don Juan?"

"Perhaps by now you know it yourself. Maybe if you were not so afraid of becoming mad, or of losing your body, you would understand this marvelous secret. But perhaps you must wait until you lose fear to understand what I mean."

11

The last event I recorded in my field notes took place in September, 1965. It was the last of don Juan's teachings. I called it "a special state of nonordinary reality" because it was not the product of any of the plants I had used before. It seemed that don Juan elicited it by means of a careful manipulation of cues about himself; that is to say, he behaved in front of me in so skillful a manner that he created the clear and sustained impression that he was not really himself, but someone impersonating him. As a result I experienced a profound sense of conflict; I wanted to believe it was don Juan, and yet I could not be sure of it. The concomitant of the conflict was a conscious terror, so acute that it impaired my health for several weeks. Afterward I thought it would have been wise to end my apprenticeship then. I have never been a participant since that time, yet don Juan has not ceased to consider me an apprentice. He has regarded my withdrawal only as a necessary period of recapitulation, another step of learning, which may last indefinitely. Since that time, however, he has never expounded on his knowledge.

I wrote the detailed account of my last experience almost a month after it happened, although I had already written copious notes on its salient points on the following day during the hours of great emotional agitation which preceded the highest point of my terror.

Friday, October 29, 1965

On Thursday, September 30, 1965, I went to see don Juan. The brief, shallow states of nonordinary reality had been persisting in spite of my deliberate attempts to end them, or slough them off as don Juan had suggested. I felt that my condition was getting worse, for the duration of such states was increasing. I became sharply aware of the noise of airplanes. The sound of their motors going overhead would unavoidably catch my attention and fix it, to the point where I felt I was following the plane as if I were inside it, or flying with it. This sensation was very annoying. My inability to shake it off produced a deep anxiety in me.

Don Juan, after listening attentively to all the details, concluded that I was suffering from a loss of soul. I told him I had been having these hallucinations ever since the time I had smoked the mushrooms, but he insisted that they were a new development. He said that earlier I had been afraid, and had just "dreamed nonsensical things," but that now I was truly bewitched. The proof was that the noise of the flying airplanes could carry me away. Ordinarily, he said, the noise of a brook or a river can trap a bewitched man who has lost his soul and carry him away to his death. He then asked me to describe all my activities during the time prior to experiencing the hallucinations. I listed all the activities I could remember. And from my account he deduced the place where I had lost my soul.

Don Juan seemed to be overly preoccupied, a state that was quite unusual for him. This naturally increased my apprehension. He said he had no definite idea as to who had trapped my soul, but whoever it was intended without doubt to kill me or make me very ill.

Then he gave me precise instructions about a "fighting form," a specific bodily position to be maintained while I remained on my beneficial spot. I *had* to maintain this posture he called a form [*una forma para pelear*].

I asked him what all that was for, and whom I was going to fight. He replied that he was going away to see who had taken my soul, and to find out if it was possible to get it back. In the meantime, I was supposed to stay on my spot until his return. The fighting form was actually a precaution, he said, in case something happened during his absence, and it had to be used if I was attacked. It consisted of clapping the calf and thigh of my right leg and stomping my left foot in a kind of dance I had to do while facing the attacker.

He warned me that the form had to be adopted only in moments of extreme crisis, but so long as there was no danger in sight I should simply sit cross-legged on my spot. Under circumstances of extreme danger, however, he said I could resort to one last means of defense —hurling an object at the enemy. He told me that ordinarily one hurls a power object, but since I did not possess any I was forced to use any small rock that would fit into the palm of my right hand, a rock I could hold by pressing it against my palm with my thumb. He said that such a technique should be used only if one was indisputably in danger of losing one's life. The hurling of the object had to be accompanied by a war cry, a yell that had the property of directing the object to its mark. He emphatically recommended that I be careful and deliberate about the outcry and not use it at random, but only under "severe conditions of seriousness."

I asked what he meant by "severe conditions of seriousness." He said that the outcry or war cry was something that remained with a man for the duration of his life; thus it had to be good from the very beginning. And the only way to start it correctly was by holding back one's natural fear and haste until one was absolutely filled with power, and then the yell would

burst out with direction and power. He said these were
the conditions of seriousness needed to launch the yell.

I asked him to explain about the power that was supposed to fill one before the outcry. He said that was
something that ran through the body coming from the
ground where one stood; it was a kind of power that
emanated from the beneficial spot, to be exact. It was
a force that pushed the yell out. If such a force was
properly managed, the battle cry would be perfect.

I asked him again if he thought something was going
to happen to me. He said he knew nothing about it
and admonished me dramatically to stay glued to my
spot for as long as it was necessary, because that was
the only protection I had against anything that might
happen.

I began to feel frightened; I begged him to be more
specific. He said all he knew was that I should not
move under any circumstances; I was not to go into
the house or into the bush. Above all, he said, I should
not utter a single word, not even to him. He said I could
sing my Mescalito songs if I became too frightened,
and then he added that I knew already too much about
these matters to have to be warned like a child about
the importance of doing everything correctly.

His admonitions produced a state of profound anguish
in me. I was sure he was expecting something to happen. I asked him why he recommended that I sing the
Mescalito songs, and what he believed was going to
frighten me. He laughed and said I might become afraid
of being alone. He walked into the house and closed
the door behind him. I looked at my watch. It was
7:00 P.M. I sat quietly for a long time. There were no
sounds coming from don Juan's room. Everything was
quiet. It was windy. I thought of making a dash for my
car to get my windbreaker, but I did not dare to go
against don Juan's advice. I was not sleepy, but tired;
the cold wind made it impossible for me to rest.

Four hours later I heard don Juan walking around
the house. I thought he might have left through the
back to urinate in the bushes. Then he called me loudly.

"Hey boy! Hey boy! I need you here," he said.

I nearly got up to go to him. It was his voice, but not his tone, or his usual words. Don Juan had never called me "Hey boy!" So I stayed where I was. A chill went up my back. He began to yell again using the same, or a similar, phrase.

I heard him walking around the back of his house. He stumbled on a woodpile as if he did not know it was there. Then he came to the porch and sat next to the door with his back against the wall. He seemed heavier than usual. His movements were not slow or clumsy, just heavier. He plunked down on the floor, instead of sliding nimbly as he usually did. Besides, that was not his spot, and don Juan would never under any circumstances sit anywhere else.

Then he talked to me again. He asked me why I refused to come when he needed me. He talked loudly. I did not want to look at him, and yet I had a compulsive urge to watch him. He began to swing slightly from side to side. I changed my position, adopted the fighting form he had taught me, and turned to face him. My muscles were stiff and strangely tense. I do not know what prompted me to adopt the fighting form, but perhaps it was because I believed don Juan was deliberately trying to scare me by creating the impression that the person I saw was not really himself. I felt he was very careful about doing the unaccustomed in order to establish doubt in my mind. I was afraid, but still I felt I was above it all, because I was actually taking stock of and analyzing the entire sequence.

At that point don Juan got up. His motions were utterly unfamiliar. He brought his arms in front of his body, and pushed himself up, lifting his backside first; then he grabbed the door and straightened out the top part of his body. I was amazed about how deeply familiar I was with his movements, and what an awesome feeling he had created by letting me see a don Juan who did not move like don Juan.

He took a couple of steps toward me. He held the lower part of his back with both hands as if he were trying to straighten up, or as if he were in pain. He whined and puffed. His nose seemed to be stuffed up. He said he was going to take me with him, and ordered me to get up and follow him. He walked toward the west side of the house. I shifted my position to face him. He turned to me. I did not move from my spot; I was glued to it.

He bellowed, "Hey boy! I told you to come with me. If you don't come I'll drag you!"

He walked toward me. I began beating my calf and thigh, and dancing fast. He got to the edge of the porch in front of me and nearly touched me. Frantically I prepared my body to adopt the hurling position, but he changed directions and moved away from me, toward the bushes to my left. At one moment, as he was walking away, he turned suddenly, but I was facing him.

He went out of sight. I retained the fighting posture for a while longer, but as I did not see him anymore I sat cross-legged again with my back to the rock. By then I was really frightened. I wanted to run away, yet that thought terrified me even more. I felt I would have been completely at his mercy if he had caught me on the way to my car. I began to sing the peyote songs I knew. But somehow I felt they were impotent there. They served only as a pacifier, yet they soothed me. I sang them over and over.

About 2:45 A.M. I heard a noise inside the house. I immediately changed my position. The door was flung open and don Juan stumbled out. He was gasping and holding his throat. He knelt in front of me and moaned. He asked me in a high, whining voice to come and help him. Then he bellowed again and ordered me to come. He made gargling sounds. He pleaded with me to come and help him because something was choking him. He crawled on his hands and knees until he was perhaps four feet away. He extended his hands to me. He said, "Come here!" Then he got up. His arms were extended toward me. He seemed ready to grab me. I stomped my foot on the ground and clapped my calf and thigh. I was beside myself with fear.

He stopped and walked to the side of the house and into the bushes. I shifted my position to face him. Then I sat down again. I did not want to sing anymore. My energy seemed to be waning. My entire body ached; all my muscles were stiff and painfully contracted. I did not know what to think. I could not make up my mind whether to be angry at don Juan or not. I thought of jumping him, but somehow I knew he would have cut me down, like a bug. I really wanted to cry. I experienced a profound despair; the thought that don Juan was going all the way out to frighten me made me feel like weeping. I was incapable of finding a reason for his tremendous display of histrionics; his movements were so artful that I became confused. It was not as if he was trying to move like a woman; it was as if a woman was trying to move like don Juan. I had the impression that she was really trying to walk and move with don Juan's deliberation, but was too heavy and did not have the nimbleness of don Juan. Whoever it was in front of me created the impression of being a younger, heavy woman trying to imitate the slow movements of an agile old man.

These thoughts threw me into a state of panic. A cricket began to call loudly, very close to me. I noticed the richness of its tone; I fancied it to have a baritone voice. The call started to fade away. Suddenly my whole body jerked. I assumed the fighting position again and faced the direction from which the cricket's call had come. The sound was taking me away; it had begun to trap me before I realized it was only cricket-like. The sound got closer again. It became terribly loud. I started to sing my peyote songs louder and louder. Suddenly the cricket stopped. I immediately sat down, but kept on singing. A moment later I saw the shape of a man running toward me from the direction opposite to that of the cricket's call. I clapped my hands on my thigh and calf and stomped vigorously, frantically. The shape went by very fast, almost touching me. It looked like a dog. I experienced so dreadful a fear that I was numb. I cannot recollect anything else I felt or thought.

The morning dew was refreshing. I felt better. Whatever the phenomenon was, it seemed to have withdrawn. It was 5:48 A.M. when don Juan opened the door quietly and came out. He stretched his arms, yawning, and glanced at me. He took two steps toward me, prolonging his yawning. I saw his eyes looking through half-closed eyelids. I jumped up; I knew then that whoever, or whatever, was in front of me was not don Juan.

I took a small, sharp-edged rock from the ground. It was next to my right hand. I did not look at it; I just held it by pressing it with my thumb against my extended fingers. I adopted the form don Juan had taught me. I felt a strange vigor filling me, in a matter of seconds. Then I yelled and hurled the rock at him. I thought it was a magnificent outcry. At that moment I did not care whether I lived or died. I felt the cry was awesome in its potency. It was piercing and prolonged, and it actually directed my aim. The figure in front wobbled and shrieked and staggered to the side of the house and into the bushes again.

It took me hours to calm down. I could not sit anymore; I kept on trotting on the same place. I had to breathe through my mouth to take in enough air.

At 11:00 A.M. don Juan came out again. I was going to jump up, but the movements were *his*. He went directly to his spot and sat down in his usual familiar way. He looked at me and smiled. He was don Juan! I went to him, and instead of being angry, I kissed his hand. I really believed then that he had not acted to create a dramatic effect, but that someone had impersonated him to cause me harm or to kill me.

The conversation began with speculations about the identity of a *female* person who had allegedly taken my soul. Then don Juan asked me to tell him about every detail of my experience.

I narrated the whole sequence of events in a very deliberate manner. He laughed all the way, as if it were a joke. When I had finished he said, "You did fine. You won the battle for your soul. But this matter is

more serious than I thought. Your life wasn't worth
two hoots last night. It is fortunate you learned something in the past. Had you not had a little training you
would be dead by now, because whoever you saw last
night meant to finish you off."

"How is it possible, don Juan, that she could take
your form?"

"Very simple. She is a *diablera* and has a good helper
on the other side. But she was not too good in assuming my likeness, and you caught on to her trick."

"Is a helper on the other side the same as an ally?"

"No, a helper is the aid of a diablero. A helper is a
spirit that lives on the other side of the world and helps
a diablero to cause sickness and pain. It helps him to
kill."

"Can a diablero also have an ally, don Juan?"

"It is the diableros who have the allies, but before a
diablero can tame an ally, he usually has a helper to
aid him in his tasks."

"How about the woman who took your form, don
Juan? Does she have only a helper and not an ally?"

"I don't know whether she has an ally or not. Some
people do not like the power of an ally and prefer a
helper. To tame an ally is hard work. It is easier to get
a helper on the other side."

"Do you think *I* could get a helper?"

"To know that, you have to learn much more. We
are again at the beginning, almost as on the first day
you came over and asked me to tell you about Mescalito, and I could not because you would not have
understood. That other side is the world of diableros.
I think it would be best to tell you my own feelings in
the same way my benefactor told me his. He was a
diablero and a warrior; his life was inclined toward the
force and the violence of the world. But I am neither
of them. That is my nature. You have seen my world
from the start. As to showing you the world of my
benefactor, I can only put you at the door, and you will
have to decide for yourself; you will have to learn about
it by your effort alone. I must admit now that I made

a mistake. It is much better, I see now, to start the way I did, myself. Then it is easier to realize how simple and yet how profound the difference is. A diablero is a diablero, and a warrior is a warrior. Or a man who only traverses the paths of life is everything. Today I am neither a warrior nor a diablero. For me there is only the traveling on the paths that have a heart, on any path that may have a heart. There I travel, and the only worthwhile challenge for me is to traverse its full length. And there I travel—looking, looking, breathlessly."

He paused. His face revealed a peculiar mood; he seemed to be unusually serious. I did not know what to ask or to say. He proceeded:

"The particular thing to learn is how to get to the crack between the worlds and how to enter the other world. There is a crack between the two worlds, the world of the diableros and the world of living men. There is a place where the two worlds overlap. The crack is there. It opens and closes like a door in the wind. To get there a man must exercise his will. He must, I should say, develop an indomitable desire for it, a single-minded dedication. But he must do it without the help of any power or any man. The man by himself must ponder and wish up to a moment in which his body is ready to undergo the journey. That moment is announced by prolonged shaking of the limbs and violent vomiting. The man usually cannot sleep or eat, and wanes away. When the convulsions do not stop the man is ready to go, and the crack between the worlds appears right in front of his eyes, like a monumental door, a crack that goes up and down. When the crack opens the man has to slide through it. It is hard to see on the other side of the boundary. It is windy, like a sandstorm. The wind whirls around. The man then must walk in any direction. It will be a short or a long journey, depending on his willpower. A strong-willed man journeys shortly. An undecided, weak man journeys long and precariously. After this journey the man arrives at a sort of plateau. It is possible to distinguish some of its features clearly. It is a plane above the ground. It is possible to recognize it by the wind, which there becomes even more violent, whipping, roaring all around. On top of that plateau is the entrance to that other world. And there stands a skin that separates the two worlds; dead men go through it without a noise, but we have to break it with an outcry. The wind gathers strength, the same unruly wind that blows on the plateau. When the wind has gathered enough force, the man has to be inflexible, too, so that he can fight the wind. All he needs is a gentle shove; he does not need to be blown to the ends of the other world. Once on the other side, the man will have to wander around. His good fortune would be to find a helper nearby—not too far from the entrance. The man has to ask him for help. In his own words he has to ask the helper to teach him and make him a diablero. When the helper agrees, he kills the man on the spot, and while he is dead he teaches him. When you make the trip yourself, depending on your luck, you may find a great diablero in the helper who will kill you and teach you. Most of the time, though, one encounters lesser brujos who have very little to teach. But neither you nor they have the power to refuse. The best instance is to find a male helper lest one become the prey of a diablera, who will make one suffer in an unbelievable manner. Women are always like that. But that depends on luck alone, unless one's benefactor is a great diablero himself, in which event he will have many helpers in the other world, and can direct one to see a particular helper. My benefactor was such a man. He directed me to encounter his spirit helper. After your return, you will not be the same man. You are committed to come back to see your helper often. And you are committed to wander farther and farther from the entrance, until finally one day you will go too far and will not be able to return. Sometimes a diablero may catch a soul and push it through the entrance and leave it in the custody of his helper until he robs the person of all his willpower. In other cases, like yours for instance, the soul belongs to a strong-willed person, and the diablero may keep it inside his pouch, because it is too hard to carry otherwise. In such instances, as in yours, a fight may resolve the problem—a fight in which the diablero either wins all, or loses all. This time she lost the combat and had to release your soul. Had she won she would have taken it to her helper, for keeps."

"But how did I win?"

"You did not move from your spot. Had you moved one inch away you would have been demolished. She chose the moment I was away as the best time to strike, and she did it well. She failed because she did not count on your own nature, which is violent, and also because you did not budge from the spot on which you are invincible."

"How would she have killed me if I had moved?"

"She would have hit you like a thunderbolt. But above all she would have kept your soul and you would have wasted away."

"What is going to happen now, don Juan?"

"Nothing. You won your soul back. It was a good battle. You learned many things last night."

Afterward we began to look for the stone I had hurled. He said if we could find it we could be absolutely sure the affair had ended. We looked for nearly three hours. I had the feeling I would recognize it. But I could not.

That same day in the early evening don Juan took me into the hills around his house. There he gave me long and detailed instructions on specific fighting procedures. At one moment in the course of repeating certain prescribed steps I found myself alone. I had run up a slope and was out of breath. I was perspiring freely, and yet I was cold. I called don Juan several times, but he did not answer, and I began to experience a strange apprehension. I heard a rustling in the underbrush as if someone was coming toward me. I listened attentively, but the noise stopped. Then it came again, louder and closer. At that moment it occurred to me that the events of the preceding night were going to be repeated. In a matter of a few seconds my fear grew out of all proportion. The rustle in the underbrush got closer, and my strength waned. I wanted to scream or weep, run away or faint. My knees sagged; I fell to the ground, whining. I could not even close my eyes. After that, I remember only that don Juan made a fire and rubbed the contracted muscles of my arms and legs.

I remained in a state of profound distress for several hours. Afterward don Juan explained my disproportionate reaction as a common occurrence. I said I could not figure out logically what had caused my panic, and he replied that it was not the fear of dying, but rather the fear of losing my soul, a fear common among men who do not have unbending intent.

That experience was the last of don Juan's teachings. Ever since that time I have refrained from seeking his lessons. And, although don Juan has not changed his benefactor's attitude toward me, I do believe that I have succumbed to the first enemy of a man of knowledge.

PART TWO

A Structural Analysis

The following structural scheme, abstracted from the data on the states of nonordinary reality presented in the foregoing part of this work, is conceived as an attempt to disclose the internal cohesion and the cogency of don Juan's teachings. The structure, as I assess it, is composed of four concepts which are the main units: (1) man of knowledge; (2) a man of knowledge had an ally; (3) an ally had a rule; and (4) the rule was corroborated by special consensus. These four units are in turn composed of a number of subsidiary ideas; thus the total structure comprises all the meaningful concepts that were presented until the time I discontinued the apprenticeship. In a sense, these units represent successive levels of analysis, each level modifying the preceding one.*

Because this conceptual structure is completely dependent on the meaning of all its units, the following clarification seems to be pertinent at this point: Throughout this entire work, meaning has been rendered as I understood it. The component concepts of don Juan's knowledge as I have presented them here could not be the exact duplicate of what he said himself. In spite of all the effort I have put forth to render these concepts as faithfully as possible, their meaning has been deflected by my own attempts to classify them.

* For the process of validating special consensus, see Appendix A.

The arrangement of the four main units of this structural scheme is, however, a logical sequence which appears to be free from the influence of extraneous classificatory devices of my own. But, insofar as the component ideas of each main unit are concerned, it has been impossible to discard my personal influence. At certain points extraneous classificatory items are necessary in order to render the phenomena understandable. And, if such a task was to be accomplished here, it had to be done by zigzagging back and forth from the alleged meanings and classificatory scheme of the teacher to the meanings and classificatory devices of the apprentice.

THE OPERATIVE ORDER

THE FIRST UNIT

MAN OF KNOWLEDGE

At a very early stage of my apprenticeship, don Juan made the statement that the goal of his teachings was "to show how to become a man of knowledge." I use that statement as a point of departure. It is obvious that to become a man of knowledge was an operational goal. And it is also obvious that every part of don Juan's orderly teachings was geared to fulfill that goal in one way or another. My line of reasoning here is that under the circumstances "man of knowledge," being an operational goal, must have been indispensable to explaining some "operative order." Then, it is justifiable to conclude that, in order to understand that operative order, one has to understand its objective: man of knowledge.

After having established "man of knowledge" as the first structural unit, it was possible for me to arrange with assurance the following seven concepts as its proper components: (1) to become a man of knowledge was a matter of learning; (2) a man of knowledge had unbending intent; (3) a man of knowledge had clarity of mind; (4) to become a man of knowledge was a matter of strenuous labor; (5) a man of knowledge was a warrior; (6) to become a man of knowledge was an unceasing process; and (7) a man of knowledge had an ally.

These seven concepts were themes. They ran through the teachings, determining the character of don Juan's entire knowledge. Inasmuch as the operational goal of his teachings was to produce a man of knowledge, everything he taught was imbued with the specific characteristics of each of the seven themes. Together they construed the concept "man of knowledge" as a way of conducting oneself, a way of behaving that was the end result of a long and hazardous training. "Man of knowledge," however, was not a guide to behavior, but a set of principles encompassing all the unordinary circumstances pertinent to the knowledge being taught.

Each one of the seven themes was composed, in turn, of various other concepts, which covered their different facets.

From don Juan's statements it was possible to assume that a man of knowledge could be a diablero, that is, a black sorcerer. He stated that his teacher was a diablero and so was he in the past, although he had ceased to be concerned with certain aspects of the practice of sorcery. Since the goal of his teaching was to show how to become a man of knowledge, and since his knowledge consisted of being a diablero, there may have been an inherent connection between man of knowledge and diablero. Although don Juan never used the two terms interchangeably, the likelihood that they were connected raised the possibility that "man of knowledge" with its seven themes and their component concepts covered, theoretically, all the circumstances that might have arisen in the course of becoming a diablero.

To Become a Man of Knowledge Was a Matter of Learning

The first theme made it implicit that learning was the only possible way of becoming a man of knowledge, and that in turn implied the act of making a resolute effort to achieve an end. To become a man of knowledge was the end result of a process, as opposed to an immediate acquisition through an act of grace or through bestowal by supernatural powers. The plausibility of learning how to become a man of knowledge warranted the existence of a system for teaching one how to accomplish it.

The first theme had three components: (1) there were no overt requirements for becoming a man of knowledge; (2) there were some covert requirements; (3) the decision as to who could learn to become a man of knowledge was made by an impersonal power.

Apparently there were no overt prerequisites that would have determined who was, or who was not, qualified to learn how to become a man of knowledge. Ideally, the task was open to anybody who wished to pursue it. Yet, in practice, such a stand was inconsistent with the fact that don Juan as a teacher selected his apprentices.

In fact, any teacher under the circumstances would have selected his apprentices by means of matching them against some covert prerequisites. The specific nature of these prerequisites was never formalized; don Juan only insinuated that there were certain clues one had to bear in mind when viewing a prospective apprentice. The clues he alluded to were supposed to reveal whether or not the candidate had a certain disposition of character, which don Juan called "unbending intent."

Nevertheless, the final decision in matters of who could learn to become a man of knowledge was left to an impersonal power that was known to don Juan, but was outside his sphere of volition. The impersonal power was credited with pointing out the right person by allowing him to perform a deed of extraordinary nature, or by creating a set of peculiar circumstances around that person. Hence, there was never a conflict between the absence of overt prerequisites and the existence of undisclosed, covert prerequisites.

The man who was singled out in that manner became the apprentice. Don Juan called him the *escogido,* the "one who was chosen." But to be an escogido meant more than to be a mere apprentice. An escogido, by the sheer act of being selected by a power, was considered already to be different from ordinary men. He was considered already to be the recipient of a minimum amount of power which was supposed to be augmented by learning.

But learning was a process of unending quest, and the power that made the original decision, or a similar power, was expected to make similar decisions on the issue of whether an escogido could continue learning or whether he had been defeated. Those decisions were manifested through omens that occurred at any point of the teachings. In that respect, any peculiar circumstances surrounding an apprentice were considered to be such omens.

A Man of Knowledge Had Unbending Intent

The idea that a man of knowledge needed unbending intent referred to the exercise of volition. Having unbending intent meant having the will to execute a necessary procedure by maintaining oneself at all times rigidly within the boundaries of the knowledge being taught. A man of knowledge needed a rigid will in order to endure the obligatory quality that every act possessed when it was performed in the context of his knowledge.

The obligatory quality of all the acts performed in such a context, and their being inflexible and predetermined, were no doubt unpleasant to any man, for which reason a modicum of unbending intent was sought as the only covert requirement needed by a prospective apprentice.

Unbending intent was composed of (1) frugality, (2) soundness of judgment, and (3) lack of freedom to innovate.

A man of knowledge needed frugality because the majority of the obligatory acts dealt with instances or with elements that were either outside the boundaries of ordinary everyday life, or were not customary in ordinary activity, and the man who had to act in accordance with them needed an extraordinary effort every time he took action. It was implicit that one could have been capable of such an extraordinary effort by being frugal with any other activity that did not deal directly with such predetermined actions.

Since all acts were predetermined and obligatory, a man of knowledge needed soundness of judgment. This concept did not imply common sense, but did imply the capacity to assess the circumstances surrounding any need to act. A guide for such an assessment was provided by bringing together, as rationales, all the parts of the teachings which were at one's command at the given moment in which any action had to be carried out. Thus, the guide was always changing as more parts were learned; yet it always implied the conviction that any obligatory act one may have had to perform was, in fact, the most appropriate under the circumstances.

Because all acts were preestablished and compulsory, having to carry them out meant lack of freedom to innovate. Don Juan's system of imparting knowledge was so well established that there was no possibility of altering it in any way.

A Man of Knowledge Had Clarity of Mind

Clarity of mind was the theme that provided a sense of direction. The fact that all acts were predetermined meant that one's orientation within the knowledge being taught was equally predetermined; as a consequence, clarity of mind supplied only a sense of direction. It reaffirmed continuously the validity of the course being taken through the component ideas of (1) freedom to seek a path, (2) knowledge of the specific purpose, and (3) being fluid.

It was believed that one had freedom to seek a path. Having the freedom to choose was not incongruous with the lack of freedom to innovate; these two ideas were not in opposition nor did they interfere with each other. Freedom to seek a path referred to the liberty to choose among different possibilities of action which were equally effective and usable. The criterion for choosing was the advantage of one possibility over others, based on one's preference. As a matter of fact, the freedom to choose a path imparted a sense of direction through the expression of personal inclinations.

Another way to create a sense of direction was through the idea that there was a specific purpose for every action performed in the context of the knowledge being taught. Therefore, a man of knowledge needed clarity of mind in order to match his own specific reasons for acting with the specific purpose of every action. The knowledge of the specific purpose of every action was the guide he used to judge the circumstances surrounding any need to act.

Another facet of clarity of mind was the idea that a man of knowledge, in order to reinforce the performance of his obligatory actions, needed to assemble all the resources that the teachings had placed at his command. This was the idea of being fluid. It created a sense of direction by giving one the feeling of being malleable and resourceful. The compulsory quality of all acts would have imbued one with a sense of stiffness or sterility had it not been for the idea that a man of knowledge needed to be fluid.

To Become a Man of Knowledge Was a Matter of
Strenuous Labor

A man of knowledge had to possess or had to develop in
the course of his training an all-around capacity for
exertion. Don Juan stated that to become a man of
knowledge was a matter of strenuous labor. Strenuous
labor denoted a capacity (1) to put forth dramatic
exertion; (2) to achieve efficacy; and (3) to meet
challenge.

In the path of a man of knowledge drama was undoubtedly the outstanding single issue, and a special
type of exertion was needed for responding to circumstances that required dramatic exploitation; that is to
say, a man of knowledge needed dramatic exertion. Taking don Juan's behavior as an example, at first glance
it may have seemed that his dramatic exertion was only
his own idiosyncratic preference for histrionics. Yet
his dramatic exertion was always much more than
acting; it was rather a profound state of belief. He
imparted through dramatic exertion the peculiar quality
of finality to all the acts he performed. As a consequence, then, his acts were set on a stage in which
death was one of the main protagonists. It was implicit
that death was a real possibility in the course of learning because of the inherently dangerous nature of the
items with which a man of knowledge dealt; then, it
was logical that the dramatic exertion created by the
conviction that death was an ubiquitous player was more
than histrionics.

Exertion entailed not only drama, but also the need
of efficacy. Exertion had to be effective; it had to possess
the quality of being properly channeled, of being suitable. The idea of impending death created not only the
drama needed for overall emphasis, but also the conviction that every action involved a struggle for survival, the conviction that annihilation would result if one's
exertion did not meet the requirement of being effica-
cious.

Exertion also entailed the idea of challenge, that is, the act of testing whether, and proving that, one was capable of performing a proper act within the rigorous boundaries of the knowledge being taught.

A Man of Knowledge Was a Warrior

The existence of a man of knowledge was an unceasing struggle, and the idea that he was a warrior, leading a warrior's life, provided one with the means for achieving emotional stability. The idea of a man at war encompassed four concepts: (1) a man of knowledge had to have respect; (2) he had to have fear; (3) he had to be wide-awake; (4) he had to be self-confident. Hence, to be a warrior was a form of self-discipline which emphasized individual accomplishment; yet it was a stand in which personal interests were reduced to a minimum, as in most instances personal interest was incompatible with the rigor needed to perform any predetermined, obligatory act.

A man of knowledge in his role of warrior was obligated to have an attitude of deferential regard for the items with which he dealt; he had to imbue everything related to his knowledge with profound respect in order to place everything in a meaningful perspective. Having respect was equivalent to having assessed one's insignificant resources when facing the Unknown.

If one remained in that frame of thought, the idea of respect was logically extended to include oneself, for one was as unknown as the Unknown itself. The exercise of so sobering a feeling of respect transformed the apprenticeship of this specific knowledge, which may otherwise have appeared to be absurd, into a very rational alternative.

Another necessity of a warrior's life was the need to experience and carefully to evaluate the sensation of fear. The ideal was that, in spite of fear, one had to proceed with the course of one's acts. Fear was supposed to be conquered and there was an alleged time in the life of a man of knowledge when it was vanquished, but first one had to be conscious of being afraid and duly to evaluate that sensation. Don Juan asserted that one was capable of conquering fear only by facing it.

As a warrior, a man of knowledge also needed to be wide-awake. A man at war had to be on the alert in order to be cognizant of most of the factors pertinent to the two mandatory aspects of awareness: (1) awareness of intent and (2) awareness of the expected flux.

Awareness of intent was the act of being cognizant of the factors involved in the relationship between the specific purpose of any obligatory act and one's own specific purpose for acting. Since all the obligatory acts had a definite purpose, a man of knowledge had to be wide-awake; that is, he needed to be capable at all times of matching the definite purpose of every obligatory act with the definite reason that he had in mind for desiring to act.

A man of knowledge, by being aware of that relationship, was also capable of being cognizant of what was believed to be the expected flux. What I have called here the "awareness of the expected flux" referred to the certainty that one was capable of detecting at all times the important variables involved in the relationship between the specific purpose of every act and one's specific reason for acting. By being aware of the expected flux one was supposed to detect the most subtle changes. That deliberate awareness of changes accounted for the recognition and interpretation of omens and of other unordinary events.

The last aspect of the idea of a warrior's behavior was the need for self-confidence, that is, the assurance that the specific purpose of an act one may have chosen to perform was the only plausible alternative for one's own specific reasons for acting. Without self-confidence, one would have been incapable of fulfilling one of the most important aspects of the teachings: the capacity to claim knowledge as power.

To Become a Man of Knowledge Was an Unceasing Process

Being a man of knowledge was not a condition entailing permanency. There was never the certainty that, by carrying out the predetermined steps of the knowledge of being taught, one would become a man of knowledge. It was implicit that the function of the steps was only to show how to become a man of knowledge. Thus, becoming a man of knowledge was a task that could not be fully achieved; rather, it was an unceasing process comprising (1) the idea that one had to renew the quest of becoming a man of knowledge; (2) the idea of one's impermanency; and (3) the idea that one had to follow the path with heart.

The constant renewal of the quest of becoming a man of knowledge was expressed in the theme of the four symbolic enemies encountered on the path of learning: fear, clarity, power, and old age. Renewing the quest implied the gaining and the maintenance of control over oneself. A true man of knowledge was expected to battle each of the four enemies, in succession, until the last moment of his life, in order to keep himself actively engaged in becoming a man of knowledge. Yet, despite the truthful renewal of the quest, the odds were inevitably against man; he would succumb to his last symbolic enemy. This was the idea of impermanency.

Offsetting the negative value of one's impermanency was the notion that one had to follow the "path with heart." The path with heart was a metaphorical way of asserting that in spite of being impermanent one still had to proceed and had to be capable of finding satisfaction and personal fulfillment in the act of choosing the most amenable alternative and identifying oneself completely with it.

Don Juan synthesized the rationale of his whole knowledge in the metaphor that the important thing for him was to find a path with heart and then travel its length, meaning that the identification with the amenable alternative was enough for him. The journey by itself was sufficient; any hope of arriving at a permanent position was outside the boundaries of his knowledge.

THE SECOND UNIT

A MAN OF KNOWLEDGE HAD AN ALLY

The idea that a man of knowledge had an ally was the most important of the seven component themes, for it was the only one that was indispensable to explaining what a man of knowledge was. In don Juan's classificatory scheme a man of knowledge had an ally, whereas the average man did not, and having an ally was what made him different from ordinary men.

Don Juan described an ally as being "a power capable of transporting a man beyond the boundaries of himself"; that is, an ally was a power that allowed one to transcend the realm of ordinary reality. Consequently, to have an ally implied having power; and the fact that a man of knowledge had an ally was by itself proof that the operational goal of the teachings had been fulfilled. Since that goal was to show how to become a man of knowledge, and since a man of knowledge was one who had an ally, another way of describing the operational goal of don Juan's teachings was to say that they also showed how to obtain an ally. The concept "man of knowledge," as a sorcerer's philosophical frame, had meaning for anyone who wanted to live within that frame only insofar as he had an ally.

I have classified this last component theme of man of knowledge as the second main structural unit because of its indispensability for explaining what a man of knowledge was.

In don Juan's teachings, there were two allies. The first was contained in the *Datura* plants commonly known as Jimson weed. Don Juan called that ally by one of the Spanish names of the plant, *yerba del diablo* (devil's weed). According to him any species of *Datura* was the container of the ally. Yet every sorcerer had to grow a patch of one species which he called his own, not only in the sense that the plants were his private property, but in the sense that they were personally identified with him.

Don Juan's own plants belonged to the species *inoxia;* there seemed to be no correlation, however, between that fact and differences that may have existed between the two species of *Datura* accessible to him.

The second ally was contained in a mushroom I identified as belonging to the genus *Psilocybe;* it was possibly *Psilocybe mexicana,* but the classification was only tentative because I was incapable of procuring a specimen for laboratory analysis.

Don Juan called this ally *humito* (little smoke), suggesting that the ally was analogous to smoke or to the smoking mixture he made with the mushroom. The smoke was referred to as if it were the real container, yet he made it clear that the power was associated with only one species of *Psilocybe;* thus special care was needed at the time of collecting in order not to confuse it with any of a dozen other species of the same genus which grew in the same area.

An ally as a meaningful concept included the following ideas and their ramifications: (1) an ally was formless; (2) an ally was perceived as a quality; (3) an ally was tamable; (4) an ally had a rule.

An Ally Was Formless

An ally was believed to be an entity existing outside and independent of oneself, yet in spite of being a separate entity an ally was believed to be formless. I have established "formlessness" as a condition that is the opposite of "having definite form," a distinction made in view of the fact there were other powers similar to an ally which had a definitely perceivable form. An ally's condition of formlessness meant that it did not possess a distinct, or a vaguely defined, or even a recognizable, form; and such a condition implied that an ally was not visible at any time.

An Ally Was Perceived as a Quality

A sequel to an ally's formlessness was another condition expressed in the idea that an ally was perceived only as a quality of the senses; that is to say, since an ally was formless its presence was noticed only by its effects on the sorcerer. Don Juan classified some of those effects as having anthropomorphic qualities. He depicted an ally as having the character of a human being, thus implying that an individual sorcerer was in the position of choosing the most suitable ally by matching his own character with an ally's alleged anthropomorphic characteristics.

The two allies involved in the teachings were presented by don Juan as having a set of antithetical qualities.

Don Juan categorized the ally contained in *Datura inoxia* as having two qualities: it was woman-like, and it was a giver of superfluous power. He thought these two qualities were thoroughly undesirable. His statements on the subject were definite, but he indicated at the same time that his value judgment on the matter was merely a personalistic choice.

The most important characteristic was undoubtedly what don Juan called its woman-like nature. The fact that it was depicted as being woman-like did not mean, however, that the ally was a female power. It seemed that the analogy of a woman may have been only a metaphorical way don Juan used to describe what he thought to be the unpleasant effects of the ally. Besides, the Spanish name of the plant, *yerba,* because of its feminine gender, may have also helped to create the female analogy. At any rate, the personification of this ally as a woman-like power ascribed to it the following anthropomorphic qualities: (1) it was possessive; (2) it was violent; (3) it was unpredictable; and (4) it had deleterious effects.

Don Juan believed that the ally had the capacity to enslave the men who became its followers; he explained this capacity as the quality of being possessive, which he correlated with a woman's character. The ally possessed its followers by bestowing power on them, by creating a feeling of dependency, and by giving them physical strength and well-being.

This ally was also believed to be violent. Its womanlike violence was expressed in its forcing its followers to engage in disruptive acts of brute force. And this specific characteristic made it best suited for men of fierce natures who wanted to find in violence a key to personal power.

Another woman-like characteristic was unpredictability. For don Juan it meant that the ally's effects were never consistent; rather, they were supposed to change erratically, and there was no discernible way of predicting them. The ally's inconsistency was to be counteracted by the sorcerer's meticulous and dramatic care of every detail of its handling. Any unfavorable turn that was unaccountable, as a result of error or mishandling, was explained as a result of the ally's woman-like unpredictability.

Because of its possessiveness, violence, and unpredictability, this ally was thought to have an overall deleterious effect on the character of its followers. Don Juan believed that the ally willfully strove to transmit its woman-like characteristics, and that its effort to do so actually succeeded.

But, alongside its woman-like nature, this ally had another facet which was also perceived as a quality: it was a giver of superfluous power. Don Juan was very emphatic on this point, and he stressed that as a generous giver of power the ally was unsurpassable. It was purported to furnish its followers with physical strength, a feeling of audacity, and the prowess to perform extraordinary deeds. In Don Juan's judgment, however, so exorbitant a power was superfluous; he stated that, for himself at least, there was no need of it anymore. Nevertheless, he presented it as a strong incentive for a prospective man of knowledge, should the latter have a natural inclination to seek power.

Don Juan's idiosyncratic point of view was that the ally contained in *Psilocybe mexicana,* on the other hand, had the most adequate and most valuable characteristics: (1) it was male-like, and (2) it was a giver of ecstasy.

He depicted this ally as being the antithesis of the one contained in *Datura* plants. He considered it to be male-like, manly. Its condition of masculinity seemed to be analogous to the female-like condition of the other ally; that is, it was not a male power, but don Juan classified its effects in terms of what he considered to be manly behavior. In this instance, too, the masculine gender of the Spanish word *humito* may have suggested the analogy to a male power.

The anthropomorphic qualities of this ally which don Juan judged to be proper to a man were the following: (1) it was dispassionate; (2) it was gentle; (3) it was predictable; and (4) it had beneficial effects.

Don Juan's idea of the dispassionate nature of the ally was expressed in the belief that it was fair, that it never actually demanded extravagant acts from its followers. It never made men its slaves, because it did not bestow easy power on them; on the contrary, Humito was hard, but just, with its followers.

The fact that the ally did not elicit overt violent behavior made it gentle. It was supposed to induce a sensation of bodilessness, and thus don Juan presented it as being calm, gentle, and a giver of peace.

It was also predictable. Don Juan described its effects on all its individual followers and in the successive experiences of any single man as being constant; in other words, its effects did not vary or, if they did, they were so similar that they were counted as being the same.

As a consequence of being dispassionate, gentle, and predictable, this ally was thought to have another manly characteristic: a beneficial effect on the character of its followers. Humito's manliness was supposed to create a very rare condition of emotional stability in them. Don

Juan believed that under the ally's guidance one would temper one's heart and acquire balance.

A corollary of all the ally's manly characteristics was believed to be a capacity to give ecstasy. This other facet of its nature was perceived also as a quality. Humito was credited with removing the body of its followers, thus allowing them to execute specialized forms of activity pertinent to a state of bodilessness. And don Juan maintained that those specialized forms of activity led unavoidably to a condition of ecstasy. The ally contained in the *Psilocybe* was said to be ideal for men whose natures predisposed them to seek contemplation.

An Ally Was Tamable

The idea that an ally was tamable implied that as a power it had the potential of being used. Don Juan explained it as an ally's innate capacity of being utilizable; after a sorcerer had tamed an ally he was thought to be in command of its specialized power which meant that he could manipulate it to his own advantage. An ally's capacity of being tamed was counterposed to the incapacity of other powers, which were similar to an ally except that they did not yield to being manipulated.

The manipulation of an ally had two aspects: (1) an ally was a vehicle; (2) an ally was a helper.

An ally was a vehicle in the sense that it served to transport a sorcerer into the realm of nonordinary reality. Insofar as my personal knowledge was concerned, the allies both served as vehicles, although the function had different implications for each of them.

The overall, undesirable qualities of the ally contained in *Datura inoxia,* especially its quality of unpredictability, turned it into a dangerous, undependable vehicle. Ritual was the only possible protection against its inconsistency, but that was never enough to ensure the ally's stability; a sorcerer using this ally as a vehicle had to wait for favorable omens before proceeding.

The ally contained in *Psilocybe mexicana,* on the other hand, was thought to be a steady and predictable vehicle as a result of all its valuable qualities. As a consequence of its predictability, a sorcerer using this ally did not need to engage in any kind of preparatory ritual.

The other aspect of an ally's manipulability was expressed in the idea that an ally was a helper. To be a helper meant that an ally, after serving a sorcerer as a vehicle, was again usable as an aid or a guide to assist him in achieving whatever goal he had in mind in going into the realm of nonordinary reality.

In their capacity as helpers, the two allies had different, unique properties. The complexity and the applicability of these properties increased as one advanced on the learning path. But, in general terms, the ally contained in *Datura inoxia* was believed to be an extraordinary helper, and this capacity was thought to be a corollary of its ability to give superfluous power. The ally contained in *Psilocybe mexicana,* however, was considered to be an even more extraordinary helper. Don Juan thought it was matchless in the function of being a helper, which he regarded as an extension of its overall valuable qualities.

THE THIRD UNIT

AN ALLY HAD A RULE

Alone among the components of the concept "ally," the idea that an ally had a rule was indispensable for explaining what an ally was. Because of that indispensability I have placed it as the third main unit in this structural scheme.

The rule, which don Juan called also the law, was the rigid organizing concept regulating all the actions that had to be executed and the behavior that had to be observed throughout the process of handling an ally. The rule was transmitted verbally from teacher to apprentice, ideally without alteration, through the sustained interaction between them. The rule was thus more than a body of regulations; it was, rather, a series of outlines of activities governing the course to be followed in the process of manipulating an ally.

Undoubtedly many elements would have fulfilled don Juan's definition of an ally as a "power capable of transporting a man beyond the boundaries of himself." Anyone accepting that definition could reasonably have conceived that anything possessing such a capability would be an ally. And logically, even bodily conditions produced by hunger, fatigue, illness, and the like could have served as allies, for they might have possessed the capacity of transporting a man beyond the realm of ordinary reality. But the idea that an ally had a rule eliminated all these possibilities. An ally was a power that had a rule. All the other possibilities could not be considered as allies because they had no rule.

As a concept the rule comprehended the following ideas and their various components: (1) the rule was inflexible; (2) the rule was noncumulative; (3) the rule was corroborated in ordinary reality; (4) the rule was corroborated in nonordinary reality; and (5) the rule was corroborated by special consensus.

The Rule Was Inflexible

The outlines of activity forming the body of the rule were unavoidable steps that one had to follow in order to achieve the operational goal of the teachings. This compulsory quality of the rule was rendered in the idea that it was inflexible. The inflexibility of the rule was intimately related to the idea of efficacy. Dramatic exertion created an incessant battle for survival, and under those conditions only the most effective act that one could perform would ensure one's survival. As individualistic points of reference were not permitted, the rule prescribed the actions constituting the only alternative for survival. Thus the rule had to be inflexible; it had to require a definite compliance to its dictum.

Compliance with the rule, however, was not absolute. In the course of the teachings I recorded one instance in which its inflexibility was canceled out. Don Juan

explained that example of deviation as a special favor
stemming from direct intervention of an ally. In this instance, owing to my unintentional error in handling
the ally contained in *Dutura inoxia,* the rule had been
breached. Don Juan extrapolated from the occurrence
that an ally had the capacity to intervene directly and
withhold the deleterious, and usually fatal, effect result-
ing from noncompliance with its rule. Such evidence of
flexibility was thought to be always the product of a
strong bond of affinity between the ally and its follower.

The Rule Was Noncumulative

The assumption here was that all conceivable methods
of manipulating an ally had already been used. Theoretically, the rule was noncumulative; there was no possibility of augmenting it. The idea of the noncumulative
nature of the rule was also related to the concept of
efficacy. Since the rule prescribed the only effective
alternative for one's personal survival, any attempt to
change it or to alter its course by innovation was considered to be not only a superfluous act, but a deadly
one. One had only the possibility of adding to one's
personal knowledge of the rule, either under the teacher's guidance or under the special guidance of the ally
itself. The latter was considered to be an instance of
direct acquisition of knowledge, not an addition to the
body of the rule.

The Rule Was Corroborated in Ordinary Reality

Corroboration of the rule meant the act of verifying it,
the act of attesting to its validity by confirming it pragmatically in an experimental manner. Because the rule
dealt with situations of ordinary and of nonordinary
reality, its corroboration took place in both areas.

The situations of ordinary reality with which the rule
dealt were most often remarkably uncommon situations,
but, no matter how unusual they were, the rule was corroborated in ordinary reality. For that reason it has

been considered to fall beyond the scope of this work, and should properly be the realm of another study. That part of the rule concerned the details of the procedures employed in recognizing, collecting, mixing, preparing, and caring for the power plants in which the allies were contained, the details of other procedures involved in the uses of such power plants, and other similar minutiae.

The Rule Was Corroborated in Nonordinary Reality

The rule was also corroborated in nonordinary reality, and the corroboration was carried out in the same pragmatic, experimental manner of validation as would have been employed in situations of ordinary reality. The idea of a pragmatic corroboration involved two concepts: (1) meetings with the ally, which I have called the states of nonordinary reality; and (2) the specific purposes of the rule.

The states of nonordinary reality.—The two plants in which the allies were contained, when used in conformity with the allies' respective rules, produced states of peculiar perception which don Juan classified as meetings with the ally. He placed extraordinary emphasis on eliciting them, an emphasis summed up in the idea that one had to meet with the ally as many times as possible in order to verify its rule in a pragmatic, experimental manner. The assumption was that the proportion of the rule that was likely to be verified was in direct correlation with the number of times one met with the ally.

The exclusive method of inducing a meeting with the ally was, naturally, through the appropriate use of the plant in which the ally was contained. Nonetheless, don Juan hinted that at a certain advanced stage of learning the meetings could have taken place without the use of the plant; that is to say, they could have been elicited by an act of volition alone.

I have called the meetings with the ally states of nonordinary reality. I chose the term "nonordinary reality" because it conformed with don Juan's assertion that such meetings took place in a continuum of reality, a reality that was only slightly different from the ordinary reality of everyday life. Consequently, nonordinary reality had specific characteristics that could have been assessed in presumably equal terms by everyone. Don Juan never formulated these characteristics in a definite manner, but his reticence seemed to stem from the idea that each man had to claim knowledge as a matter of personal nature.

The following categories, which I consider the specific characteristics of nonordinary reality, were drawn from my personal experience. Yet, in spite of their seemingly idiosyncratic origin, they were reinforced and developed by don Juan under the premises of his knowledge; he conducted his teachings as if these characteristics were inherent in nonordinary reality: (1) nonordinary reality was utilizable; (2) nonordinary reality had component elements.

The first characteristic—that nonordinary reality was utilizable—implied that it was fit for actual service. Don Juan explained time and time again that the encompassing concern of his knowledge was the pursuit of practical results, and that such a pursuit was pertinent in ordinary as well as in nonordinary reality. He maintained that in his knowledge there were the means of putting nonordinary reality into service, in the same way as ordinary reality. According to that assertion, the states induced by the allies were elicited with the deliberate intention of being used. In this particular instance don Juan's rationale was that the meetings with the allies were set up to learn their secrets, and this rationale served as a rigid guide to screen out other personalistic motives that one may have had for seeking the states of nonordinary reality.

The second characteristic of nonordinary reality was that it had component elements. Those component elements were the items, the actions, and the events that one perceived, seemingly with one's senses, as being the content of a state of nonordinary reality. The total picture of nonordinary reality was made up of elements that appeared to possess qualities both of the elements of ordinary reality and of the components of an ordinary dream, although they were not on a par with either one.

According to my personal judgment, the component elements of nonordinary reality had three unique characteristics: (1) stability, (2) singularity, and (3) lack of ordinary consensus. These qualities made them stand on their own as discrete units possessing an unmistakable individuality.

The component elements of nonordinary reality had stability in the sense that they were constant. In this respect they were similar to the component elements of ordinary reality, for they neither shifted nor disappeared, as would the component elements of ordinary dreams. It seemed as if every detail that made up a component element of nonordinary reality had a concreteness of its own, a concreteness I perceived as being extraordinarily stable. The stability was so pronounced that it allowed me to establish the criterion that, in nonordinary reality, one always possessed the capacity to come to a halt in order to examine any of the component elements for what appeared to be an indefinite length of time. The application of this criterion permitted me to differentiate the states of nonordinary reality used by don Juan from other states of peculiar perception which may have appeared to be nonordinary reality, but which did not yield to this criterion.

The second exclusive characteristic of the component elements of nonordinary reality—their singularity—meant that every detail of the component elements was a single, individual item; it seemed as if each detail was isolated from others, or as if details appeared one at a time. The singularity of the component elements seemed further to create a unique necessity, which may have been common to everybody: the imperative need, the urge, to amalgamate all isolated details into a real scene, a total composite. Don Juan was obviously aware of that need and used it on every possible occasion.

The third unique characteristic of the component elements, and the most dramatic of all, was their lack of ordinary consensus. One perceived the component elements while being in a state of complete solitude, which was more like the aloneness of a man witnessing by himself an unfamiliar scene in ordinary reality than like the solitude of dreaming. As the stability of the component elements of nonordinary reality enabled one to stop and examine any of them for what appeared to be an indefinite length of time, it seemed almost as if they were elements of everyday life; however, the difference between the component elements of the two states of reality was their capacity for ordinary consensus. By ordinary consensus I mean the tacit or the implicit agreement on the component elements of everyday life which fellowmen give to one another in various ways. For the component elements of nonordinary reality, ordinary consensus was unattainable. In this respect nonordinary reality was closer to a state of dreaming than to ordinary reality. And yet, because of their unique characteristics of stability and singularity, the component elements of nonordinary reality had a compelling quality of realness which seemed to foster the necessity of validating their existence in terms of consensus.

The specific purpose of the rule.—The other component of the concept that the rule was verified in nonordinary reality was the idea that the rule had a specific purpose. That purpose was the achievement, by using an ally, of a utilitarian goal. In the context of don Juan's teachings, it was assumed that the rule was learned by corroborating it in ordinary and nonordinary reality. The decisive facet of the teachings was, however, corroboration of the rule in the states of nonordinary reality; and what was corroborated in the actions and elements perceived in nonordinary reality was the specific purpose of the rule. That specific purpose dealt with the ally's power, that is, with the manipulation of an ally first as a vehicle and then as a helper, but don Juan always treated each instance of the specific purpose of the rule as a single unit implicitly covering these two areas.

Because the specific purpose referred to the manipulation of the ally's power, it had an inseparable sequel —the manipulatory techniques.

The manipulatory techniques were the actual procedures, the actual operations, undertaken in each instance involving the manipulation of an ally's power. The idea that an ally was manipulatable warranted its usefulness in the achievement of pragmatic goals, and the manipulatory techniques were the procedures that supposedly rendered the ally usable.

Specific purpose and manipulatory techniques formed a single unit which a sorcerer had to know exactly in order to command his ally with efficacy.

Don Juan's teachings included the following specific purposes of the two allies' rules. I have arranged them here in the same order in which he presented them to me.

The first specific purpose that was verified in nonordinary reality was testing with the ally contained in *Datura inoxia*. The manipulatory technique was ingesting a potion made with a section of the root of the *Datura* plant. Ingesting that potion produced a shallow state of nonordinary reality, which don Juan used for testing me in order to determine whether or not, as a prospective apprentice, I had affinity with the ally contained in the plant. The potion was supposed to produce either a sensation of unspecified physical well-being or a feeling of great discomfort, effects that don Juan judged to be, respectively, a sign of affinity or the lack of it.

The second specific purpose was divination. It was also part of the rule of the ally contained in *Datura inoxia*. Don Juan considered divination to be a form of specialized movement, on the assumption that a sorcerer was transported by the ally to a particular compartment of nonordinary reality where he was capable of divining events that were otherwise unknown to him.

The manipulatory technique of the second specific purpose was a process of ingestion-absorption. A potion made with *Datura* root was ingested, and an unguent made with *Datura* seeds was rubbed on the temporal and frontal areas of the head. I have used the term "ingestion-absorption" because ingestion might have been aided by skin absorption in producing a state of nonordinary reality, or skin absorption might have been aided by ingestion.

This manipulatory technique required the utilization of other elements besides the *Datura* plant, in this instance two lizards. They were supposed to serve the sorcerer as instruments of movement, meaning here the peculiar perception of being in a particular realm in which one was capable of hearing a lizard talk and then of visualizing whatever it had said. Don Juan explained such phenomena as the lizards answering the questions that had been posed for divination.

The third specific purpose of the rule of the ally contained in the *Datura* plants dealt with another specialized form of movement, bodily flight. As don Juan explained, a sorcerer using this ally was capable of flying bodily over enormous distances; the bodily flight was the sorcerer's capacity to move through nonordinary reality and then to return at will to ordinary reality.

The manipulatory technique of the third specific purpose was also a process of ingestion-absorption. A potion made with *Datura* root was ingested, and an unguent made with *Datura* seeds was rubbed on the soles of the feet, on the inner part of both legs, and on the genitals.

The third specific purpose was not corroborated in depth; don Juan implied that he had not disclosed other aspects of the manipulatory technique which would permit a sorcerer to acquire a sense of direction while moving.

The fourth specific purpose of the rule was testing, the ally being contained in *Psilocybe mexicana*. The testing was not intended to determine affinity or lack of affinity with the ally, but rather to be an unavoidable first trial, or the first meeting with the ally.

The manipulatory technique for the fourth specific purpose utilized a smoking mixture made of dried mushrooms mixed with different parts of five other plants, none of which was known to have hallucinogenic properties. The rule placed the emphasis on the act of inhaling the smoke from the mixture; the teacher thus used the word *humito* (little smoke) to refer to the ally contained in it. But I have called this process "ingestion-inhalation" because it was a combination of ingesting first and then of inhaling. The mushrooms, because of their softness, dried into a very fine dust which was rather difficult to burn. The other ingredients turned into shreds upon drying. These shreds were incinerated in the pipe bowl while the mushroom powder, which did not burn so easily, was drawn into the mouth and ingested. Logically, the quantity of dried mushrooms ingested was larger than the quantity of shreds burned and inhaled.

The effect of the first state of nonordinary reality elicited by *Psilocybe mexicana* gave rise to don Juan's brief discussion of the fifth specific purpose of the rule. It was concerned with movement—moving with the help of the ally contained in *Psilocybe mexicana* into and through inanimate objects or into and through animate beings. The complete manipulatory technique may have included hypnotic suggestion besides the process of ingestion-inhalation. Because don Juan presented this specific purpose only as a brief discussion which was not further verified, it was impossible for me to assess correctly any of its aspects.

The sixth specific purpose of the rule verified in nonordinary reality, also involving the ally contained in *Psilocybe mexicana*, had the inherent capacity to cause the sorcerer's body to disappear; thus the idea of adopting an alternate form was a logical possibility for achieving movement under the conditions of bodilessness. Another logical possibility for achieving movement was, naturally, moving through objects and beings, which don Juan had discussed briefly.

The manipulatory technique of the sixth specific purpose of the rule included not only ingestion-inhalation but also, according to all indications, hypnotic suggestion. Don Juan had put forth such a suggestion during the transitional stages into nonordinary reality, and also during the early part of the states of nonordinary reality. He classified the seemingly hypnotic process as being only his personal supervision, meaning that he had not revealed to me the complete manipulatory technique at that particular time.

The adoption of an alternate form did not mean that a sorcerer was free to take, on the spur of the moment, any form he wanted to take; on the contrary, it implied a lifelong training to achieve a preconceived form. The preconceived form don Juan had prefered to adopt was that of a crow, and consequently he emphasized that particular form in his teachings. He made it very clear, nonetheless, that a crow was his personal choice, and that there were innumerable other possible preconceived forms.

THE FOURTH UNIT

THE RULE WAS CORROBORATED BY SPECIAL CONSENSUS

Among the component concepts forming the rule, the one that was indispensable for explaining it was the idea that the rule was corroborated by special consensus; all the other component concepts were insufficient by themselves for explaining the meaning of the rule.

Don Juan made it very clear that an ally was not bestowed on a sorcerer, but that a sorcerer learned to manipulate the ally through the process of corroborating its rule. The complete learning process involved verification of the rule in nonordinary reality as well as in ordinary reality. Yet the crucial facet of don Juan's teachings was corroboration of the rule in a pragmatic and experimental manner in the context of what one perceived as being the component elements of nonordinary reality. But those component elements were not subject to ordinary consensus, and if one was incapable of obtaining agreement on their existence, their perceived realness would have been only an illusion. As a man would have to be by himself in nonordinary reality, by reason of his solitariness whatever he perceived would have to be idiosyncratic. The solitariness and the idiosyncrasies were a consequence of the assumed fact that no fellowman could give one ordinary consensus on one's perceptions.

At this point don Juan brought in the most important constituent part of his teachings: he provided me with special consensus on the actions and the elements I had perceived in nonordinary reality, actions and elements that were believed to corroborate the rule. In don Juan's teachings, special consensus meant tacit or implicit agreement on the component elements of nonordinary reality, which he, in his capacity as teacher, gave me as the apprentice of his knowledge. This special consensus was not in any way fraudulent or spurious, such as the one two persons might give each other in describing the component elements of their individual dreams. This special consensus don Juan supplied was systematic, and to provide it he may have needed the totality of his knowledge. With the acquisition of systematic consensus the actions and the elements perceived in nonordinary reality became consensually real, which meant, in don Juan's classificatory scheme, that the rule of the ally had been corroborated. The rule had meaning as a concept, then, only inasmuch as it was subject to special consensus, for without special agreement about its corroboration the rule would have been a purely idiosyncratic construct.

Because of its indispensability for explaining the rule, I have made the idea that the rule was corroborated by special consensus the fourth main unit of this structural scheme. This unit, because it was basically the interplay between two individuals, was composed of (1) the benefactor, or the guide into the knowledge being taught, the agent who supplied special consensus; (2) the apprentice or the subject for whom special consensus was provided.

Failure or success in achieving the operational goal of the teachings rested on this unit. Thus, special consensus was the precarious culmination of the following process: A sorcerer had a distinctive feature, possession of an ally, which differentiated him from ordinary men. An ally was a power that had the special property of having a rule. And the unique characteristic of the rule was its corroboration in nonordinary reality by means of special consensus.

The Benefactor

The benefactor was the agent without whom the corroboration of the rule would have been impossible. In order to provide special consensus, he performed the two tasks of (1) preparing the background for special consensus on the corroboration of the rule, and (2) guiding special consensus.

Preparing Special Consensus

The benefactor's first task was to set the background necessary for bringing forth special consensus on corroboration of the rule. As my teacher, don Juan made me (1) experience other states of nonordinary reality which he explained as being quite apart from those elicited to corroborate the rule of the allies; (2) participate with him in certain special states of ordinary reality which he seemed to have produced himself; and (3) recapitulate each experience in detail. Don Juan's task of preparing special consensus consisted of strengthening and confirming the corroboration of the rule by giving special consensus on the component elements of these new states of nonordinary reality, and on the component elements of the special states of ordinary reality.

The other states of nonordinary reality which don Juan made me experience were induced by the ingestion of the cactus *Lophophora williamsii,* commonly known as peyote. Usually the top part of the cactus was cut off and stored until it had dried, and then it was chewed and ingested, but under special circumstances the top part was ingested while it was fresh. Ingestion, however, was not the only way to experience a state of nonordinary reality with *Lophophora williamsii.* Don Juan suggested that spontaneous states of nonordinary reality occurred under unique conditions, and he categorized them as gifts from or bestowals by the power contained in the plant.

Nonordinary reality induced by *Lophophora williamsii* had three distinctive features: (1) it was believed to be produced by an entity called "Mescalito"; (2) it was utilizable; and (3) it had component elements.

Mescalito was purported to be a unique power, similar to an ally in the sense that it allowed one to transcend the boundaries of ordinary reality, but also quite different from an ally. Like an ally, Mescalito was contained in a definite plant, the cactus *Lophophora williamsii.* But unlike an ally, which was merely *contained in* a plant, Mescalito and the plant in which it was contained were the same; the plant was the center of overt manifestations of respect, the recipient of profound veneration. Don Juan firmly believed that under certain conditions, such as a state of profound acquiescence to Mescalito, the simple act of being contiguous to the cactus would induce a state of nonordinary reality.

But Mescalito did not have a rule, and for that reason it was not an ally even though it was capable of transporting a man outside the boundaries of ordinary reality. Not having a rule not only barred Mescalito from being used as an ally, for without a rule it could not conceivably be manipulated, but also made it a power remarkably different from an ally.

As a direct consequence of not having a rule, Mescalito was available to any man without the need of a long apprenticeship or the commitment to manipulatory techniques, as with an ally. And because it was available without any training, Mescalito was said to be a protector. To be a protector meant that it was accessible to every man, and with some individuals it was not compatible. According to don Juan, such incompatibility was caused by the discrepancy between Mescalito's "unbending morality" and the individual's own questionable character.

Mescalito was also a teacher. It was supposed to exercise didactic functions. It was a director, a guide to proper behavior. Mescalito taught the right way. Don Juan's idea of the right way seemed to be a sense of propriety, which consisted not of righteousness in terms of morality, but of a tendency to simplify behavioral patterns in terms of the efficacy promoted by his teachings. Don Juan believed Mescalito taught simplification of behavior.

Mescalito was believed to be an entity. And as such it was purported to have a definite form that was usually not constant or predictable. This quality implied that Mescalito was perceived differently not only by different men, but also by the same man on different occasions. Don Juan expressed this idea in terms of Mescalito's ability to adopt any conceivable form. For individuals with whom it was compatible, however, it adopted an unchanging form after they had partaken of it over a period of years.

The nonordinary reality produced by Mescalito was utilizable, and in this respect was identical with that induced by an ally. The only difference was the rationale don Juan used in his teachings for eliciting it: one was supposed to seek "Mescalito's lessons on the right way."

The nonordinary reality produced by Mescalito also had component elements, and here again the states of nonordinary reality induced by Mescalito and by an ally were identical. In both, the characteristics of the component elements were stability, singularity, and lack of consensus.

The other procedure don Juan used to prepare the background for special consensus was to make me the coparticipant in special states of ordinary reality. A special state of ordinary reality was a situation that could be described in terms of the properties of everyday life, except that it might have been impossible to obtain ordinary consensus on its component elements. Don Juan prepared the background for special consensus on the corroboration of the rule by giving special consensus on the component elements of the special states of ordinary reality. These component elements were elements of everyday life whose existence could be confirmed only by don Juan through special agreement. This was a supposition on my part, because as coparticipant in the special states of ordinary reality I believed that only don Juan, as the other coparticipant, would know which component elements made up the special state of ordinary reality.

In my own personal judgment, the special states of ordinary reality were produced by don Juan, although he never claimed to have done so. It seemed that he produced them through a skillful manipulation of hints and suggestions to guide my behavior. I have called that process the "manipulation of cues." It had two aspects: (1) cuing about the environment, and (2) cuing about behavior.

During the course of the teachings don Juan made me experience two such states. He may have produced the first through the process of cuing about the environment. Don Juan's rationale for producing it was that I needed a test to prove my good intentions, and only after he had given me special consensus on its component elements did he consent to begin his teachings. By "cuing about the environment" I meant that don Juan led me into a special state of ordinary reality by isolating, through subtle suggestions, component elements of ordinary reality which were part of the immediate physical surroundings. Elements isolated in such a manner created in this instance a specific visual perception of color, which don Juan tacitly verified.

The second state of ordinary reality may have been produced by the process of cuing about behavior. Don Juan, through close association with me and through the exercise of a consistent way of behaving, had succeeded in creating an image of himself, an image that served me as an essential pattern by which I could recognize him. Then, by performing certain specific choice responses, which were irreconcilable with the image he had created, don Juan was capable of distorting this essential pattern of recognition. The distortion may in turn have changed the normal configuration of elements associated with the pattern into a new and incongruous pattern which could not be subjected to ordinary consensus; don Juan, as the coparticipant of that special state of ordinary reality, was the only person who knew which the component elements were, and thus he was the only person who could give me agreement on their existence.

Don Juan set up the second special state of ordinary reality also as a test, as a sort of recapitulation of his teachings. It seemed that both special states of ordinary reality marked a transition in the teachings. They seemed to be points of articulation. And the second state may have marked my entrance into a new stage of learning characterized by more direct coparticipation between teacher and apprentice for purposes of arriving at special consensus.

The third procedure that don Juan employed to prepare special consensus was to make me render a detailed account of what I had experienced as an aftermath of each state of nonordinary reality and each special state of ordinary reality, and then to stress certain choice units which he isolated from the content of my account. The essential factor was directing the outcome of the states of nonordinary reality, and my implicit assumption here was the characteristics of the component elements of nonordinary reality—stability, singularity, and lack of ordinary consensus—where inherent in them and were not the result of don Juan's guidance. This assumption was based on the observation that the component elements of the first state of nonordinary reality I underwent possessed the same characteristics, and yet don Juan had hardly begun his directing. Assuming, then, that these characteristics were inherent in the component elements of nonordinary reality in general, don Juan's task consisted of utilizing them as the basis for directing the outcome of each state of nonordinary reality elicited by *Datura inoxia, Psilocybe mexicana,* and *Lophophora williamsii.*

The detailed account that don Juan made me render as the aftermath of each state of nonordinary reality was a recapitulation of the experience. It entailed a meticulous verbal rendition of what I had perceived during the course of each state. A recapitulation had two facets: (1) the recollection of events and (2) the description of perceived component elements. The recollection of events was concerned with the incidents I had seemingly perceived during the course of the experience I was narrating: that is, the events that seemed to have happened and the actions I seemed to have performed. The description of the perceived component elements was my account of the specific form and the specific detail of the component elements I seemed to have perceived.

From each recapitulation of the experience don Juan selected certain units by means of the processes of (1) attaching importance to certain appropriate areas of my account and (2) denying all importance to other areas of my account. The interval between states of nonordinary reality was the time when don Juan expounded on the recapitulation of the experience.

I have called the first process "emphasis" because it entailed a forceful speculation on the distinction between what don Juan had conceived as the goals I should have accomplished in the state of nonordinary reality and what I had perceived myself. Emphasis meant, then, that don Juan isolated an area of my narrative by centering on it the bulk of his speculation. Emphasis was either positive or negative. Positive emphasis implied that don Juan was satisfied with a particular item I had perceived because it conformed with the goals he had expected me to achieve in the state of nonordinary reality. Negative emphasis meant that don Juan was not satisfied with what I had perceived because it may not have conformed with his expectations or because he judged it insufficient. Nonetheless, he still placed the bulk of speculation on that area of my recapitulation in order to emphasize the negative value of my perception.

The second selective process that don Juan employed was to deny all importance to some areas of my account. I have called it "lack of emphasis" because it was the opposite and the counterbalance of emphasis. It seemed that by denying importance to the parts of my account pertaining to component elements which don Juan judged to be completely superfluous to the goal of his teachings, he literally obliterated my perception of the same elements in the successive states of nonordinary reality.

Guiding Special Consensus

The second aspect of don Juan's task as a teacher was to guide special consensus by directing the outcome of each state of nonordinary reality and each special state of ordinary reality. Don Juan directed that outcome through an orderly manipulation of the extrinsic and the intrinsic levels of nonordinary reality, and of the intrinsic level of the special states of ordinary reality.

The extrinsic level of nonordinary reality pertained to its operative arrangement. It involved the mechanics, the steps leading into nonordinary reality proper. The extrinsic level had three discernible aspects: (1) the preparatory period, (2) the transitional stages, and (3) the teacher's supervision.

The preparatory period was the time that elapsed between one state of nonordinary reality and the next. Don Juan used it to give me direct instructions and to develop the general course of his teachings. The preparatory period was of critical importance in setting up the states of nonordinary reality, and because it pivoted on them it had two distinct facets: (1) the period prior to nonordinary reality, and (2) the period following nonordinary reality.

The period prior to nonordinary reality was a relatively short interval of time, twenty-four hours at the most. In the states of nonordinary reality induced by *Datura inoxia* and *Pscilocybe mexicana* the period was characterized by don Juan's dramatic and accelerated direct instructions on the specific purpose of the rule and on the manipulatory techniques I was supposed to corroborate in the oncoming state of nonordinary reality. With *Lophophora williamsii* the period was essentially a time of ritual behavior, since Mescalito had no rule.

The period following nonordinary reality, on the other hand, was a long span of time; usually lasting for months, it allowed time for don Juan's discussion and clarification of the events that had taken place during the preceding state of nonordinary reality. This period was especially important after the use of *Lophophora williamsii*. Because Mescalito did not have a rule, the goal pursued in nonordinary reality was the verification of Mescalito's characteristics; don Juan delineated those characteristics during the long interval following each state of nonordinary reality.

The second aspect of the extrinsic level was the transitional stages, which mean the passage from a state of ordinary reality into a state of nonordinary reality, and vice versa. The two states of reality overlapped in these transitional stages, and the criterion I used to differentiate the latter from either state of reality was that their component elements were blurred. I was never able to perceive them or to recollect them with precision.

In terms of perceived time, the transitional stages were either abrupt or slow. In the instance of *Datura inoxia*, ordinary and nonordinary states were almost juxtaposed, and the transition from one to the other took place abruptly. The most noticeable were the passages into nonordinary reality. *Psilocybe mexicana,* on the other hand, elicited transitional stages that I perceived to be slow. The passage from ordinary into nonordinary reality was specially long-drawn-out and perceivable. I was always more aware of it, perhaps because of my apprehension about forthcoming events.

The transitional stages elicited by *Lophophora williamsii* seemed to combine features of the other two. For one thing, both the passages into and out of nonordinary reality were very noticeable. The entering into nonordinary reality was slow, and I experienced it with hardly any impairment of my faculties; but reverting back into ordinary reality was an abrupt transitional stage, which I perceived with clarity, but with less facility to assess every detail of it.

The third aspect of the extrinsic level was the teacher's supervision or the actual help that I, as the apprentice, received in the course of experiencing a state of nonordinary reality. I have set up supervision as a category by itself because it was implied that the teacher would have to enter nonordinary reality with his apprentice at a certain point of the teachings.

During the states of nonordinary reality elicited by *Datura inoxia* I received minimal supervision. Don Juan placed heavy stress on fulfilling the steps of the preparatory period, but after I had complied with that requirement he let me proceed by myself.

In the nonordinary reality induced by *Psilocybe mexicana,* the degree of supervision was the complete opposite, for here, according to don Juan, the apprentice needed the most extensive guidance and help. The corroboration of the rule necessitated the adoption of an alternate form, which seemed to suggest that I had to undergo a series of very specialized adjustments in perceiving the surroundings. Don Juan produced those necessary adjustments through verbal commands and suggestions during the transitional stages into nonordinary reality. Another aspect of his supervision was to direct me during the early part of the states of nonordinary reality by commanding me to focus my attention on certain component elements of the preceding state of ordinary reality. The items he focused upon were apparently chosen at random, as the important issue was the act of perfecting the adopted alternate form. The final aspect of supervision was restoring me back to ordinary reality. It was implicit that this operation also required maximal supervision from don Juan, although I could not recall the actual procedure.

The supervision necessary for the states induced by *Lophophora williamsii* was a blend of the other two. Don Juan remained at my side for as long as he could, yet he did not attempt in any way to direct me into or out of nonordinary reality.

The second level of differentiative order in nonordinary reality was the seemingly internal standards of the seemingly internal arrangement of its component elements. I have called it the "intrinsic level," and I have assumed here that the component elements were subject to three general processes, which seemed to be the product of don Juan's guidance: (1) a progression toward the specific; (2) a progression toward a more extensive range of appraisal; and (3) a progression toward a more pragmatic use of nonordinary reality.

The progression toward the specific was the apparent advance of the component elements of each successive state of nonordinary reality toward being more precise, more specific. It entailed two separate aspects: (1) a progression toward specific single forms; and (2) a progression toward specific total results.

The progression toward specific single forms implied that the component elements were amorphously familiar in the early states. The progression seemed to encompass two levels of change in the component elements of nonordinary reality: (1) a progressive complexity of perceived detail; and (2) a progression from familiar to unfamiliar forms.

Progressive complexity of detail meant that in each successive state of nonordinary reality, the minute particulars I perceived as constituting the component elements became more complex. I assessed complexity in terms of my being aware that the structure of the component elements grew more complicated, yet the details did not become exceedingly or perplexingly entangled. The increasing complexity referred rather to the harmonious increase of perceived detail, which ranged from my impressions of vague forms during the early states to my perception of massive, elaborate arrays of minute particulars in the late states.

The progression from familiar to unfamiliar forms implied that at first the forms of the component elements either were familiar forms found in ordinary reality, or at least evoked the familiarity of everyday life. But in successive states of nonordinary reality the specific forms, the details making up the form, and the patterns in which the component elements were combined became progressively unfamiliar, until I could not put them on a par with, nor could they even evoke, in some instances, anything I had ever perceived in ordinary reality.

The progression of the component elements toward specific total results was the gradually closer approximation of the total result I accomplished in each state of nonordinary reality to the total result don Juan sought, in matters of corroborating the rule; that is, nonordinary reality was induced to corroborate the rule, and the corroboration grew more specific in each successive attempt.

The second general process of the intrinsic level of nonordinary reality was the progression toward a more extensive range of appraisal. In other words, it was the gain I perceived in each successive state of nonordinary reality toward the expansion of the area over which I could have exercised my capacity to focus attention. The point in question here was either that there existed a definite area that expanded, or that my capacity to perceive seemed to increase in each successive state. Don Juan's teachings fostered and reinforced the idea that there was an area that expanded, and I have called that alleged area the "range of appraisal." Its progressive expansion consisted of a seemingly sensorial appraisal I made of the component elements of nonordinary reality which fell within a certain range. I evaluated and analyzed these component elements, it seemed, with my senses, and to all appearances I perceived the range in which they occurred as being more extensive, more encompassing, in each successive state.

The range of appraisal was of two kinds (1) the dependent range and (2) the independent range. The dependent range was an area in which the component elements were the items of the physical environment which had been within my awareness in the preceding state of ordinary reality. The independent range, on the other hand, was the area in which the component elements of nonordinary reality seemed to come into existence by themselves, free of the influence of the physical surroundings of the preceding ordinary reality.

Don Juan's clear allusion in matters of the range of appraisal was that each of the two allies and Mescalito possessed the property of inducing both forms of perception. Yet it seemed to me that *Datura inoxia* had a greater capacity to induce an independent range, although in the facet of bodily flight, which I did not perceive long enough to assess it, the range of appraisal was implicitly a dependent one. *Psilocybe mexicana* had the capacity to produce a dependent range. *Lophophora williamsii* had the capacity to produce both.

My assumption was that don Juan used those different properties in order to prepare special consensus. In other words, in the states produced by *Datura inoxia* the component elements lacking ordinary consensus existed independently of the preceding ordinary reality. With *Psilocybe mexicana*, lack of ordinary consensus involved component elements that depended on the environment of the preceding ordinary reality. And with *Lophophora williamsii*, some component elements were determined by the environment, whereas others were independent of the environment. Thus the use of the three plants together seemed to have been designed to create a broad perception of the lack of ordinary consensus on the component elements of nonordinary reality.

The last process of the intrinsic level of nonordinary reality was the progression I perceived in each successive state toward a more pragmatic use of nonordinary reality. This progression seemed to be correlated with the idea that each new state was a more complex stage of learning, and that the increasing complexity of each new stage required a more inclusive and pragmatic use of nonordinary reality. The progression was most noticeable when *Lophophora williamsii* was used; the simultaneous existence of a dependent and an independent range of appraisal in each state made the pragmatic use of nonordinary reality more extensive, for it covered both ranges at once.

Directing the outcome of the special states of ordinary reality seemed to produce an order in the intrinsic level, an order characterized by the progression of the component elements toward the specific; that is to say, the component elements were more numerous and were isolated more easily in each successive special state of ordinary reality. In the course of his teachings, don Juan elicited only two of them, but it was still possible for me to detect that in the second it was easier for don Juan to isolate a large number of component elements, and the facility for specific results affected the rapidity with which the second special state of ordinary reality was produced.*

---

* For an outline of the units of my structural analysis, see Appendix B.

THE CONCEPTUAL ORDER

THE APPRENTICE

The apprentice was the last unit of the operative order. The apprentice was in his own right the unit that brought don Juan's teachings into focus, for he had to accept the totality of the special consensus given on the component elements of all the states of nonordinary reality and all the special states of ordinary reality, before special consensus could become a meaningful concept. But special consensus, by force of being concerned with the actions and elements perceived in nonordinary reality, entailed a peculiar order of conceptualization, an order that brought such perceived actions and elements into accordance with corroboration of the rule. Therefore the acceptance of special consensus meant for me, as the apprentice, the adoption of a certain point of view validated by the totality of don Juan's teachings; that is, it meant my entrance into a conceptual level, a level comprising an order of conceptualization that would render the teachings understandable in their own terms. I have called it the "conceptual order" because it was the order that gave meaning to the unordinary phenomena that formed don Juan's knowledge; it was the matrix of meaning in which all individual concepts brought out in his teachings were embedded.

Taking into account, then, that the apprentice's goal consisted of adopting that order of conceptualization, he had two alternatives: he could either fail in his efforts or he could succeed.

The first alternative, failure to adopt the conceptual order, meant also that the apprentice had failed to achieve the operational goal of the teachings. The idea of failure was explained in the theme of the four symbolic enemies of a man of knowledge; it was implicit that failure was not merely the act of discontinuing pursuit of the goal, but the act of abandoning the quest completely under the pressure created by any one of the four symbolic enemies. The same theme also made it clear that the first two enemies—fear and clarity— were the cause of a man's defeat at the apprentice's level, that defeat at that level signified failure to learn how to command an ally, and that as a consequence of such failure the apprentice had adopted the conceptual order in a shallow, fallacious manner. That is, his adoption of the conceptual order was fallacious in the sense of being a fraudulent affiliation with or commitment to the meaning propounded by the teachings. The idea was that upon being defeated an apprentice, besides being incapable of commanding an ally, would be left with only the knowledge of certain manipulatory techniques, plus the memory of the perceived component elements of nonordinary reality, but he would not identify with the rationale that might have made them meaningful in their own terms. Under these circumstances any man might be forced to develop his own explanations for idiosyncratically chosen areas of the phenomena he had experienced, and that process would entail the fallacious adoption of the point of view propounded by don Juan's teachings. Fallacious adoption of the conceptual order, however, was apparently not restricted to the apprentice alone. In the theme of the enemies of a man of knowledge, it was also implicit that a man, after having achieved the goal of learning to command an ally, could still succumb to the onslaughts of his other two enemies—power and old age. In don Juan's categorization scheme, such a defeat implied that a man had fallen into a shallow or fallacious adoption of the conceptual order, as had the defeated apprentice.

The successful adoption of the conceptual order, on the other hand, meant that the apprentice had achieved the operational goal—a bona fide adoption of the point of view propounded in the teachings. That is, his adoption of the conceptual order was bona fide in that it was a complete affiliation with, a complete commitment to, the meaning expressed in that order of conceptualization.

Don Juan never clarified the exact point at which, or the exact way in which, an apprentice ceased to be an apprentice, although the allusion was clear that once he had achieved the operational goal of the system— that is, once he knew how to command an ally—he would no longer need the teacher for guidance. The idea that the time would come when a teacher's directions would be superfluous implied that the apprentice would succeed in adopting the conceptual order, and in so doing he would acquire the capacity to draw meaningful inferences without the teacher's aid.

Insofar as don Juan's teachings were concerned, and until I discontinued my apprenticeship, the acceptance of special consensus seemed to entail the adoption of two units of the conceptual order: (1) the idea of a reality of special consensus; (2) the idea that the reality of ordinary, everyday-life consensus, and the reality of special consensus, had an equally pragmatic value.

Reality of Special Consensus

The main body of don Juan's teachings, as he himself stated, concerned the use of the three hallucinogenic plants with which he induced states of nonordinary reality. The use of these three plants seems to have been a matter of deliberate intent on his part. He seems to have employed them because each of them possessed different hallucinogenic properties, which he interpreted as the different inherent natures of the powers contained in them. By directing the extrinsic and intrinsic levels of nonordinary reality, don Juan exploited the different hallucinogenic properties until they created in me, as the apprentice, the perception that nonordinary reality was a perfectly defined area, a realm separate from ordinary, everyday life whose inherent properties were revealed as I went along.

Nevertheless, it was also possible that the allegedly different properties might have been merely the product of don Juan's own process of directing the intrinsic order of nonordinary reality, although in his teachings he exploited the idea that the power contained in each plant induced states of nonordinary reality which differed from one another. If the latter was true, their differences in terms of the units of this analysis seem to have been in the range of appraisal which one could perceive in the states elicited by each of the three. Owing to the peculiarities of their range of appraisal, all three contributed to producing the perception of a perfectly defined area or realm, consisting of two compartments: the independent range, called the realm of the lizards, or of Mescalito's lessons; and the dependent range, referred to as the area where one would move by one's own means.

I use the term "nonordinary reality," as already noted, in the sense of extraordinary, uncommon reality. For a beginner apprentice such a reality was by all means unordinary, but the apprenticeship of don Juan's knowledge demanded my compulsory participation and my commitment to pragmatic and experimental practice of whatever I had learned. That meant that I, as the apprentice, had to experience a number of states of nonordinary reality, and that firsthand knowledge would, sooner or later, make the classifications "ordinary" and "nonordinary" meaningless for me. The bona fide adoption of the first unit of the conceptual order would have entailed, then, the idea that there was another separate, but no longer unordinary, realm of reality, the "reality of special consensus."

Accepting as a major premise that the reality of special consensus was a separate realm would have explained meaningfully the idea that the meetings with the allies or with Mescalito took place in a realm that was not illusory.

The Reality of Special Consensus Had Pragmatic Value

The same process of directing the extrinsic and intrinsic levels of nonordinary reality, which seemed to have created the recognition of the reality of special consensus as a separate realm, appeared also to have been responsible for my perception that the reality of special consensus was practical and usable. The acceptance of special consensus on all the states of ordinary reality, and on all the special states of ordinary reality, was designed to consolidate the awareness that it was equal to the reality of ordinary, everyday-life consensus. This equality was based on the impression that the reality of special consensus was not a realm that could be equated with dreams. On the contrary, it had stable component elements that were subject to special agreement. It was actually a realm where one could perceive the surroundings in a deliberate manner. Its component elements were not idiosyncratic or whimsical, but concise items or events whose existence was attested to by the whole body of teachings.

The implication of the equality was clear in the treatment don Juan accorded to the reality of special consensus, a treatment that was utilitarian and matter of course; not at any time did he refer to it, nor was I required to behave toward it in any but a utilitarian, matter-of-course way. The fact that the two areas were considered equal, however, did not mean that at any moment one could have behaved in exactly the same way in either area. On the contrary, a sorcerer's behavior had to be different since each area of reality had qualities that rendered it utilizable in its own way. The defining factor in terms of meaning seems to have been the idea that such an equality could be measured on the grounds of practical utility. Thus, a sorcerer had to believe that it was possible to shift back and forth from one area to the other, that both were inherently utilizable, and that the only dissimilarity between the two was their different capacity for being used, that is, the different purposes they served.

Yet their separateness seemed to be only an appropriate arrangement that was pertinent to my particular level of apprenticeship, which don Juan used for making me aware that another realm of reality could exist.

But from his acts, more than from his statements, I was led to believe that for a sorcerer there was but one single continuum of reality which had two, or perhaps more than two, parts from which he drew inferences of pragmatic value. The bona fide adoption of the idea that the reality of special consensus had pragmatic value would have given a meaningful perspective to movement.

If I had accepted the idea that the reality of special consensus was usable because it possessed inherently utilizable properties which were as pragmatic as those of the reality of everyday consensus, then it would have been logical for me to understand why don Juan exploited the notion of movement in the reality of special consensus at such great length. After accepting the pragmatic existence of another reality, the only thing a sorcerer had to do would be to learn the mechanics of movement. Naturally, movement in that instance had to be specialized because it was concerned with the inherent, pragmatic properties of the reality of special consensus.

SUMMARY

The issues of my analysis have been the following:

1. The fragment of don Juan's teachings which I have presented here consisted of two aspects: the operative order or the meaningful sequence in which all the individual concepts of his teachings were linked to one another, and the conceptual order or the matrix of meaning in which all the individual concepts of his teaching were embedded.

2. The operative order had four main units with their respective component ideas: (1) the concept "man of knowledge"; (2) the idea that a man of knowledge had the aid of a specialized power called an ally; (3) the idea that an ally was governed by a body of regulations

called the rule; and (4) the idea that the corroboration of the rule was subject to special consensus.

3. These four units were related to one another in the following manner: the goal of the operative order was to teach one how to become a man of knowledge; a man of knowledge was different from ordinary men because he had an ally; an ally was a specialized power, which had a rule; one could acquire or tame an ally through the process of verifying its rule in the realm of nonordinary reality and through obtaining special consensus on that corroboration.

4. In the context of don Juan's teachings, becoming a man of knowledge was not a permanent accomplishment, but rather a process. That is to say, the factor that made a man of knowledge was not solely the possession of an ally, but the man's lifelong struggle to maintain himself within the boundaries of a system of beliefs. Don Juan's teachings, however, were aimed at practical results, and his practical goal, in relation to teaching how to become a man of knowledge, was to teach how to acquire an ally through learning its rule. Thus the goal of the operative order was to provide one with special consensus on the component elements perceived in nonordinary reality, which were considered to be the corroboration of the ally's rule.

5. In order to provide special consensus on the corroboration of the ally's rule, don Juan had to provide special consensus on the component elements of all the states of nonordinary reality and the special states of ordinary reality elicited in the course of his teachings. Special consensus, therefore, dealt with unordinary phenomena, a fact that permitted me to assume that any apprentice, by accepting special consensus, was led into adopting the conceptual order of the knowledge being taught.

6. From the point of view of my personal stage of learning, I could deduce that up to the time when I withdrew from the apprenticeship don Juan's teachings had fostered the adoption of two units of the conceptual order: (1) the idea that there was a separate realm

of reality, another world, which I have called the "reality of special consensus"; (2) the idea that the reality of special consensus, or that other world, was as utilizable as the world of everyday life.

Nearly six years after I had begun the apprenticeship, don Juan's knowledge became a coherent whole for the first time. I realized that he had aimed at providing a bona fide consensus on my personal findings, and although I did not continue because I was not, nor will I ever be, prepared to undergo the rigors of such a training, my own way to meet his standards of personal exertion was my attempt to understand his teachings. I felt it was imperative to prove, if only to myself, that they were not an oddity.

After I had arranged my structural scheme, and was capable of discarding many data that were superfluous to my initial effort to uncovering the cogency of his teachings, it became clear to me that they had an internal cohesion, a logical sequence that enabled me to view the entire phenomenon in a light that dispelled the sense of bizarreness which was the mark of all I had experienced. It was obvious to me then that my apprenticeship had been only the beginning of a very long road. And the strenuous experiences I had undergone, which were so overwhelming to me, were but a very small fragment of a system of logical thought from which don Juan drew meaningful inferences for his day-to-day life, a vastly complex system of beliefs in which inquiry was an experience leading to exultation.

Appendix A

THE PROCESS OF VALIDATING SPECIAL CONSENSUS

Validating special consensus involved, at every point, the cumulation of don Juan's teachings. For the purpose of explaining the cumulative process, I have arranged the validation of special consensus according to the sequence in which the states of nonordinary reality and special ordinary reality occurred. Don Juan did not seem to have fixed the process of directing the intrinsic order of nonordinary and special ordinary reality in an exact manner; he seemed to have isolated the units for direction in a rather fluid way.

Don Juan began to prepare the background for special consensus by producing the first special state of ordinary reality through the process of manipulating cues about the environment. He isolated by that method certain component elements from the range of ordinary reality, and by isolating them, he directed me to perceive a progression toward the specific, in this instance the perception of colors that seemed to emanate from two small areas on the ground. Upon being isolated those areas of coloration became deprived of ordinary consensus; it seemed that only I was capable of seeing them, and thus they created a special state of ordinary reality.

Isolating those two areas on the ground by depriving them of ordinary consensus served to establish the first link between ordinary and nonordinary reality. Don Juan directed me to perceive a portion of ordinary reality in an unaccustomed manner; that is, he changed certain ordinary elements into items that needed special consensus.

239

The aftermath of the first special state of ordinary reality was my recapitulation of the experience; from it don Juan selected the perception of different areas of coloration as the units for positive emphasis. He isolated for negative emphasis the account of my fear and fatigue, and the possibility of my lacking persistence.

During the subsequent preparatory period he placed the bulk of speculation on the units he had isolated, and he carried over the idea that it was possible to detect in the surroundings more than the usual. From the units drawn from my recapitulation don Juan also introduced some of the component concepts of man of knowledge.

As the second step in preparing special consensus on the corroboration of the rule, don Juan induced a state of nonordinary reality with *Lophophora williamsii*. The total content of that first state of nonordinary reality was rather vague and disassociated, yet the component elements were very well defined; I perceived its characteristics of stability, singularity, and lack of ordinary consensus almost as clearly as in later states. These characteristics were not so obvious, perhaps because of my lack of proficiency; it was the first time I had experienced nonordinary reality.

It was impossible to ascertain the effect of don Juan's previous directing on the actual course of the experience; however, his mastery in directing the outcome of subsequent states of nonordinary reality was very clear from that point on.

From my recapitulation of the experience, he selected the units to direct the progression toward specific single forms and specific total results. He took the account of my actions with a dog and connected it with the idea that Mescalito was a visible entity. It was capable of adopting any form; above all it was an entity outside oneself.

The account of my actions also served don Juan in setting the progression toward a more extensive range of appraisal; in this instance the progression was toward a dependent range. Don Juan placed positive emphasis on the notion that I had moved and acted in nonordinary reality almost as I would have in everyday life.

The progression toward a more pragmatic use of non-ordinary reality was set by giving negative emphasis to the account of my incapacity to pay logical attention to the perceived component elements. Don Juan hinted that it would have been possible for me to examine the elements with detachment and accuracy; this idea brought forth two general characteristics of nonordinary reality, that it was pragmatic and that it had component elements that could be assessed sensorially.

The lack of ordinary consensus for the component elements was brought forth dramatically by an interplay of positive and negative emphasis placed on the views of onlookers who observed my behavior during the course of that first state of nonordinary reality.

The preparatory period following the first state of nonordinary reality lasted more than a year. Don Juan employed that time to introduce more component concepts of man of knowledge, and to disclose some parts of the rule of the two allies. He elicited also a shallow state of nonordinary reality in order to test my affinity with the ally contained in *Datura inoxia*. Don Juan used whatever vague sensations I had in the course of that shallow state to delineate the general characteristics of the ally by contrasting it with what he had isolated as Mescalito's perceivable characteristics.

The third step in preparing the special consensus on the corroboration of the rule was to elicit another state of nonordinary reality with *Lophophora williamsii*. Don Juan's previous directing seems to have guided me to perceiving this second state of nonordinary reality in the following manner:

The progression toward the specific created the possibility of visualizing an entity whose form had changed remarkably, from the familiar shape of a dog in the first state to the completely unfamiliar form of an anthropomorphic composite that existed, seemingly, outside myself.

The progression toward a more extensive range of

appraisal was evident in my perception of a journey. In the course of that journey the range of appraisal was both dependent and independent, although a majority of the component elements depended on the environment of the preceding state of ordinary reality.

The progression toward a more pragmatic use of nonordinary reality was, perhaps, the most outstanding feature of my second state. It became evident to me, in a complex and detailed manner, that one could move around in nonordinary reality.

I also examined the component elements with detachment and accuracy. I perceived their stability, singularity, and lack of consensus very clearly.

From my recapitulation of the experience, don Juan emphasized the following: For the progression toward the specific he gave positive emphasis to my account that I had seen Mescalito as an anthropomorphic composite. The bulk of speculation on this area was centered on the idea that Mescalito was capable of being a teacher, and also a protector.

In order to direct the progression toward a more extensive range of appraisal, don Juan placed positive emphasis on the account of my journey, which obviously had taken place in the dependent range; he also put positive emphasis on my version of the visionary scenes I viewed on the hand of Mescalito, scenes that seemed to be independent of the component elements of the preceding ordinary reality.

The account of my journey, and the scenes viewed on Mescalito's hand, also enabled don Juan to direct the progression toward a more pragmatic use of nonordinary reality. He first put forth the idea that it was possible to obtain direction; second, he interpreted the scenes as lessons concerning the right way to live.

Some areas of my recapitulation which deal with the perception of superfluous composites were not emphasized at all, because they were not useful for setting the direction of the intrinsic order.

The next state of nonordinary reality, the third one, was induced for the corroboration of the rule with the ally contained in *Datura inoxia*. The preparatory period was important and noticeable for the first time. Don Juan presented the manipulatory techniques and disclosed that the specific purpose I had to corroborate was divination.

His previous directing of the three aspects of the intrinsic order seemed to have produced the following results: The progression toward the specific was manifested in my capacity to perceive an ally as a quality; that is, I verified the assertion that an ally was not visible at all. The progression toward the specific also produced the peculiar perception of a series of images very similar to those I had viewed on Mescalito's hand. Don Juan interpreted these scenes as divination, or the corroboration of the specific purpose of the rule.

Perceiving that series of scenes entailed also a progression toward a more extensive range of appraisal. This time the range was independent of the environment of the preceding ordinary reality. The scenes did not appear to be superimposed on the component elements, as had the images I viewed on Mescalito's hand; in fact, there were no other component elements besides those that were part of the scenes. In other words, the total range of appraisal was independent.

The perception of a completely independent range also exhibited progression toward a more pragmatic use of nonordinary reality. Divining implied that one could give a utilitarian value to whatever had been seen.

For the purpose of directing the progression toward the specific, don Juan put positive emphasis on the idea that it was impossible to move by one's own means in the independent range of appraisal. He explained movement there as being indirect, and as being accomplished, in this particular instance, by the lizards as instruments. In order to set the direction of the second aspect of the intrinsic level, the progression toward a more extensive range of appraisal, he centered the bulk of speculation on the idea that the scenes I had perceived, which were the answers to divination, could have been examined and extended for as long as I wanted. For guiding the progression toward a more pragmatic use of nonordinary reality, don Juan placed positive emphasis on the idea that the topic to be divined had to be simple and direct in order to obtain a result that could be usable.

The fourth state of nonordinary reality was elicited also for the corroboration of the rule of the ally contained in *Datura inoxia*. The specific purpose of the rule to be corroborated had to do with bodily flight as another aspect of movement.

A result of directing the progression toward the specific may have been the perception of soaring bodily through the air. That sensation was acute, although it lacked the depth of all the earlier perceptions of acts that I had presumably performed in nonordinary reality. Bodily flight appeared to have taken place in a dependent range of appraisal, and it appeared to have entailed moving by one's own power, which may have been the result of a progression toward a wider range of appraisal.

Two other aspects of the sensation of soaring through the air may have been the product of directing the progression toward a more pragmatic use of nonordinary reality. They were, first, the perception of distance, a perception that created the feeling of an actual flight, and second, the possibility of acquiring direction in the course of that alleged movement.

During the subsequent preparatory period don Juan speculated on the supposedly deleterious nature of the ally contained in *Datura inoxia*. And he isolated the following areas of my account: For directing the progression toward the specific, he placed positive emphasis on my recollection of having soared through the air. Although I did not perceive the component elements of that state of nonordinary reality with the clarity that was customary by then, my sensation of movement was very definite, and don Juan used it to reinforce the specific result of movement. The progression toward a more pragmatic use of nonordinary reality was established by centering the bulk of speculation on the idea that sorcerers could fly over enormous distances, a speculation that gave rise to the possibility that one could move in the dependent range of appraisal and then switch such movement over into ordinary reality.

The fifth state of nonordinary reality was produced by the ally contained in *Psilocybe mexicana*. It was the first time that the plant was used, and the state that ensued was more in line with a test than with an attempt to corroborate the rule. In the preparatory period don Juan presented only a manipulatory technique; as he did not disclose the specific purpose to be verified I did not believe the state was elicited to corroborate the rule. Yet the direction of the intrinsic level of nonordinary reality set earlier appeared to have terminated in the following results.

Directing the progression toward specific total results produced in me the perception that the two allies were different from each other, and that each was different from Mescalito. I perceived the ally contained in *Psilocybe mexicana* as a quality—formless and invisible, and producing a sensation of bodilessness. The progression toward a more extensive range of appraisal resulted in the sensation that the total environment of the preceding ordinary reality, which remained within my awareness, was usable in nonordinary reality; that is, the expansion of the dependent range seemed to have covered everything. The progression toward a more pragmatic use of nonordinary reality produced the peculiar perception that I could go through the component elements within the dependent range of appraisal, in spite of the fact that they appeared to be ordinary elements of everyday life.

Don Juan did not demand the usual recapitulation of the experience; it was as if the absence of a specific purpose had made this state of nonordinary reality only a prolonged transitional stage. During the subsequent preparatory period, however, he speculated on certain observations he had made on my behavior during the course of the experience.

He placed negative emphasis on the logical impasse

nat prevented my believing that one could go through things or beings. With that speculation he directed the progression toward a specific total result of movement through the component elements of nonordinary reality perceived within the dependent range of appraisal.

Don Juan used those same observations to direct the second aspect of the intrinsic level, a more extensive range of appraisal. If movement through things and beings was possible, then the dependent range had to expand accordingly; it had to cover the total environment of the preceding ordinary reality which was within one's awareness at any given time, since movement entailed a constant change of surroundings. In the same speculation it was also implicit that nonordinary reality could have been used in a more pragmatic manner. Moving through objects and beings implied a definite point of advantage which was inaccessible to a sorcerer in ordinary reality.

Don Juan next used a series of three states of nonordinary reality, elicited by *Lophophora williamsii,* to prepare further the special consensus on the corroboration of the rule. These three states have here been treated as a single unit because they took place during four consecutive days, and during the few hours in between them I had no communication whatsoever with don Juan. The intrinsic order of the three states has also been considered a single unit with the following characteristics. The progression of Mescalito as a visible, anthropomorphic entity capable of teaching. The ability to give lessons implied that Mescalito was capable of acting toward people.

The progression toward a more extensive range of appraisal reached a point where I perceived both ranges at the same time, and I was incapable of establishing the difference between them except in terms of movement. In the dependent range it was possible for me to move by my own means and volition, but in the independent range I was able to move only with the aid of Mescalito as an instrument. For example, Mescalito's lessons comprised a series of scenes that I could only watch. The progression toward a more pragmatic use of nonordinary reality was implicit in the idea that Mescalito could actually deliver lessons on the right way to live.

During the preparatory period that followed the last state of nonordinary reality in this series, don Juan selected the following units. For the progression toward the specific, he placed positive emphasis on the ideas that Mescalito was instrumental in moving one through the independent range of appraisal, and that Mescalito was a didactic entity capable of delivering lessons by allowing one to enter into a visionary world. He also speculated on the implication that Mescalito had voiced its name and had supposedly taught me some songs; those two instances were constructed as examples of Mescalito's capacity to be a protector. And the fact that I had perceived Mescalito as a light was emphasized as the possibility that it might at last have adopted an abstract, permanent form for me.

Stressing these same units also served don Juan in directing the progression toward a more extensive range of appraisal. During the course of the three states of nonordinary reality I clearly perceived that the dependent range and the independent range were two separate aspects of nonordinary reality which were equally important. The independent range was the area where Mescalito delivered its lessons, and since these states of nonordinary reality were supposed to have been elicited only to seek such lessons, the independent range was, logically, an area of special importance. Mescalito was a protector and a teacher, which meant that it was visible; yet its form had nothing to do with the preceding state of ordinary reality. On the other hand, one was supposed to journey, to move in nonordinary reality, in order to seek Mescalito's lessons, an idea that implied the importance of the dependent range.

The progression toward a more pragmatic use of nonordinary reality was set by devoting the bulk of speculation to Mescalito's lessons. Don Juan constructed these lessons as being indispensable to a man's life; it was a clear inference that nonordinary reality could have

been used in a more pragmatic manner to draw points
of reference which had value in ordinary reality. It was
the first time don Juan had verbalized such an implication.

The subsequent state of nonordinary reality, the ninth
in the teachings, was induced in order to corroborate the
rule of the ally contained in *Datura inoxia.* The specific
purpose to be corroborated in that state was concerned
with divination, and the previous direction of the intrinsic level ended in the following points. The progression toward a specific total result created the perception
of a coherent set of scenes, which were purported to
be the voice of the lizard narrating the events to be
divined, and the sensation of a voice that actually
described such scenes. The progression toward an independent range of appraisal resulted in the perception of
an extensive and clear independent range that was free
from the extraneous influence of ordinary reality. The
progression toward a more pragmatic use of nonordinary
reality ended in the utilitarian possibilities of exploiting
the independent range. That particular trend was set
up by don Juan's speculation on the possibility of draw-
ing points of reference from the independent range and
using them in ordinary reality. Thus the divinatory
scenes had an obvious pragmatic value, for they were
thought to represent a view of acts performed by others,
acts to which one would have had no access by ordinary
means.

In the following preparatory period, don Juan emphasized more of the component themes of man of
knowledge. He seemed to be getting ready to shift
to the pursuit of only one of the two allies, the ally
humito. Yet he gave positive emphasis to the idea that
I had a close affinity with the ally contained in *Datura
inoxia,* because it had allowed me to witness an inci-
dence of flexibility of the rule when I had made an
error in performing a manipulatory technique. My assumption that don Juan was ready to abandon teaching
the rule of the ally contained in *Datura inoxia* was fostered by the fact that he did not isolate any areas of my

recapitulation of the experience to account for directing the intrinsic level of the subsequent states of nonordinary reality.

Next was a series of three states of nonordinary reality elicited to corroborate the rule of the ally contained in *Psilocybe mexicana*. They have been treated here as a single unit. And although a considerable time elapsed in between them, during those intervals don Juan made no attempt to speculate on any aspect of their intrinsic order.

The first state of the series was vague; it ended rapidly and its component elements were not precise. It had the appearance of being more like a state of nonordinary reality proper.

The second state had more depth. I perceived the transitional stage into nonordinary reality separately for the first time. During the course of that first transitional stage don Juan revealed that the specific purpose of the rule, which I had to corroborate, dealt with another aspect of movement, an aspect requiring his exhaustive supervision; I have rendered it as "moving by adopting an alternate form." As a consequence, two aspects of the extrinsic level of nonordinary reality became evident for the first time: the transitional stages, and the teacher's supervision.

Don Juan used his supervision during that first transitional stage to pinpoint the subsequent direction of the three aspects of the intrinsic level. His efforts were channeled, in the first place, to produce a specific total result by guiding me to experience the precise sensation of having adopted the shape of a crow.

The possibility of adopting an alternate form in order to achieve movement in nonordinary reality entailed in turn an expansion of the dependent range of appraisal, the only area where such movement could take place.

The pragmatic use of nonordinary reality was determined by directing me to focus my attention on certain component elements of the dependent range, in order to use them as points of reference for moving.

During the preparatory period that followed the

second state of the series, don Juan refused to speculate on any part of my experience. He treated the second state as if it had been merely another prolonged transitional stage.

The third state of the series, however, was paramount in the teachings. It was a state in which the process of directing the intrinsic level culminated in the following results: The progression toward the specific created the easy perception that I had adopted an alternative form so completely that it even induced precise adjustments in the way I focused my eyes and in my way of seeing. A result of those adjustments was my perception of a new facet of the dependent range of appraisal—the minutiae that formed the component elements—and that perception definitely enlarged the range of appraisal. The progression toward a more pragmatic use of nonordinary reality culminated in my awareness that it was possible to move in the dependent range as pragmatically as one walks in ordinary reality.

In the preparatory period following the last state of nonordinary reality, don Juan introduced a different type of recapitulation. He selected the areas for recollection before he had heard my account; that is, he demanded to hear only the accounts that pertained to the pragmatic use of nonordinary reality and to movement.

From such accounts he set the progression toward the specific by giving positive emphasis to the version of how I had exploited the crow's form. Yet he attached importance only to the idea of moving after having adopted that form. Movement was the area of my recapitulation on which he placed an interplay of positive and negative emphasis. He gave the account positive emphasis when it enhanced the idea of the pragmatic nature of nonordinary reality, or when it dealt with the perception of component elements which had permitted me to obtain a general sense of orientation, while seemingly moving in the dependent range of appraisal. He placed negative emphasis on my incapacity to recollect with precision the nature or the direction of such movement.

In directing the progression toward a wider range of appraisal, don Juan centered his speculation on my account of the peculiar way in which I had perceived the minutiae that formed the component elements that were within the dependent range. His speculation led me to the assumption that, if it were possible to see the world as a crow does, the dependent range of appraisal had to expand in depth and had to extend to cover the whole spectrum of ordinary reality.

To direct the progression toward a more pragmatic use of nonordinary reality, don Juan explained my peculiar way of perceiving the component elements as being a crow's way of seeing the world. And, logically, that way of seeing presupposed entrance into a range of phenomena beyond normal possibilities in ordinary reality.

The last experience recorded in my field notes was a special state of ordinary reality; don Juan produced it by isolating component elements of ordinary reality through the process of cuing about his own behavior.

The general processes used in directing the intrinsic level of nonordinary reality produced the following results during the course of the second special state of ordinary reality. The progression toward the specific resulted in the easy isolation of many elements of ordinary reality. In the first special state of ordinary reality, the very few component elements that were isolated through the process of cuing about the environment were also transformed into unfamiliar forms deprived of ordinary consensus; however, in the second special state of ordinary reality its component elements were numerous, and, although they did not lose their quality of being familiar elements, they may have lost their capacity for ordinary consensus. Such component elements covered, perhaps, the total environment that was within my awareness.

Don Juan may have produced this second special state in order to strengthen the link between ordinary and nonordinary reality by developing the possibility that most, if not all, of the component elements of ordinary reality could lose their capacity to have ordinary consensus.

From my own point of view, however, that last special state was the final summation of my apprenticeship. The formidable impact of terror on the level of sober consciousness had the peculiar quality of undermining the certainty that the reality of everyday life was implicitly real, the certainty that I, in matters of ordinary reality, could provide myself with consensus indefinitely. Up to that point the course of my apprenticeship seemed to have been a continuous building toward the collapse of that certainty. Don Juan used every facet of his dramatic exertion to accomplish the collapse during that last special state, a fact prompting me to believe that complete collapse of that certainty would have removed the last barrier that kept me from accepting the existence of a separate reality: the reality of special consensus.

Appendix B

OUTLINE FOR STRUCTURAL ANALYSIS

THE OPERATIVE ORDER

THE FIRST UNIT
MAN OF KNOWLEDGE
  TO BECOME A MAN OF KNOWLEDGE WAS A
  MATTER OF LEARNING
    There were no overt requirements
    There were some covert requirements
    An apprentice was selected by an impersonal power
      The one that was chosen (*escogido*)

The power's decisions were indicated through omens

A MAN OF KNOWLEDGE HAD UNBENDING INTENT

Frugality

Soundness of judgment

Lack of freedom to innovate

A MAN OF KNOWLEDGE HAD CLARITY OF MIND

Freedom to seek a path

Knowledge of the specific purpose

Being fluid

TO BECOME A MAN OF KNOWLEDGE WAS A MATTER OF STRENUOUS LABOR

Dramatic exertion

Efficacy

Challenge

A MAN OF KNOWLEDGE WAS A WARRIOR

He had to have respect

He had to have fear

He had to be wide-awake

    Awareness of intent

    Awareness of the expected flux

He had to be self-confident

TO BECOME A MAN OF KNOWLDGE WAS AN UNCEASING PROCESS

He had to renew the quest of becoming a man of knowledge

He was impermanent

He had to follow the path with heart

THE SECOND UNIT

A MAN OF KNOWLEDGE HAD AN ALLY

AN ALLY WAS FORMLESS

AN ALLY WAS PERCEIVED AS A QUALITY

The ally contained in *Datura inoxia*

    It was woman-like

        It was possessive

        It was violent

        It was unpredictable

        It had a deleterious effect on the character of its followers

It was a giver of superfluous power
The ally contained in *Psilocybe mexicana*
It was male-like
It was dispassionate
It was gentle
It was predictable
It was beneficial to the character of its followers
It was a giver of ecstasy
AN ALLY WAS TAMABLE
An ally was a vehicle
The ally contained in *Datura inoxia* was unpredictable
The ally contained in *Psilocybe mexicana* was predictable
An ally was a helper

THE THIRD UNIT
AN ALLY HAD A RULE
THE RULE WAS INFLEXIBLE
Exception due to ally's direct intervention
THE RULE WAS NONCUMULATIVE
THE RULE WAS CORROBORATED IN ORDINARY REALITY
THE RULE WAS CORROBORATED IN NONORDINARY REALITY
The states of nonordinary reality
Nonordinary reality was utilizable
Nonordinary reality had component elements
The component elements had stability
They had singularity
They lacked ordinary consensus
The specific purposes of the rule
First specific purpose, testing (*Datura inoxia*)
Manipulatory technique, ingestion
Second specific purpose, divination (*Datura inoxia*)
Manipulatory technique, ingestion-absorption
Third specific purpose, bodily flight (*Datura inoxia*)

Manipulatory technique, ingestion-absorption
Fourth specific purpose, testing *(Psilocybe mexicana)*
Manipulatory technique, ingestion-inhalation
Fifth specific purpose, movement *(Psilocybe mexicana)*
Manipulatory technique, ingestion-inhalation
Sixth specific purpose, movement by adopting an alternate form *(Psilocybe mexicana)*
Manipulatory technique, ingestion-inhalation

THE FOURTH UNIT
THE RULE WAS CORROBORATED BY SPECIAL CONSENSUS
THE BENEFACTOR
Preparing special consensus
The other states of nonordinary reality
They were produced by Mescalito
It was contained
The container was the power itself
It did not have a rule
It did not need apprenticeship
It was a protector
It was a teacher
It had a definite form
Nonordinary reality was utilizable
Nonordinary reality had component elements
The special states of ordinary reality
They were produced by the teacher
Cuing about the environment
Cuing about behavior
The recapitulation of the experience
The recollection of events
The description of the component elements
Emphasis
Positive emphasis
Negative emphasis
Lack of emphasis
Guiding special consensus
The extrinsic level of nonordinary reality
The preparatory period